CONTENTS

PART ONE

CREATING COUNTRY STYLE

Introducing the look

Making the right choice of pattern and colour is the key to creating the 'country look'. That doesn't mean the choice is limited – far from it. There are florals and trellises, stripes and checks, leafy designs and mini-prints, and traditional motifs such as paisley and bows. But it is the combinations of colours and patterns that count.

There are two characteristic looks. One is based on a single pattern – usually for upholstery or curtains – combined with plain walls in 'country colours'. Alternatively, several large and small patterns are combined for a rich, cosy, warm feeling. Whichever of these

strategies you prefer will depend on your personal taste: some people prefer to work with one or two patterns in a room, others love a rich medley of colour and pattern. Patterned and plain surfaces can be used in many combinations depending on personal taste, the function of the room and the effect you wish to create.

This and the following chapters introduce you to all the patterns, as well as the broad palette of colours that fit into the country style. Dozens of swatches, photographs and diagrams will help you develop an eye for judging how a snippet of fabric will look when it is covering a large area; how a small sample

of wallpaper will look when it is up; and how to combine patterns and colours to achieve pleasing effects.

Pattern with plain

The straightforward way of creating a scheme is to start with a pattern in colours that please you and then build the colour scheme for the room around that – choosing plain colours for walls, flooring and other fabrics that match the colours in the pattern. To carry the principle further, plain curtains can be trimmed with the patterned fabric, or a patterned sofa can be edged with a matching plain piping in a toning or accent colour.

A

B

◀ **The starting point** The sofa fabric (**A**) is the basis for this scheme. The soft leafy print is also used for the blind and a cushion.

Plain accent colours – green (**B**) and deep pink (**C**) – are picked out of the pattern for the curtains, lampshade and cushions.

Co-ordinated ranges

Manufacturers' pattern books are full of lovely co-ordinated ranges of patterns for fabrics and wallpapers. For example, many floral wallpapers are designed to team with a mini print, the two papers being linked by colour or motif. The same pattern theme may also be available in furnishing fabrics, bed and table linen, even kitchen accessories, giving limitless mix-and-match opportunities. These co-ordinated ranges give you the confidence to use two or three patterns knowing that they will combine successfully.

The pictures here show how country-style co-ordinates can be handled in different ways to create a welcoming look – light and airy as in the bedroom, or cosy and warm, as in the dining area. The common denominator in both these ranges is a larger design pulled together and combined with a smaller, all-over pattern – much easier on the eye than combining large-scale patterns.

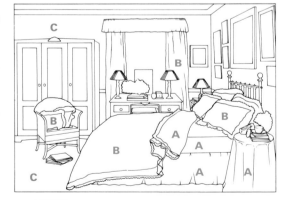

▲ **Co-ordinated bedroom range** A summery bedroom features different but related fabrics, both linked by the same colours and a rosy motif. The small pattern (**A**) is densely packed. The larger floral pattern (**B**) has a more open design. The plain colours (**C**) on the carpet and walls contribute to a restful, all-over effect.

▲ **Mix-and-match fabrics** *This range shows how well large motifs combine with an all-over design. The tablecloth, napkins, and tea cosy are all made up in the smaller design, while the curtains take up the theme with a larger, posy motif in the same colouring.*

◄ **Wallpapers and borders** *Flowery sprigs, borders, and an all-over pattern blend to create the total country ambience. (Note how the piping on the cushions picks up the red to provide a plain accent.)*

One colour, many patterns

If you enjoy the idea of combining different patterns, but don't want to work with a manufacturer's range of co-ordinates, the simplest approach is to work with a single colour theme. This way you are free to pick up remnants, market bargains or recycle old furnishings. The secret is to settle on one single colour and stick to that. Suppose, for example, that you like pink and that you wish to create a 'pink' bedroom. First, you should choose one item. It might be the bed cover, the curtains or the wallpaper. If you've fallen in love with a floral duvet set in several shades of pink, you might buy curtains in exactly the same fabric, or in another pattern, a

check or a mini-print, but with the same combination of colours.

Next, you might look at the walls. By now you are linking three elements: the bed linen, the window dressing and the wall surface. The easiest and most predictable way forward would be a plain wallpaper or paint in the same sort of pink but matching one of the lighter or darker shades in the pattern. But a more exciting solution would be to find yet another pattern, a stripe for example, in the same colour. Accessories such as china decorations and rugs on the floor can also be included in the colour scheme. By choosing the right combinations, you can bring the comfortable, mellow style of the country house into your own home.

▲ **One colour theme** Here several blue and white florals and checks on wallpapers and fabrics combine to produce a deliciously fresh effect. It doesn't matter if the colours don't match exactly – some can be lighter, some darker. What makes it work is that one basic colour theme is used throughout for walls, cushions and the seat. Even the decorative plates on the wall are blue and white.

Identifying country patterns

There are many different sorts of country-style patterns for fabrics and wallcoverings which group into broad categories. These include florals and mini-prints, spots and stripes, ginghams and checks, as well as traditional designs such as paisley and William Morris. Many of these patterns can be mixed together successfully as later chapters show. Here the patterns that evoke the country style are shown in the form of samples of fabrics and wallpapers.

▲ **Florals and stripes** A traditional floral design – lovely old-fashioned roses and peonies in a bold colourway – teams handsomely with toning stripes. The same mixture of florals and stripes looks just as effective in a paler or cooler colour scheme.

Large florals

These are an important part of the country look. The range of designs is extensive including large splashy watercolour patterns, naturalistic leaves and flowers and stylized designs such as those by William Morris. In some a single colour predominates, in others there are several dominant colours, allowing you freedom in your colour scheme.

Large florals should be handled with care as they can overwhelm in a small room. They are best used for full-length curtains, bedspreads or sofas – but not all at once. In the right context, such as a hall, a rich floral wallpaper can create a warm and welcoming space.

Glazed cottons with colourful designs of flowers and birds are often loosely known as 'chintzes'.

Small all-over florals and leaves

These are available in an abundance of designs and colours. These smaller designs are often well suited to the proportions of contemporary homes. This all-over quality in wallpapers helps to link furniture or furnishings together, and creates a friendly, welcoming feeling in a room.

Sprigs

These are small sprays of flowers or foliage, or even single flowers or leaves, scattered on a plain or subtly textured background. The lighter sprigs are fresh and clean – ideal for bedrooms and bathrooms. Sprigs can seem a bit spotty if there is a lot of plain background between the motifs.

Mini-prints

A mini-print is a very small repeating pattern. It can be any type of pattern including florals and little geometric motifs. Because mini-prints are small they are not overwhelming and when you stand back from them they look more like a textural design. They are useful where you want to introduce a subtle pattern, or in confined spaces such as corridors and cloakrooms. They team successfully with larger patterns, above a picture rail, for example.

Provençal and paisley prints

Originally from the French Mediterranean, Provençal patterns (right) are complex, colourful and often floral. They evolved from imitations of the motifs on Indian cottons, which reached France as exclusive imports in the seventeenth century. In time the Provençal designs became less oriental and more French. Saffron yellow, brilliant red and indigo blue are among the vibrant colours associated with Provençal prints, but they also come in muted, delicate colours.

Paisley patterns (left) are based on the small, familiar Indian teardrop shape. These can be small and neat or large, flowing and filled with flowers to give a distinctly eastern feel to fabrics and wallcoverings.

Textural

These designs are printed to imitate materials such as wood grain and paint effects such as sponging, dragging or spattering. These 'paint effects' are useful where you want to keep your walls simple but not plain. Textural fabrics include cotton damask with its slightly raised surfaces reflecting different light and lace with its more obvious visual texture. Moiré fabrics and wallpapers have a smooth, shiny surface which also reflects light differently in each of the lengthwise directions.

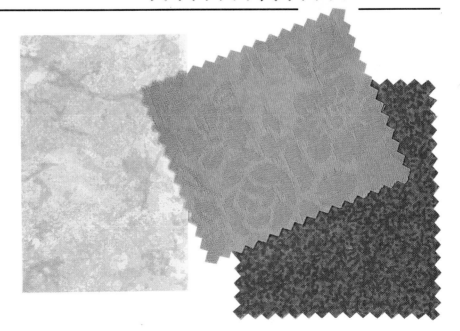

Checks, ginghams and tartans

A check is a pattern of crossed lines forming squares, either woven or printed. Checks can be used on wallpapers, furnishing fabrics and floor coverings. They can be in any colour combination and the effect created depends entirely on the combination of colours. For example, blue and white looks crisp and clean, while a mixture of heathery pastels is gentle and pretty.

Gingham – a cotton material woven from coloured yarns into checks – is a classic fabric that is never out of fashion. The most popular ginghams are red and white or blue and white, though black, green and yellow ginghams can also be found. These are inexpensive fabrics – easy to wash, they always look fresh and clean. Traditionally they are associated with farmhouse kitchens, especially in red and white.

Tartan is a distinctive type of woven check, Celtic in origin, it is created by multiple bands crossing at right angles. The most common tartan materials, such as those used in Scottish kilts, are woven from wool. In the home, tartan patterns have been adapted for use on furnishing fabrics and also wallpapers. Tartan has a timeless quality that never seems to date. Tartan wallpapers tend to be fairly dark and so are best used to give a dining room a cosy quality.

Trellis

These are patterns based on a diagonal lattice or ribbon motif which have a distinctly garden flavour. Sometimes a floral or leafy motif is incorporated, trailing around the trellis. These patterns are usually fresh and clean, ideal for a bedroom, bathroom, hallway or conservatory, or to co-ordinate with floral patterns.

Spots

A popular and traditional pattern which is easy to live with, polka-dots on a white background are bright and cheerful, and work well in small rooms such as bathrooms, kitchens and children's bedrooms. White dots on a coloured background look more grown up, and spotted voiles make charming sheers.

Stripes

Stripes have always been popular, especially for walls and curtains. There are many kinds of stripes – stripes in a single colourway and multi-coloured stripes, broad stripes, narrow stripes and Regency stripes. Candy stripes are narrow, with the white and coloured stripes nearly equal in width.

Country motifs

These tend to be single-colour pictorial patterns. The pictures are inspired by country life and nature: farming and hunting scenes, images of birds, butterflies and plants. William Morris bird patterns fit into this category, as does the French *toile de Jouy*, an unglazed cotton fabric which continues to be made at Jouy outside Paris after 200 years in production.

Using samples

When selecting patterned fabric or wallpaper, try at least to get a small sample, about 10cm (4 in) square, to take home. You may find that the colour looks entirely different in natural light or by electric light compared with the strip lights used in the shop.

If you really can't decide if you like a pattern it's a good idea to buy a metre of fabric or a roll of wallpaper, pin it up in the room it is planned for and leave it for a few days. If you don't like the effect you can always use the fabric for cushion covers and the wallpaper for drawer linings.

Better still, allow time to get the shop to order a large sample from the manufacturer for you to take home. You will have to leave a returnable deposit and it may take a few weeks to come, but it's well worth taking the trouble rather than make an expensive mistake.

▲ **Co-ordinating patterns** Small samples can be quite misleading. Here the contrast between the floral and the stripe looks quite strong in the samples. But they blend happily in a larger piece because the colours are gentle and the stripes fairly narrow.

Small florals

For the country look floral patterns are a key element. They are very popular, and have been so for hundreds of years. This chapter looks at the way small florals can be used as wall coverings, curtain and upholstery fabrics, carpets and accessories.

The term floral is loosely used to describe a wide variety of prints from the familiar cabbage rose designs to leafy prints in a single colour. Yet within each floral category there is a huge range of subjects, styles and colourways. Within the broad category of rose prints, for example, you will find trailing roses, clusters of roses, roses scattered on a background, roses mixed with other flowers, large roses, botanically correct roses and highly stylized, almost abstract roses.

Small florals are pretty and this is, perhaps, their most obvious quality. It makes them easy to live with and particularly appropriate for the country look. In living rooms bright or pale florals can be used to create a sunny, cheerful feel. Darker patterns can be used to create a richer look, or a cosy, traditional room. The softer, paler small florals look lovely in bedrooms.

In recent years florals have become very popular for co-ordinating ranges,

▲ *A small floral collection* A floral design can be interpreted in many ways. The flowers can be stylized, as shown in the fabrics across the top; with leaves and flowers all in one colour as in the blue fabric; an all-over leaf design; or drawn from nature as the decoration used on the china plate and sugar bowl.

manufacturers offering matching bedlinen, wallpaper, curtains, cushion covers, and sometimes china. The patterns chosen may not, at first, seem to work together but they can be surprisingly successful as shown in the co-ordinated range in the bedroom on page 20.

Choosing florals

Florals can be divided into two groups – large and small – and the overall effect of these patterns is quite different. In general big and bold patterns should only be used for large lofty rooms. Small patterns – and patterns composed of pale or closely related colours – work best in modern homes, which tend to be smaller and have lower ceilings.

Small florals are easier and safer to use than large florals. Basically, small patterns, or no pattern at all, make a room look bigger and are less overwhelming in today's smaller homes. If the ceiling height is 2.6m (8ft 6in) or less, or the room is smaller than 3 x 3.6m (10 x 12ft), it is easier to use a small floral pattern than a large one.

Economy is another factor. With small florals there is less of the waste involved in matching large-drop patterned wallpapers.

By choosing a small, all-over floral, you can unify diverse elements in the room, such as furniture and decoration. The pattern complements rather than fights with the other decorative objects used in the scheme.

▶ **Florals for upholstery** *All-over designs look inviting and are practical for upholstery fabrics. This classic William Morris willow pattern works well with a range of country colours such as peach, buff and blue.*

▶ **A matter of scale** *The little sample (above right) looks bright and clear. The same design seen in a larger area (right) provides a gentle all-over pattern that links furniture, pictures and other decorative elements.*

◀ **Small-scale floral patterns** *The pattern on the tablecloth and curtain is small enough to enhance, rather than compete with, the pretty china and collection of baskets. Note how the green in the pattern is used for the door frame.*

◀ *Floral floors* *Floral prints can also be used on floors. Here a modern carpet design in pale pinks and grey co-ordinates with a flowers-and-stripes wallpaper and spotted drapes. These pale colours and subtle designs introduce a flowery theme while allowing the rich honey tones of old pine to dominate.*

▼ *A feast of florals* *For this cosy bedroom, a floral pattern in several colourways has been used to warm and pretty effect. The bedlinen, curtain fabric and wallpaper come from a co-ordinated range, but you can achieve this effect by mixing patterns with similar colours and scale. Patterns in rich colours may need to be tempered by neutral areas – like the cream walls and plain floor in this room.*

A rich palette

Most floral patterns incorporate several colours, giving you plenty of 'hooks' for your over-all decorating schemes. Some patterns lean towards a particular colour, while others give equal emphasis to several colours. This means that a floral wallpaper is highly adaptable. You can pick out one colour for the carpet and another for the woodwork.

Optical illusions

A pattern is not a fixed thing in the eye of the beholder. Viewed from close-up or in a sample, you may be able to see each flower, each petal, maybe even the stamens of a floral print. But from the middle of the room the same pattern begins to blur and soften. It becomes a pattern of, say, blue and white rather than white flowers against a blue ground.

If the print starts as a soft-edged design against a neutral background, without a great contrast in the colours, the detail dissolves and the eye sees a soft pattern of colours. But if the design is outlined in a dark colour or contrasts strongly with the background, the eye still 'reads' the flowers at a distance.

When you are thinking about pattern in a room, such optical effects are important considerations. Usually people do not want the walls to dominate, they are merely a background to set off the furniture and furnishings to best advantage. So a small pattern with pale colours in similar tones will intrude less than a larger pattern with highly contrasted colours. Strong contrast is best kept for halls and dining rooms where you spend less time; softer, less contrasting patterns for bedrooms and living rooms where you spend more time.

Sprigs

Floral patterns with their suggestion of country lanes and cottage gardens are a delightful way of bringing the countryside into our homes. While the large and small floral patterns discussed in earlier chapters sum up the country look, you'll find that sprigs are actually more popular. Sprigs are not, however, confined to floral motifs – bows, foliage and abstract motifs all come under this grouping. In fact sprigs are quite widespread, once you start looking for them you'll find them everywhere – in magazines, shops and in other people's homes, used on walls, curtains, carpets, tiles and ceramics.

Identifying sprigs
The difference between a sprig and other floral designs is the amount of background which shows between each motif. In a sprigged design the flowers, leaves, twigs or abstract motifs are scattered over the background so that when you stand back and view the

pattern from a distance, the overall impression is rather spotty. Individual motifs dance around the wall surface, rather than blending together to create a continuous pattern.

They are popular because they are easy to use and effortless to live with – they allow you to introduce a floral motif without overwhelming the room. The motifs may be naturalistic, simplified or so abstracted that their origins are barely recognizable – the fleur-de-lys is derived from the iris, for example.

The most common type of sprigged pattern has a pale background – often white, sometimes cream. These are fresh and springlike, ideal for small rooms to which they give a bright cottagey feel.

They can also be found with textured, spotted, striped or trellised backgrounds, but these background patterns are subtle with the sprig as the dominant feature.

Different motifs create different effects and you should bear this in mind

when selecting wallcoverings or fabric. Carefully rendered sprigs of formal flowers on a pale background look elegant and suit a formal setting such as a living room, or dining room, in a well-proportioned home.

Looser groups of wild flowers suit a less sophisticated setting – for example, bedrooms or living rooms with low ceilings, small windows and a generally rustic feel.

Simple, rather graphic motifs look extremely elegant used as part of a restrained, but pretty decorative scheme in a dining room – this type of pattern offering a compromise between the flowery and the abstract.

▼ *Simply sprigs*
Although the typical sprigged fabric or paper shows flowers on a plain white or cream background, plenty of other motifs and backgrounds are around – there's certainly a sprig for every occasion.

Sprigs for floors

Sprigged designs are becoming increasingly popular for floor coverings. Plain carpets are undoubtedly very attractive and also provide a useful setting for heavily patterned walls and furnishings, but they do show marks and wear and tear, especially the paler shades. A small, sprigged pattern will act as a camouflage and whilst it will not hide marks, it will distract from them by breaking up the surface. A single stain will jump out of a plain continuous surface, but will not be so apparent on a patterned surface because the eye will move to and fro from one motif to another, rather than lingering at a single point.

Halls and stairways

Because they are light and pretty these patterns are particularly suitable for walls in halls, landings, staircases, lobbies and dark nooks and crannies. They can be used to brighten dark corners and provide a decorative surface without being overwhelming. This is particularly important in a restricted space where the pattern will be seen close to. Sprigged carpets work well in these locations for the same reasons.

Kitchens

Sprigs, especially those on a white background are popular in kitchens because they offer a white surface which looks clean and hygienic, but also pro-

▲ Flowers underfoot

A sprigged carpet looks particularly pretty in a bedroom. Here the motif is in muted shades to complement the walls and curtains.

vide little accents of colour which can be used to tie together a colour scheme. They can either be used on wallpapers or on tiles. In the latter case the patterned tiles may be scattered amongst plain ones, preventing an otherwise plain surface from being too severe. Choose bright primary colours – reds, yellows or blues are good kitchen colours – and team the tiles with checked, striped or plain curtains and kitchen accessories in a co-ordinating colour.

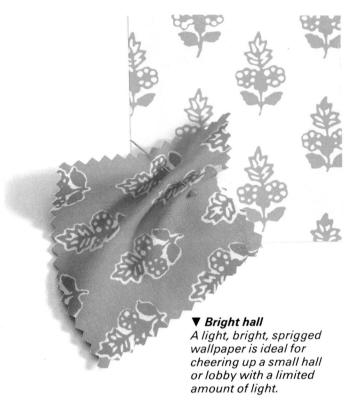

▼ Bright hall
A light, bright, sprigged wallpaper is ideal for cheering up a small hall or lobby with a limited amount of light.

▲ Old world charm
In an old-fashioned, country kitchen a red and white fir tree sprig makes a cheerful background for pine cupboards and lovely traditional, floral curtains.

▲ Sprigged tiles
Sprigged tiles with a bright blue and yellow motif on a white background look fresh and sparky in the kitchen.

Bathrooms

Sprigs on a white background are often used in bathrooms for the same reason as they are used in kitchens – the white is associated with cleanliness while the motif adds a touch of colour. Many manufacturers produce ranges of co-ordinating tiles and fabric. For a really pretty effect choose pastel colours; ideally the pattern should incorporate both warm and cool shades – pinks, blues and greens. Tile around the splashbacks, combining plain tiles with patterned ones, and use the sprigged fabric to make Austrian blinds. A plain carpet in one of the pastel shades will add a slab of solid colour.

▲ Sprigs and swags
A sprigged fabric in pinks and greens with a co-ordinating wallpaper border is attractively swagged with bows in a matching striped fabric.

◄ Keep it cool
Two frilled, sprigged fabrics in blue, green and white, set against a delicately patterned blue wallpaper, create a restful atmosphere.

walls, and at the window, will hold the whole scheme together.

For another simple bedroom treatment start with a range of sprigged bed linens – there are many to choose from. Match one of the colours in the motif and use that on the walls – applying the paint as a simple colour-wash, or sponge it on. The effect should be subtle, so that the colour is delicate and does not create a distracting pattern. At the windows either use pale curtains in a co-ordinating fabric, or choose plain roller blinds in a neutral colour taken from the pattern – cream or a golden straw colour for example. Natural floor materials would look good – either bare floorboards, coir or sisal matting. A few rugs in a similar colour range would soften the look. Rich, golden pine furniture would look particularly pretty with this scheme.

◄ Pale prettiness
This unusual bedroom has been decorated with fabrics and papers from a co-ordinated range. Sprigs in both the canopy and on the wallpaper are in identical green and yellow, while the canopy background of pale grey moir matches the wallpaper below the dado. Striped jade lining for the canopy, enhances the theme.

Sprigs in the bedroom

Use a pink and green rosebud motif on the walls of a small bedroom. Team it with curtains in the same fabric, or a co-ordinating range, lined with pink to give the room a rosy glow. Choose a crushed raspberry carpet, and plain white bed linen with broderie anglaise frills and details. The cool whites will be balanced by the warm pinks and the sprigs on the

Co-ordinating sprigs

Sprigs can be mixed and matched with other patterns, with mini-prints and large florals, for example, and also with plains. Sprigged curtains with a plain lining look very pretty, especially if you turn the lining back when draping the curtains into the tiebacks. Or use a large sprigged motif for cushions, with a smaller design for the frills. There are lots of wallpaper and fabric collections which have mix and match schemes that include large and small sprigs designed to co-ordinate.

Sprigs on a textured background

Small sprigs, widely scattered over a white background, can be distracting if used on a large unbroken surface. Because there is such a strong contrast between the background and the motif the eye jumps from one element to another and never finds anywhere to rest. The closer in tone the motif is to the background, the less this happens, so if, for example, you are going to wallpaper a big room, choose a design which has less background showing, or one in which the background is quite strongly coloured or textured.

There are many patterns which have a light, but textured background – a subtle sponged or marbled effect, for example. Others have a spotted or trellis background pattern. These reduce the contrast between motif and background, making these designs suitable for large rooms where a plain background would not be so effective.

▲▶ **Mixing and matching**
Combining sprigged fabrics and papers with other patterns can be rewarding. Above, a sprigged wallpaper is set above a striped one and a sprigged blind makes a lining for the pretty floral curtains. Right, a harmony of blues is created by using a small sprig with a blue background for tablecloth and curtains, and one with a creamy background for the walls.

Mini-prints

Mini-prints are incredibly versatile and easy to use, and are particularly well suited to country homes, especially those with smaller rooms and lower ceilings. Their popularity goes back to the very early days of printed wallpapers and fabrics in the 18th century. Their scale suited the elegant proportions and restrained decor of contemporary Georgian homes. The early Victorians also favoured the tiny, all-over sprigged designs, usually in darker, richer colours. Towards the end of the 19th century, however, mini-prints dwindled in popularity as the larger, bolder, stylized patterns that we now associate with Liberty prints became the latest craze.

Mini-prints came back into fashion in the 1970s. The trend was spearheaded by Laura Ashley, whose designs were based on 18th century and Indian woodblocks. Laura Ashley designs – tiny repeating motifs and small sprigs – became the rage for wallpapers, furnishing fabrics and high fashion clothes. Laura Ashley's influence was immense, and many of her designs have become classics. Mini-prints seem to have become a permanent part of the design repertoire.

People who had used plain colours throughout the 1960s started to introduce pattern into their homes, they even began to mix patterns: mini-prints with mini-prints and then mini-prints with

▲ Mini selection
Choose from a wide range of mini prints for your country home. They can be used anywhere around the home from tiling to curtains. This selection shows some of the varieties of mini-prints which are available in the shops.

large prints. Manufacturers responded to demand by developing co-ordinated ranges with plains, large prints and miniprints. Tile manufacturers and carpet manufacturers followed suit with ranges of tiny and sprigged prints.

Choosing patterns and colours

Mini-print wallpapers, fabrics, tiles and floorcoverings are available in a huge range of designs and colourways, so where do you start? If you want to mix patterns there are several ways of finding designs which will go together. The easiest method is to stick to one family of colours, blues, for instance. The pretty

◄ A cool blue room
Co-ordinating wallpaper and fabric in a blue foliage print combine attractively with a geometric print in another shade of blue.

blue bedroom on the facing page shows how successful this approach can be. If, however, you want to use more than one colour, find a linking colour which appears in every pattern – it may be the dominant colour in one pattern but only a minor theme in another. When working with large multi-coloured prints select one or two colours from the main print and find a mini-print in these colours. In the room at the bottom of this page a delicate sage green mini-print has been teamed with large florals – it is used above the dado rail and also in the panels below.

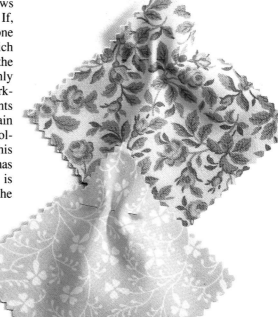

◄ On a pink theme
Offcuts have been used to make these pretty scatter cushions – pink links the different patterns.

▼ Large and small
A subtle green mini-print is teamed with floral curtains and an exuberant rose border.

◄ **Strong colour**
This bright sunshine yellow miniprint 'reads' as a single colour from a distance because the background colour is so strong and the dots are close together.

How we see mini-prints

Because they are small, mini-prints tend to 'read' as a single colour when viewed from a distance – in a large room, or down a corridor, for example. Denser patterns will read as a dark shade of the colour, while those with more white background showing will read as pale.

If you intend to use a mini-print on a large surface, stand back from it to see what the overall colour is – it may well be different from the colour which dominates when you look at it close-to. Half-closing your eyes will help you see how it will look.

The way you see a mini-print also depends on the degree of contrast within the pattern. If the colours in the pattern are close in tone they will tend to merge together. If, however, the colours are highly contrasted, blue on a white background for example, the individual motifs will hold their form for a greater distance.

The space between the motifs is also important: if the sprigs are close together they will tend to merge, but if they are widely scattered on a plain background they will be seen as separate elements for a greater distance. If the motifs are both widely spaced and in strong colour contrast to the background they will remain separate even longer – for example, black stars on a white ground will remain distinct, whereas grey stars on a cream background will quickly merge to create a single colour.

Practical uses

Because they are small and dainty, mini-prints will not overwhelm a small room. They are often used very effectively in small bathrooms, bedrooms or hallways, where, teamed with a plain colour, they can make the room feel quite spacious, especially if pale, cool colours are selected.

One great advantage of mini-prints is that the small scale of the patterns means that they are easy to use in those oddly-shaped rooms so characteristic of older homes. A wallpaper with a small pattern and a small repeat can be used where there are sloping ceilings, uneven walls and corners which aren't square. The pattern will hide any unevenness in

> **tip**
>
> **Mixing mini-prints**
> Take the worry out of mixing patterns and colours by choosing from a fully co-ordinated range of wallpapers, curtain fabrics and bedlinens.

◄ **Strong pattern**
By contrast this relatively subtle pattern holds its form at a distance because there is a strong contrast between the widely spaced motifs and the pale background.

the wall surface where a plain colour would show it up.

Small overall patterns also help to break up large areas and, by distracting the eye, camouflage awkward spots. A large pattern with a large repeat is both difficult to match when walls are out of the true and would draw attention to any structural irregularities in the room.

Mini-print designs are also practical for carpets in rooms and hallways that get heavy use, as they tend not to show the dirt in the way that plain carpets do. They can be teamed with plain walls or walls with a small pattern.

On walls you could even take a mini-print up to dado level with a plain colour above.

Checks and ginghams

This large group of traditional patterns is bright, cheerful, easy to use and generally cheap. They appeal in particular to people who prefer a simple, uncluttered interpretation of the country look as a satisfactory way of introducing pattern, texture and colour without using the more obvious florals.

Gingham, madras, prince of wales and hound's-tooth checks are all traditional check patterns. Gingham was always made from a sturdy woven cotton, madras from a much finer, thinner cotton, while prince of wales and hound's-tooth checks were woven wool fabrics. However, modern weaving and printing methods mean that it is now possible to have a hound's-tooth check printed on, say, linen; or a gingham type check in fine wool.

Using checks and ginghams

Checks and ginghams are fresh, crisp and cheerful, and they are an ideal way to capture the simplicity of a rustic country cottage. They can be mixed together on cushions, chair seats and small armchairs. They aren't normally used on large items like sofas as the pattern would look too busy and would be visually disturbing. However, there are exceptions to every rule and in a room with a lot of strong flat colours a gingham sofa can look dramatic. Checks and ginghams can also be used for curtains, and for small items such as table cloths and lampshades.

Checked fabrics and wallpapers can be used to brighten up a plain room or as the starting point for a room design, pulling out colours from the pattern in the same way as can be done with floral patterns (see pages 17–20). They can also be used in a single-colour room – combining green and white checks with green walls and white woodwork, for example. Finally you can, with care, mix a selection of checks of different sizes – and even different colours – together to create a bright, rather jolly effect. This would be fun in a children's room, a family room or a kitchen.

◀ A checked collection
The traditional gingham check comes in a range of sizes and colours, each fabric using a single colour with white. Checked patterns are equally diverse in size and they can also introduce two, three or more colours into the pattern.

Checks in the kitchen

Checks and ginghams which combine white with one other colour look particularly good in kitchens and kitchen diners. Patterns containing a large proportion of white always look fresh and clean, a quality we instinctively seek in a room where food is prepared. The white in the pattern also works well with white enamelled and glazed surfaces, the traditional finishes for sinks, tiles and stoves. These days electrical goods such as cookers, dishwashers and fridges are available in a whole range of colours, but fashion is very fickle and you may find you tire of brown or red kitchen equipment, while white never goes out of fashion.

Checks and ginghams look particularly attractive with the woods used for traditional kitchen furniture – pine, oak and beech, but they also work well with darker woods.

The use of checks with plain washed walls, bare wooden floors and country furniture can be traced back to cottage interiors of the past. This image of the typical cosy country kitchen has been kept alive in many ways, particularly in the illustrations in traditional children's books. They have re-appeared in recent years in television advertisements for products that the manufacturers wish us to associate with traditional values – with naturalness and wholesomeness.

The reason for the historic popularity of these cotton materials was above all practicality; they were tough, easy to wash, and cheap. This country style can also be seen in French provincial homes and in another form in the interiors of American colonial homes. In the American interpretation of the style, checked fabrics were often combined with naturally darker woods or dark wood finishes. All these styles have a long history and have never entirely dropped out of fashion.

Checks for a quick lift

Checks are simple patterns, but they nevertheless have an impact which is out of all proportion to the amount of the pattern used. Even in a room full of patterns, checks and ginghams will stand out because of the simple geometry of the design motif – repeating squares, straight lines and right angles – which the eye can read and retain very easily. Stripes also have this quality.

Less geometric designs such as florals are more complex, and less direct. So a small floral will tend to merge into the background, whereas a check on the same scale will demand attention. Floral and other asymmetrical patterns rely on colour and scale for their impact. For

▲ **Kitchen charm**
This very simple white-walled country kitchen is taken out of the ordinary by its cheerful gingham curtains, blue and white china and the bright splashes of red in flowers and pepperpots.

◀ **Mix and match**
You need to be bold to use a check on a large piece of furniture – but it works beautifully, teaming confidently with the blue and white patterns on the walls, curtains and lampshade and china.

▶ Checks for impact
A checked curtain in warm shades of russet, olive and cream hung across the garden door gives a warm, dramatic glow to the hall, which is otherwise simply decorated in matching shades.

this reason checks can be used to give a quick, inexpensive lift to the way a room feels – the most appropriate applications, however, are in the kitchen. Choose a predominant colour, it might be a red floor, or even red trims and knobs on built-in units, and find a fabric that matches. Use it to make cottage-style curtains tied back with bows. Make up some flat squab cushions for your kitchen chairs, finishing them off with bows.

Finally, you can use the same fabric to make a table cloth and a few small items such as oven mitts, tea cloths and perhaps a tea cosy or apron. You will find that you have achieved a transformation and given your kitchen a new lease of life for very little expenditure of either time or effort.

Checks for children

Checks and ginghams are ideal for children's rooms, where bright, stimulating colours and cheap but hardwearing materials are essential. Brilliant primary reds and blues work well, but any combination of strong clear colours will look equally good. The checks can be combined with patterns designed for children – these are sometimes based on motifs such as trains, cars, toys or on

their favourite story book characters. Their simple flat colours on plain, often white, backgrounds team easily with checks or plains in bright colours.

Blue and white

Of all the colours used in the country home, the combination of blue and white is the most popular and persistent. This is particularly reflected in the ranges of blue and white chinaware and tiles, in designs derived from almost every part of the world and every period of history – think of delft tiles, and the willow pattern. Similarly, blue and white gingham is ever popular – and can be used creatively in any kitchen to suggest that country look, especially if you already have a collection of blue and white china.

Large and small checks

Many fabric companies produce the same check in large or small versions. This gives you a great deal of flexibility in devising treatments for soft furnishings. You could, for example, use a large check for curtains or roman blinds, and a smaller version for cushions, chairs and tablecloths. You can even use large and small checks on the same item. Use the small check to make a border and tie-backs for curtains in a large check,

▲*Checking it up*
This room cleverly combines different types of blue and white checks – on the bed curtains, the valance and the wallpaper – with blue and white striped sheeting and an abstract patterned rug. The surprise is the floor, stained in checks of warm brown and the natural wood.

▲ Floor check
An Edwardian tiled hall floor strikingly mixes squared patterns with diagonal patterns in a rich yet subtle combination of rust, black, grey and cream, mellowed with age.

▼ Sitting ducks
The bright primary colours of the sunny check wallpaper and the great bowls of scarlet pelargoniums make this old fashioned, stone-floored sitting room seem very warm and welcoming.

▲ Chequerboard
One of the oldest floor designs in the world must be the black and white chequerboard, set here on the diagonal. The design is popular in halls and kitchens, and can be done in tiles, lino or painted wood.

▲ Cheerful china
Perk up a modern, streamlined kitchen with rustic plates in bold blue and white checks.

◄ Bathroom tiles
Tiny check tiles make a welcome break for the eye in a blue and yellow floral bathroom.

▼ Childish checks
A dream bedroom for a little girl teams floral curtains with wallpaper in tiny pink and white checks, with matching larger checks for the mirror frame and dressing table curtain.

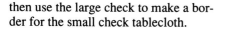

then use the large check to make a border for the small check tablecloth.

Lining up
Checks and ginghams can be used straight-on or on the diagonal. Cut the fabric on the diagonal to add interest to the borders, cushions or tie-backs. Experiment to see what happens when you gather the check in one direction – the horizontal lines along the gather show more strongly as the vertical lines disappear into the folds. Use this phenomenon for shirred tie-backs or for a ruched band at the top of a valance.

Trellis

Trellis patterns in all their forms are a useful addition to the collection of country motifs. In its simplest form trellis consists of a basic geometric diamond or lattice-work pattern, usually drawn with thin lines on a plain, pale background. On wallpaper and furnishing fabrics, however, trellis is often combined with a floral motif, either sprigs scattered within the rectangles, or with floral or leafy motifs twining around the basic geometric structure. It is also a popular design woven in self-coloured, textured fabrics like damask, jacquard or cotton twill.

Trellis patterns may be large or small, simple or complicated, but apart from a few rather severe or violently coloured designs they are almost always appropriate in a country style home.

▲ Trellis variety
Just a few of the immense variety of trellis patterns: trellis with a formal flower design inside the diamond; a mini-print trellis; a trellis with a large floral superimposed on it, and, on the table, a double trellis with a floral motif.

▲ Cane, pine and bamboo
A green bamboo trellis wallpaper is used to great effect in a hall with stripped pine doors and an interesting bamboo display cabinet. The wildflower curtain fabric adds vital touches of scarlet and mustard to the scheme.

◄ Basic style
A really simple trellis pattern can be used as a neutral background: here it works as a restful complement to floral curtains, a mini-print blind and some rather exotic cane furniture.

Types of trellis pattern

Basic lattice pattern These simple geometric patterns – a line against a pale background – are particularly useful in situations where you want to introduce a bit of surface interest and colour, but retain a formal feel. In a basically neutral room a creamy wallpaper with a trellis motif in a pale ochre would add a touch of colour and texture so subtle that it would only become apparent on close inspection. A pale, widely spaced stripe would have a similar effect, but stripes seem grand and formal, whereas a trellis suggests the controlled informality of a well-managed garden.

Bold contrasts Be careful how you use plain, wide trellis in a dark colour against a pale background or the other way around. On their own on a large surface they can set up disturbing visual effects, so only use them in a room in which the wall surface will be broken up by furniture, shelving and paintings, or above a dado, perhaps rather than on a mass of wall.

Implied trellis In some patterns the trellis is implied rather than drawn, so the design forms are organised in repeating diamond shapes, but the actual trellis is missing. Nevertheless, the eye interprets the pattern as a trellis.

Double trellis Another variation on the trellis motif are the double trellis patterns in which the straight lines are duplicated. There are also various kinds of basket-weave designs, generally found in brown and green colours, which have a distinctly rustic feel like real trellis.

▼ Garden illusion
Designed to give the effect of nailed white garden trellis, this paper creates a striking background for a garden room complete with cane furniture and trailing plants.

▲ Implied trellis
The trellis pattern in this deep glowing paper is actually formed by the spaces between the motifs. Its rich colours give the room a high Victorian feel.

Trellis with floral or leafy motifs

These trellis patterns are a happy combination of floral or leafy patterns, with an underlying geometric structure that holds them together and gives them a more formal feel.

The patterns may be large or small scale, simple or complicated. Generally they are on a white or light background which gives the pattern a light and airy feel. The scale of the pattern should be chosen for the space in which it will be seen – a large open trellis would work in a large room but not in a narrow hallway. A small trellis on the other hand will look like a small floral when seen at a distance in a large room.

The trellis can be big, bold and quite ornate with curls and twirls like wrought iron grills. This could well be the dominant feature of the room, and should be used with care, for curtains perhaps, using plainer patterns elsewhere in the room.

All the climbing plants have been used as trellis motifs at some time, either in a natural form or in a simpler, more abstract interpretation. The most popular is the rose, followed by ivy, but wisteria, passion-flower and honeysuckle feature too. Sometimes the trellis is lightly scattered with plant tendrils, sometimes they are massed so that the framework is obscured by the buds, leaves and flower heads.

In some particularly pretty forms of the pattern the diamond-shaped structure is provided by loops of ribbon, with exuberant swags of flowers dotted about, either at the intersections or in the centre of the spaces. Other popular trellis patterns can be made up with bamboo and cane which give the room a slightly oriental flavour.

▲ The cottage look
A very pretty and informal version of trellis in primrose, blue and green looks charming in a cottage living room with pine furniture, baskets and rustic trappings.

▼ Hothouse trellis
A deep-diamond trellis, patterned with luxuriant foliage, gives an exotic planthouse feel to a bathroom rich in hanging baskets and interesting ornaments.

Ways of using trellis

Floral or leafy trellis patterns are a lovely way of introducing a light, bright, spring-like feel into a room. It works particularly well in living rooms, especially those which connect directly to the garden or a conservatory where the suggestion of garden architecture would be particularly appropriate. They can also look very pretty in bedrooms.

The lozenge form of the trellis pattern is a useful device, because you can use it to modify the optical proportions of a room. If the ceilings are low, consider using a trellis pattern to give it height. To do this effectively the pattern should be taller than it is broad and the pattern small enough to allow plenty of repeats between floor and ceiling. It can also be used to give width – to a short wall at the end of a hall for example. In that case the lozenges should be wider than they are high.

The size of a trellis pattern is an important factor in the way in which it is used. Very small patterns are useful as co-ordinating patterns which can be used as a contrast to more eye-catching designs, providing a subtle contrast which is neither plain nor boring. A wallpaper with a small trellis and flower motif could, for example, be teamed with curtains and furnishings in a large floral design.

A wallpaper in a larger pattern would work well teamed with a splash of a good strong colour – in curtains for example. Remember that if you do choose a large scale pattern you must allow enough for matching the repeats which may make decorating a room expensive.

The background in most trellis patterns is pale, and the contrast between the motif and the background holds the pattern even at quite small sizes. This means that most trellis patterns are strong and will 'read' even when the trellis itself is quite small and seen at a distance. The greater the contrast the more the pattern holds.

▼ **Large and small**
This leaf trellis looks clean and fresh on two sizes of glazed tiles.

▶ **Summer bower**
A wildflower trellis gives the sitting room a year-round summer feel.

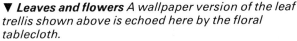
▼ **Leaves and flowers** A wallpaper version of the leaf trellis shown above is echoed here by the floral tablecloth.

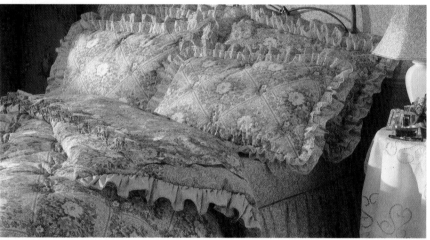

▲ Touches of trellis
A formal country bedroom has a green and cream trellis carpet, an interesting Chinese lacquer work chest with a trellis front, and a black and gold trellis lampshade.

▲ Trellis with frills
Exuberant flowers and frills rampage over trellis patterned bed-linen.

▼ Country trellis
This trellis pattern on the curtains will only be apparent when drawn.

Trellis on furnishings

If the background is a more definite colour, there will be less contrast between the motif and the background, making the pattern less visually busy. This type of trellis is particularly useful on furnishings where a large, contrasting pattern can be very distracting. You'll also find that on furnishing fabrics with pale backgrounds the floral motif wanders across the spaces between the trellis, another device which breaks up the spaces and makes them less distracting.

Be careful when matching patterns and allow for the extra material you will need to get it right. A badly matched trellis or diamond pattern will look dreadful if the apex of the diamond runs unevenly along the top of curtains, for example.

The more elaborate designs are best used in small quantities in situations which show off the design – perhaps on a roller blind, or for dramatic effect on a hall wall.

Diamond, double diamond and trellis patterns are traditional patterns for quilted bedspreads, particularly in Italian quilting, a decorative form of corded quilting.

Stripes

From the simplicity of ticking to the sophistication of Regency, stripes offer the decorator plenty of styles, designs and colourways to choose from. Slender and restrained, or big and bold, the stripes may be alone or combined with a pattern, and they may be alternated with floral motifs, or decorated with entwined foliage and flowers for a very fresh country look.

Stripes are not only very varied, but they are also extremely versatile. They can be used horizontally or vertically to enhance or restrain the proportions of a room by making it look taller or wider, or used on the diagonal to create unusual borders or trimmings for other fabrics. They can enhance other plain or patterned fabrics, and add depth without rivalling the other designs used.

▲ **Striped variations**
There are many ways in which stripes are used in fabrics and wallpapers: they may be vertical or horizontal, broad or narrow, monochrome or multi-coloured, and they may be combined with other patterns or motifs, for a wealth of styles and effects.

▲ *Bright delight*
A printed fabric with wide, multi-coloured stripes and bold, floral motifs, makes a bright and cheerful curtain. The fabric is so eye-catching that an ornate curtain style is not required.

▼ *Elegant option*
In contrast to the picture above, the stripes here are designed to be very subtle, adding interest to the walls and linking the colours of the curtains with the bedding and paintwork.

Printed, woven or embossed?

On wallpapers, stripes may be printed, or they may be embossed in order to achieve a self-coloured effect – sometimes a combination of both is used to give the design depth and interest. Stripes are also printed on to fabrics, or they may be woven, either in a self-colour with a difference in texture defining the stripe, in a contrast colour, or a combination of both.

The dyed yarn in woven designs becomes an integral part of the cloth, so these fabrics often have more texture and depth of colour than printed fabrics, where the dye sits on the surface of the cloth. This is not always the case, however, and many printed fabrics have incredibly vivid and intense colours. Texture is obviously an important element in self-coloured textiles in which the stripes are created by changes of weave and texture.

◀ **Using stripes**
A *The horizontal lines of the painted cornicing, picture rail, dado and skirting make this room look more spacious by emphasizing the wall-to-wall dimensions.*
B *Wide stripes can be difficult to use on soft covers because it is essential to match them well, but used, as here, with a formal style, they create a very neat look.*
C *Although stripes are usually used vertically on soft furnishings, they are positioned horizontally on the back of this chair to emphasize the shape and to create a smooth line rolling round the arms and down on to the seat. A cushion in the wide stripe of the sofa provides a link.*
D *Checked fabrics at the windows provide new elements of colour and pattern, but their straight lines tie in with the stripes used elsewhere.*

Printed stripes tend to be smoother than woven stripes as the dye 'takes' better on an even surface. Sometimes stripes are printed on to a textured fabric to deliberately exploit the way the uneven surface breaks up and softens the printed design.

Playing tricks with stripes

There are all sorts of ways in which you can deceive the eye with colour and pattern – stripes, for example, can be used to modify the appearance of a room. Thin, vertical stripes emphasize height rather than width and can therefore make a room look taller. Narrow stripes can be used to draw attention to a particularly tall window, or, if you find the height excessive, wide stripes can be used to make it look less tall.

Horizontal stripes, provided by border wallpapers, or even strongly linear devices like dado rails and picture rails,

make a tall room seem broader by drawing attention to the wall-to-wall dimension rather than the height.

Working with stripes

Stripes are most easy to use on flat, rectangular surfaces, so that you avoid the problems associated with working straight lines round irregular shapes and surfaces, creating odd joins and converging lines – flat blinds like roller blinds and Roman blinds are therefore an ideal application. In either case a striped fabric works well without any further embellishment.

If you want to add interest to striped blinds, you can play with their linear qualities. On a Roman blind, for example, you can make a border in a plain contrasting material, or you can use the same stripes at right angles, or even a stripe in a contrasting colour.

When heading curtains with pinch or

goblet pleats, it is usually possible to make the pleats follow the pattern of the stripes – spend some time working out how the stripes will fall before you finish the side seams so that you can make adjustments to the width if necessary. One of the joys of these cheaper fabrics is that you can afford to be lavish with quantities – use two or even two and a half times the width of the curtain track or pole and make the curtains longer by about 5cm (2in) so that they cascade on to the floor.

Stripes can be used on soft furnishings, but be careful as there will be a lot of wastage with certain kinds of patterns. Choose very narrow or simple stripes in which the matching problems are minimal, or wider stripes overlaid with a tracery of floral motifs, so that the underlying stripes are partially masked, again avoiding too obvious mismatches of repeats.

Use stripes as piping, binding, borders and frills for all sorts of soft furnishings, as a contrast to plain or spotted fabrics. For cushions that combine stripes and florals, place a floral motif in the centre of the cushion cover and make a mitred frame in a matching striped fabric. Striped fabrics also work well for the whole cushion, particularly in one colour plus white which is very fresh and clean when combined with floral or plain fabrics and furnishings.

You could have fun in the kitchen by teaming red and white spots with stripes. Trim a spotted cushion with piping and a 2.5cm (1in) striped frill. Curtains in the same spotted fabric can also be trimmed with a 2.5cm (1in) border of the same, and the striped fabric can be used to make bow tie-backs. The effect is fresh, jolly and very country.

Striped rugs and runners are useful for bringing the flooring into a room's decorative scheme, by picking out the colours of the main flooring and those of the walls or

◄ **Refreshing stripe**
A stripe of one colour plus white, makes a fresh and appealing Austrian blind, and the scalloped shape is highlighted by a frill in the same fabric. The stripe also lines the white curtains.

▼ **Have a break**
Wallpapers with narrow stripes add height to a room, but if the effect is too dramatic, the horizontal elements of a dado or picture rail and wallpaper border will temper the effect.

▲ Light relief
*Striped cushions, trimmed
with lace to soften their
hard lines, help to break up
the overall effect of the
pattern on the bedspread.
The window dressing
combines both fabrics.*

▼ Easy elegance
*Ticking has an understated
elegance and simplicity
which is easy to live with.
It's an inexpensive fabric,
so use it in lavish
quantities, with curtains
spilling on to the floor.*

furnishings. For floors in halls and on staircases, use striped runners in a flat herringbone or ribbed weave. These are traditional, hard-wearing and relatively inexpensive. They will protect the main flooring, and at the same time provide important decorative interest.

Country farmhouse

For a rustic, farmhouse look, choose plain stripes with simple wallpapers and natural materials. Plain, candy-striped wallpaper is ideal, and looks particularly attractive when used in conjunction with a dado rail. Use the stripe either above or below the dado rail, and team it with a plain version of the same colour.

Ticking, an old-fashioned utility cloth, with a characteristic herringbone weave, is an excellent fabric to use for this look. Originally hand-woven in linen as a covering for feather mattresses, it had to be sturdy and dense to keep the feathers in and, presumably, to keep the ticks out. Like many of the fabrics which have been with us a long time, ticking has been revamped in recent times to give it new qualities and is now available in many other colours besides the traditional black on white.

Coloured ticking looks just right made up as squab cushions on kitchen chairs. For a stunning, but unfussy bedroom treatment, a four-poster bed can be dressed in blue and white ticking – add a self-border with the stripes at right angles for a final flourish. A similarly dramatic effect can be achieved by using a plain fabric and lining it with ticking in the same colour plus white. This combination of plain and striped fabrics will work just as well for window treatments.

Striped tea cloth fabric, also known as glass cloth, is usually made of cotton, linen, or a mixture of both. It has a fresh, crisp texture which suits the simple country look, with colour-washed walls, and old pine or painted and distressed furniture. It is very effective for fresh bedroom curtains and valances, or you could use it in the kitchen for fresh curtains or tablecloths.

Muslin is another natural fabric which is just right for the informal country look. It comes self-striped or plain, natural or white. A self-striped ivory muslin, ideally with a silky finish, would make lovely billowing draperies on a four-poster bed and at the window.

Cottage stripes

For the country cottage look, co-ordinate stripes and florals, or choose combined stripe and floral designs. There are lots of co-ordinating ranges of fabrics and wallpapers available which include plain stripes, stripes with florals, small florals, mini-prints and plains. It is the combination of these which will achieve this look.

In cosy cottage rooms, where florals mixed with other florals would be too much, stripes provide pattern and texture without being overwhelming. You could combine a large floral print in strong or fresh colours with a sprig and stripe which includes two colours from the main fabric.

Sophisticated stripes

The illusion of height given by stripes adds elegance to any room, and they are an ideal wall treatment for the more sophisticated country house look. On walls, however, avoid bumpy or uneven surfaces and rooms with odd angles as it will be difficult to get the stripes to line up, and irregularities will be only too obvious.

Stripes became very popular in the Regency period, around the end of the eighteenth century and the beginning of the nineteenth century. This style was essentially light and graceful, but suited to domestic interiors, unlike some of the rather grand styles which had preceded it. If you prefer antique or reproduction furniture and rather restrained surroundings, a Regency stripe or any fine multiple stripe will look wonderful in the reception areas of your home. Used in your living room it will create a light and airy atmosphere.

Keep the walls uncluttered – just one or two framed prints or paintings on each wall – and choose rather elaborate window treatments in plain or striped fabrics. The linear quality of elegant striped fabrics is particularly suited to elaborate draperies with lots of loops, gathers and swags, emphasizing the movement and flow of the fabric.

Textural stripes are ideal for upholstery because they add depth without fussiness. Used in these formal surroundings they look extremely smart.

▲ Elegant stripes
Striped wallpapers have an elegance which is perfect for the sophisticated country house look. Here, where stripes on the whole wall would make the room look too high, the effect is tempered with border papers and plainer paper.

▶ Rose-bud co-ordinates
A fine example of how to use a range of co-ordinated striped and floral fabrics: the main, rose-bud fabric is used for the curtains, and the motif is used again on the bedding with a striped background; the stripe alone makes a fine sheet and valance.

Country~style motifs

Animals and birds, fruits and vegetables, flowers and trees are just some of the images which fall into the category of country motifs. The images are everywhere in the country-style home: on textiles, wallpapers, tiles and china, and on purely decorative items like wooden cut-outs, ornaments, prints and paintings.

Sometimes a motif is used singly, but it may also make up part of a larger design, perhaps mixed with other country motifs or used with geometrics. Large designs may capture a whole country scene, such as the lovely Toile de Jouy fabrics from France, which are both charming and elegant.

Traditional patterns

Many of the most familiar country motifs have been used for hundreds of years to decorate the home, changing their form slightly to suit the fashion of each period of history. Classical motifs of horses, cats and mythological creatures were taken from the Ancient World. From Mediaeval paintings and tapestries came images of hunting scenes, animals and flowers, some of which, such as squirrels, thistles, strawberries and snails, are still familiar motifs in the contemporary country-style home.

Ideas were taken from China, India and the Middle East – all areas which had strong trading links with Europe. From China came peacocks, sprigs of peach and cherry blossom, waterlilies, tumbling mountain streams and scenes of everyday life. From India came designs of leaves and vines, and the 'tree of life' motif which is still widely used. From the Middle East came many of the

▲ **In the farmyard**
Farmyard animals and birds are some of the most popular country motifs. They can be found around the country-style home in a range of guises: on wallpapers, plates, tiles, and even as wooden cut-outs.

naturalistic designs we know, including scenes of flowers, birds and animals, gardens and trees.

At the end of the last century, the brilliant designers of the Arts and Crafts movement incorporated many motifs from Asia and the Middle East into their own flowing designs. The well-known peacock feather design, still produced by Liberty's, for example, is reminiscent of the peacock designs of China. Leafy images and the pine motif from India. which is now the basic motif in paisley

▲ *Cockerel tapestry cushion*

designs, were also widely adopted and modified by many designers.

These designs were taken from all sorts of things: rugs, fine hand-painted prints and wallpapers, decorative furniture and porcelain, which were all imported into Europe. Designers quickly adopted motifs taken from these imports, not just because they were attractive, but because they were popular and, by the late 19th century, some of these had been compiled in encyclopedias of ornamentation, providing inspiration for decorators and designers.

Popular interpretations

As designers continue to produce new products, decorative motifs are constantly being updated, so that most of the country motifs seen today are not replicas of the original designs, but modified versions adapted for the popular market.

The story of chintz makes a fine example of how motifs were copied, modified and developed. Chintz originally featured colourful Indian designs of plants and animals, but the fabric was such a huge success in Britain that local manufacturers started to produce imitations. They copied the overall feel of the designs and adopted some of the original motifs, such as exotic birds and hothouse flowers, but they also included their own motifs, based on British plants and flowers, birds, butterflies and small mammals.

Animals, birds and insects

Today's country-style homes contain motifs reflecting the countryside around them. Country manors abound with images of horses, dogs and hunting scenes, and of freshwater fish like trout and salmon – all images of favourite outdoor pursuits. Farmhouse or cottage style homes contain images of pigs, sheep and chickens, and of small country

creatures from the hedgerows, like field mice, hedgehogs, rabbits and squirrels.

Many of these animal motifs appear in new forms, but as a result of the increased interest in traditional styles, some of the old motifs are being copied or emulated. Wooden cut-outs of sheep, pigs and cows can be hung on the wall or propped up at the back of a shelf or kitchen worktop. These wooden cut-outs are often naively painted, sometimes following traditional designs and colours for a simple, rustic look.

Bird motifs, symbolizing life, peace and freedom, have been popular in many cultures and periods of the past. In Mediaeval times, the dove, with its biblical symbolism, was used in tapestries and even stained glass, as were common European birds like the wren. Later, the exotic birds depicted on Indian chintzes caught on, and today there is a wide range of motifs to choose from. Motifs of common birds, like robins or blue tits work well in a rustic, farmhouse style, as well as farmyard ducks, chickens and roosters, while more exotic birds like peacocks look best in the country house style.

The insects most commonly depicted

▲ *Spot the stencil*
A very rustic tablecloth, stencilled with a cockerel motif to match the spotted blue and white china, transforms an old pine table into a delightful place for tea. Large spots, also stencilled on to the cloth, emphasize the connection.

▼ *Flying ducks?*
A group of large china ducks makes a novel and rather special kitchen collection particularly as more can be added to the group as time goes by. Placed by an open window, they look as if they could take off into the sunshine.

in the country-style home are bees and butterflies. These colourful creatures recall sunny summer days, fresh breezes and the freedom of open spaces. For the kitchen, look out for bee and honey pot motifs on tea towels and china – these motifs will also go down well in a child's room. Choose pale wallpapers with butterfly motifs for a fresh, airy feel in bedrooms and bathrooms. For an elegant effect, choose two or three colour fabrics with bee or butterfly motifs, and combine them with fabrics depicting flowers or even vines.

Flowers, fruits and vegetables

Flowers have an enduring appeal which has made them popular motifs since early times. In the Mediaeval period, a type of tapestry called *mille fleur* was developed, which got its name from the millions of flowers that filled in the background. The famous Lady and the Unicorn tapestries from France belong

▼ Butterfly elegance
An elegant fabric in ivory and plum with motifs of butterflies, leaves and flowers complements the dark wood of this formal dining table and gives the room a fresh country feel.

▲ Hopping mad
Co-ordinated bunny fabrics on the valance, cushion cover and bedhead are combined with a matching wallpaper to make this an endearing country bedroom for a young girl.

◀ *Fruity tile and border*

to this group. Kits for making copies of these tapestries for wall hangings and cushion covers are available today and, because of their detailed backgrounds, they are fun to make as well as a pleasure to look at.

Spring flowers make excellent subjects for fresh fabrics like chintz, for painted fire screens and tiles. Use a flowery chintz with a pale background for bedroom curtains to create a delicate freshness, and place a tapestry cushion featuring similar flowers on a bedroom chair to continue the theme. If there is a fireplace, white tiles with spring flower motifs or a painted flower screen will complete the look.

Autumnal fruits like apples, peaches and plums, with their rich colours ranging from greeny-yellow and pale orange to deep purple, make wonderful, mouthwatering country motifs, which

are particularly appropriate in kitchens and dining rooms. Use fruity fabrics in these rooms for curtains and chair covers, or for a colourful tablecloth. Look out for tea towels with fruit motifs and kitchen accessories like oven gloves, tea cosies or even an apron.

For the dining room, look for wallpaper borders which pick up the fruity theme, or make a stencil by tracing motifs from fabric, and use this to make your own borders. Coloured drawings or botanical prints of fruits are another option, and will look particularly good in a formal dining room. For the table, you could have pretty china or earthenware with fruit motifs, like the Portmeirion ranges.

Vegetable motifs are often used in the kitchen on wallpapers and tea towels, but tapestries with vegetable motifs will make eccentric cushion covers for a sofa or armchair, and can be combined with fruit, flower, bird or animal tapestry cushions for a country feel. Bowls and plates, which have vegetable motifs or which are textured to look like vegetables, can be used to hold pot plants, store pot pourri or simply as decoration.

◀ *Dining room delight*
A luscious fruit fabric with a fresh, white background transforms the window into a blaze of colour, and calls attention to the fruit china on the window-sill. The same fabric in another colour-way is used for a co-ordinated tablecloth.

▲ Kitchen kit
A glorious red, yellow and green tapestry panel of apples and apple blossom makes a striking wall decoration. The panel is made from a tapestry kit.

▼ Mouthwatering
A collection of fruity china makes a mouthwatering display in the kitchen, highlighted by the dark wood shelves. The china will also look nice when it's in use in the dining room.

▲ Fruits, flowers and vines
A striking grape vine fabric, used for the curtains and chair cover, provides the most obvious country motifs here, but close inspection reveals that the carpet covered with its fern and ivy designs also has its own country style. The small box under the table adds emphasis to the fruity theme, and fresh fruits and flowers complete the look.

◀ **Daisy ways**
Traditional large country motifs are still popular in the country-style home: this fabric, of the Michaelmas daisy, is an original William Morris design. Notice the clever trimming idea on the cushion where the decorative buttons have each been covered with a daisy motif.

▼ **Tile style**
The large pattern on the blue and green tiles creates a striking effect and provide a colour link with the vegetable china on the wall. Used as a border, the tiles add life to this farmhouse kitchen.

Toile de Jouy

These pictorial designs were developed in 1770 at the Jouy factory near Versailles, in France, and depict scenes like merry milkmaids, shepherds watching their sheep, or lovers strolling arm in arm through the countryside.

The fabrics are printed in a single colour on a white, off-white or creamy background, and the colours are soft and mellow, based on the original natural dyes. Pinks and pinky-reds, blues and rusts, earth green, brown and black are the traditional colours. The misty colours of the fabric and the pale backgrounds combine to create an elegant effect which can look lovely in formal bedrooms or dining rooms.

Toile de Jouy fabrics are large prints, and like other large prints should be used carefully. Use them for curtains, flat blinds and bedspreads where the whole pattern can be seen.

◀ **Toile de Jouy**
A traditional Toile de Jouy fabric, showing romantic figures ambling through the countryside, looks delightful used on extensive soft furnishings. The large pattern on these traditional fabrics can make them difficult to use. They tend to look best in a spacious room where you can stand back to admire the design.

▼ **Traditional blue motif**

PART TWO

WALL AND FLOOR FINISHES

Hanging wallpaper

A fresh patterned wallpaper can bring a room to life, with the added advantage that an all-over pattern helps disguise imperfections. For the most satisfying effects, wallpapering requires planning and attention to detail. (If you haven't wallpapered before, gain confidence by starting with a small room.)

This chapter deals with squared-up walls in good condition. Pages 23–26 show how to hang wallpaper borders, and pages 27–28 explain how to cope with switches, sockets, doors and windows.

Preparing the surface
The surface to be decorated should be as clean and smooth as possible. Usually, it is best to remove old wallpaper but if you know that the plaster underneath is in poor condition, and the existing wallpaper is plain, you could leave it in place to serve as a lining paper.

If you intend wallpapering on to new plaster, you must first brush on size. This is a watered-down adhesive which seals the fresh plaster and provides 'slip' so that the wallpaper can slide into position more easily. Sizing can be done days or hours before papering.

Choosing wallpaper
Don't be tempted to buy inexpensive wallpaper – a mediumweight quality is best because thin, cheap papers absorb

▲ **Difficult corners** *Floral wallpapers suit the cosiness of this attic bedroom. The walls are papered in an all-over small floral paper, with a complementary sprig pattern on the ceiling. Note how the two papers are clearly separated with a cornice in an accent colour.*

the paste and stretch and tear too easily.

For a first attempt, avoid flock wallcoverings, which have fibres attached to parts of the pattern, and fabric wallcoverings such as hessian or silk. Relief wallcoverings, such as anaglypta, need care when smoothing into place and painting after hanging.

Measuring up

Before buying the wallpaper, measure the area to be covered. First, measure the height of the room from the floor or skirting board to cornice or ceiling – this is the length or 'drop'. Then measure the distance around the walls. Don't deduct the space taken up by doors and windows. With the two figures you can use the charts to calculate the number of rolls. Buy all the paper you need at the same time and check that all the rolls have the same batch number as the colour may vary slightly between batches.

If your paper has a large pattern, check it for the depth of the pattern repeat. If the repeat is, for example, 30cm (12in), then you need to multiply 30cm by the number of drops you need. If this comes to more than 10m (33ft) you will need to add an extra roll of paper to the total.

How many rolls?

Use the charts to calculate the number of rolls needed. The standard roll of wallpaper is 10m (33ft) long by 53cm (21in) wide.

Wallpaper calculator

The following charts are designed to help you calculate how many rolls of wallpaper are needed to cover a room.

METRIC								IMPERIAL							
Wall height from skirting in metres								Wall height from skirting in feet							
2-2.2	2.2-2.4	2.4-2.6	2.6-2.8	2.8-3	3-3.2	3.2-3.4		6'6"-7'2"	7'2"-7'10"	7'10"-8'6"	8'6"-9'2"	9'2"-9'10"	9'10"-10'6"	10'6"-11'2"	
5	5	5	6	6	6	7	10m	5	5	5	6	6	6	7	33'
5	5	6	6	7	7	7	11m	5	5	6	6	7	7	7	36'
5	6	6	7	7	8	8	12m	5	6	6	7	7	8	8	39'
6	6	7	7	8	8	9	13m	6	6	7	7	8	8	9	43'
6	7	7	8	8	9	9	14m	6	7	7	8	8	9	9	46'
7	7	8	8	9	10	10	15m	7	7	8	8	9	10	10	49'
7	8	8	9	9	10	11	16m	7	8	8	9	9	10	11	52'
7	8	9	9	10	11	11	17m	7	8	9	9	10	11	11	56'
8	9	9	10	11	11	12	18m	8	9	9	10	11	11	12	59'
8	9	10	11	11	12	13	19m	8	9	10	11	11	12	13	62'
9	10	10	11	12	13	13	20m	9	10	10	11	12	13	13	66'
9	10	11	12	12	13	14	21m	9	10	11	12	12	13	14	69'
10	10	11	12	13	14	15	22m	10	10	11	12	13	14	15	72'

Measurement round room in metres (including doors and windows) ▲

Measurement round room in feet (including doors and windows) ▲

Newly hung paper

When you have just finished wallpapering, it may look unattractively blistered and patchy. But the irregularities smooth out as the wallpaper dries and after a day it will be flat and wrinkle free.

► **Wallpaper medley** A carefully positioned large floral border bridges the gap between the busy mini-print above and the cool stripes below. The wallpapers are hung first and then the border covers the join.

WHERE TO START

The first drop Nearly all modern wallpapers are designed so that the drops simply butt up against each other rather than overlapping; this means you can start to hang paper virtually anywhere in a room. Still, there is something to be said for the traditional technique of starting alongside the largest window and working away from it. Any shadows cast at the joins won't show because you will be working away from the light source. When using a wallpaper with a large, bold pattern, the first drop should be centred on a focal point in the room, such as a chimney breast. Subsequent drops are hung working outwards in both directions.

Use a plumbline This is a weight tied to a piece of string that is stuck to the top of the wall with masking tape. Pencil a vertical line down the wall against which the first drop will be hung. This will ensure the first drop hangs absolutely straight.

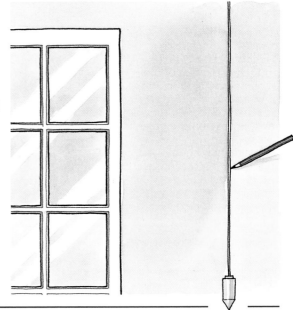

PAPERING WALLS

1 Measure the drop When you have decided on your starting point, measure for length, adding 10cm (4in) to allow for trimming at the top and bottom. This measurement can be used for all the full lengths of paper. Lay wallpaper face up on the pasting table and measure out the first length. Decide where the pattern will be placed. If the paper has a dominant print, make sure that a full pattern repeat is at the top of the wall where it is most obvious.

2 Cutting the drop Mark the cutting line in light pencil across the paper, check that it is at right angles to the edges, and cut along the line.

3 Match the pattern Now check the next length against this one to match the pattern before cutting. Mark the top of each length on the wrong side to avoid hanging patterns upside down and number as you cut.

4 Pasting the paper Lay the first length face down on the pasting table. Align the top and the far edge with the edges of the table, allowing the paper to overlap the table slightly. This prevents paste getting all over the table and on to the next length. Start pasting from the centre, working outwards and away from you, spreading the paste evenly right out to the far edges.

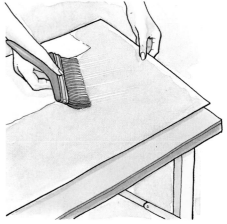

5 Paste the other half Move the length towards you, this time overlapping on the near edge of the table and paste the rest of the wallpaper.

6 **Folding the paper** Fold the paper up concertina fashion as you paste. Move the folded section along the table and paste the rest of the paper, continuing to fold in the same way. Some papers must be left for a few minutes for the paste to soak in or they will wrinkle when hung – follow the instructions on the roll label. Lay this folded paper to one side and paste the next length in the meantime.

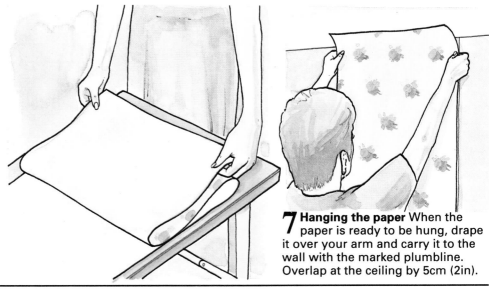

7 **Hanging the paper** When the paper is ready to be hung, drape it over your arm and carry it to the wall with the marked plumbline. Overlap at the ceiling by 5cm (2in).

9 **Finishing off** With a pair of scissors, make a crease at the ceiling angle and pull the paper back from the wall to cut along this crease. Dab the end of the paper back into place. If necessary add a little extra paste to the top edge first. Repeat this at the floor or skirting board and brush the paper back on to the wall. Remove any paste from the ceiling or woodwork with a damp sponge.

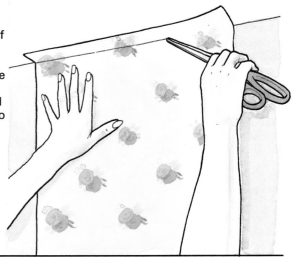

8 **Removing air bubbles** Unfold the remainder of the paper and working from the centre brush it on to the wall, removing any air bubbles as you brush.

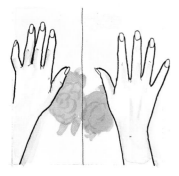 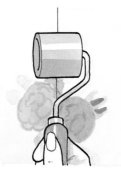

10 **The next drop** Paste and hang the next drop as numbered, matching the pattern exactly. To do this, slide the paper up or down using the palms of your hands. Brush into place and trim as before.

11 **For a perfect finish** Run a seam roller over the join about 20 minutes after hanging. Do not roll embossed papers – dab the seams firmly

12 **Turning a corner** Measure the distance from the last drop of paper to the corner. For internal corners, add 12mm ($\frac{1}{2}$in) to this measurement; for external corners, such as round a chimney breast, add 4cm (1$\frac{1}{2}$in). Cut a length of paper to this width and hang it with the cut edge brushed into (or around) the corner. Measure the width of the remainder of the paper and then measure this distance from the corner. Hang a plumbline from this point and mark the wall with pencil. Paste and hang the paper to this line, overlapping the amount carried round – any slight mismatch should not show.

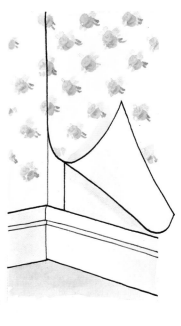

Wallpaper borders

Wallpaper borders have an assured place in a country-style home. They can be used to emphasize traditional architectural features such as cornices, covings, picture and dado rails, or – in modern or renovated houses – they can substitute where there are none.

A pretty floral border around the room just below ceiling level will soften the contours of even the most featureless modern room. Borders can be applied over almost any sound surface with the exception of heavily embossed wallpapers and textured plaster such as Artex. They can be used on top of wallpaper, including low-relief woodchip papers (although here the results will be less perfect), or on painted walls and woodwork. You can even use them on painted furniture to give it a co-ordinated look.

Borders are also a quick and simple way of introducing a splash of pattern and colour into a plain room. So for maximum impact with minimum effort and expenditure, just study the simple step-by-step guide on the following pages.

Self adhesive borders are available in some ranges. With these borders you can dispense with paste.

▲ *Introducing flowers* A wide floral border used at both picture rail and dado rail level brings a hint of the cottage rose garden into a hallway.

WHERE TO PUT BORDERS

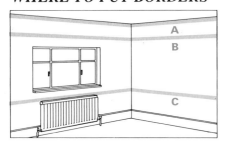

Just below ceiling level A border at the top of the wall finishes a wall neatly. It sits below the coving or cornice (if present) or butts up against the ceiling.

Picture-rail level In pre-1940s houses there was usually a picture rail – a wooden moulding fixed 30-45cm (12-18in) down from the ceiling. Many have been removed, which can leave a room looking badly proportioned since they helped to 'reduce' its height.

Dado-rail height A dado rail was often used by Victorians to prevent chairs from knocking against their costly wallcoverings. Also, the rail could cover the join between the fragile and expensive paper or fabric above, and a more hardwearing painted surface, such as anaglypta, below. The usual height was 90cm (3ft) from the floor – a third of the way between floor and picture rail.

Border placements *A dado rail can be simulated by a wallpaper border (above), creating two separate areas for decoration. A picture rail border (below) is used to link two contrasting walpapers. Notice how the cornice has been picked out in a stronger colour to add definition to the decor. The ceiling border (left), positioned just below the cornice, co-ordinates with the floral motif of the bed linen and curtains.*

Preparing to paste

The special **paste** used for borders contains more adhesive than ordinary wallpaper paste. Border pastes are sold in tubes for small jobs and tubs for bigger jobs.

An **ordinary paint brush** is used to apply the paste: use a brush that is about the same width as the border.

A **pasting table** or kitchen table, ideally 1.5m (5ft) long, will make your work easier.

You will also need a pair of **scissors**, a **paperhanger's brush** and a **seam roller** (optional).

Self-adhesive borders make the work even simpler. Lay them lightly in place and when you are happy with the result, press them firmly against the wall. They cannot then be moved.

How many rolls?

Most borders are sold in rolls 10m (11yd) long and in a range of widths from 21mm (1in) to 240mm (9$\frac{1}{2}$in). Around 50-90mm (2-3 in) is a useful size for most purposes – it is wide enough to show if used along the top of the wall in an average 2.5m (8$\frac{1}{2}$ft) high room, but not overwhelming.

To work out how many rolls you need to run a border around the top of a room, simply measure the long wall and the short wall and work out the combined length of all four. The measurements for a border at dado rail level, or at skirting board level are just the same.

If you intend to run the border around a door, or a window as well, you will have to measure them and add that to your total.

When you have the total length, round up the figure to the nearest whole roll. Allow a reasonable margin for error – if your sum works out to exactly five rolls, you should buy six as you will undoubtedly waste some.

Preparing the surface

Make sure the wall surface is smooth, clean and dry. If you are applying a border to freshly hung wallpaper you should leave it for at least 48 hours before hanging the border.

Establishing a guideline

It is difficult to get a border straight by eye alone, so draw a guideline in pencil to lay the border against.

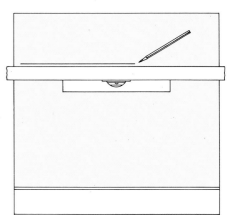

To draw a straight line against which to place the border, you will need a spirit level, a pencil and a long wooden batten.

Place a spirit level just below the height you want the border and rest a long batten on the top. Hold the batten in one hand and draw a pencil line along it to extend the spirit level line.

If you don't have a spirit level, mark the distance from the floor or ceiling at intervals along the wall. Then join up these points using a faint pencil line. This method is necessary if you are continuing the border up a stairway.

HANGING A BORDER

Hanging borders is easiest when you are laying the border against an existing feature – a coving or picture rail, for example.

If you are laying your first border around the top of a room, simply align it against the ceiling. Unfortunately walls are rarely straight, so in practice you will have to use your judgement and rely on your eye. In fact these imperfections will not show.

Often the junction of the wall and ceiling isn't perfectly straight. If the border doesn't butt up against the ceiling all along its length, fill in any spaces with paint that is the same colour as the ceiling. Use a small brush and a steady hand.

1 Unwind a sufficient length of paper to cover one wall but, before you cut it to length, hold it up and check that you have got the best positions at the corners. If possible, try to avoid cutting motifs. If you do have to cut a motif you will find that some cuts look better than others. Cut the length you require, allowing a small overlap (12mm/$\frac{1}{2}$in) at either end.

2 Lay the border face down on the pasting table and apply a strip of paste down the centre of the reverse side. Use the paint brush to feather the paste out to the edges, ensuring that the whole area is evenly and liberally covered.

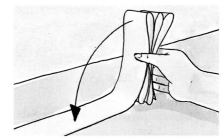

3 Fold the border up concertina-fashion, with the pasted sides together, so that you can hold it in one hand. With a long run you will have to repeat this process several times to get the whole length pasted. Wipe the table before pasting the next strip.

4 If you are right-handed, hold the concertina of paper in your left hand and work from right to left. This leaves your right hand free to work. Using your line as a guide (or the edge you are working up to), unfold a length of border, lay it on to the wall and press it lightly into place with the flat of your hand. Smooth it down firmly with a paperhanger's brush, working from the centre to the outer edges to expel air bubbles. Wipe off any paste.

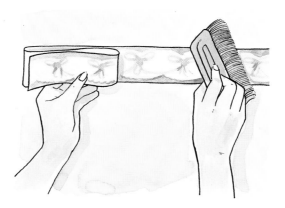

5 Continue in this way along one side of the room. Take the paper around the corner on the first side. On the second side start with a slight overlap, adjusting and trimming if necessary so that you get the best pattern match. If you have one, roll the seam with a seam roller to get a good, flat seal.

Mitring corners

A well-mitred corner around a window, door or panel finishes off a job neatly. This is especially important where you have vertical stripes meeting horizontal stripes. Once mastered, the craft of mitring has many applications, increasing the decorative possibilities of borders. They can be used to outline mirrors, for example, or they can break up a large area of wall by creating 'panels'.

▶ **A narrow border** *This has been used to create rectangular wall 'panels' on the plain coloured walls and to frame the mirror.*

tip **Disguising corners**

With some borders, you can buy special decorative corner motifs to disguise corners. Alternatively, cut a motif from the border and paste it over the corner.

HOW TO CUT A MITRED CORNER

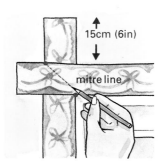

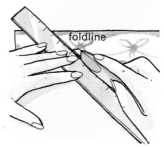

1 Cut and paste the vertical section in place, leaving a 15cm (6in) overlap more than the width of the border. Lay the horizontal strip and mark in pencil on the vertical strip where they intersect at the inner and outer points. Join these lines to make the angle of the mitre. On the vertical section, cut along the line and repaste.

2 Fold along the pencil line of the horizontal strip and place it against the pasted strip to get the right pattern match. When you are satisfied, make a sharp crease at the foldline to match the pencil line.

3 Cut along the foldline on the horizontal section with sharp scissors or a craft knife held against a ruler. Measure up and cut the full length of the horizontal strip, allowing 15cm (6in) overlap at the other end.

4 Paste the horizontal section and butt it up to the other strip. Press firmly in place and wipe surplus adhesive from the wall. Secure the join with a seam roller.

Wallpapering solutions

Even the smallest room can present obstacles to a perfect finish. Though it might seem simple to wallpaper a cloakroom, for example, the small space is likely to have nooks and crannies, recessed windows, a cistern and a small radiator to paper behind. But for each little deviation there is a tried and tested technique.

The most traditional-looking rooms often have complicated interiors. Sloping walls, recessed windows and irregularly shaped rooms present an obvious challenge. Even modern interiors have their own complications, most obviously in the form of fixtures and fittings to do with the conveniences of a contemporary lifestyle. Increasing numbers of electrical appliances in every room mean there is a need for several sockets. Light switches, too, need to be fitted into a wallpapering scheme. Luckily, most of these fitments can be removed – after turning off the electricity – and papered smoothly behind before replacing them.

Even in today's standardized homes doors, windows and recesses come in a variety of shapes and sizes and present their own problems to the decorator. Radiators can be tackled in one of two ways. If they are of the older type of design, or if you feel unsure of how to remove them from the wall bracket, simply paper as far behind them as possible. Alternatively, the newer types can be loosened and swung forward to allow you to paper behind them.

With a little care, all these problem features can be overcome to give a smooth, professional finish to the room.

▼ **Papering a bathroom** *Small rooms, with the conveniences of modern life, can be the most difficult to paper because there isn't a lot of space to work in. This Victorian-style bathroom has a towel rail, window sills that jut out on to the adjacent wall and sanitary ware with its associated plumbing – all are tricky shapes needing care to paper around successfully.*

SOCKETS AND SWITCHES

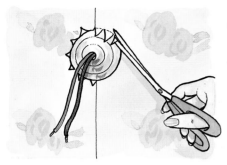

Papering around wall switches If the faceplate is removable, turn off the power at the mains and then unscrew the plate. Make the diagonal cuts but instead of trimming off the flaps, tuck them behind the plate. Do not use this method with foil paper.

Papering around sockets Turn off power at the mains and remove any light fittings. Paper straight over the the light socket and then use a sharp knife to make diagonal cuts to the corners (or several cuts if it is round). Press the flaps back into position and trim.

DOORS AND WINDOWS

1 Hanging the paper Hang the drop in the normal way, allowing it to hang over the face of the door. Trim paper roughly to the shape of the frame, allowing about 2.5cm (1in) overlap, and make a 12mm (1/2in) diagonal cut into corner.

2 Trimming to the corner Brush the paper into the angle between wall and frame, mark a crease line with the back of the scissors and trim.

WINDOW RECESS

Where to begin Paper the inside of the recess first, turning a 12mm (1/2in) flap on to the surrounding wall. Then paper the wall round the window, cutting out the shape exactly.

RADIATORS

Behind a fixed radiator Let the paper hang over the face of the radiator and cut a slit up from the bottom of the length so that the paper can pass either side of the radiator bracket. Across the centre you may find it easier to cut the paper to 20-30cm (8-12in). Tuck the paper behind the radiator and smooth it around the bracket with a long ruler or similar implement to allow you to reach down behind the radiator.

Removing the radiator Hang the paper over the brackets. Make a vertical cut up the bracket and horizontal slits at top and bottom. Smooth the paper each side of the bracket and trim off the excess.

Painting techniques

A room decorated in true cottage style should be simple and unsophisticated. A few coats of paint in fresh country colours on walls and woodwork are all you need, and act as the perfect foil for fabrics, pictures and rugs. Paint is cheaper than wallpaper and easy to apply with a roller or brush. It's not hard to achieve a professional finish, and highly satisfying results can be gained relatively quickly.

Choosing the paint
It's important to select the right paint for the job before you start, and this will depend on whether the paint needs to be washable and which type of finish you prefer.

Matt vinyl Suitable for interior walls and ceilings, this paint gives a smooth finish and helps to disguise uneven wall surfaces. It should not be used in kitchens or bathrooms where condensation may damage the finish.
Silk vinyl This paint has a low sheen which helps to reflect light. It is ideal for highlighting the relief pattern of textured wallpapers and plaster, and its waterproof finish means that it is suitable for kitchens and bathrooms.
Solid emulsion This paint comes in a paint tray ready to roll on to the wall. It is a good choice for beginners since it does not drip and is easy to use. Choose either the matt or silk variety depending on the finish required.

▲ *Good morning sunshine*
Sunny yellow paint on walls and woodwork is bright and cheerful.

How much to buy
Check the information given on the side of the tin or tray to check the covering capacity of each type of paint. Coverage will vary with the brand and the absorbency of the surface but, as a rough guide, 1 litre (2pt) of emulsion covers about 13sq m (15sq yd).

You can calculate the approximate area of wall surface to be painted by multiplying the width of each wall by its height and adding the totals for each wall together. Remember to double up if you're likely to need two coats.

◀ **Equipment**
From the top: roller tray with radiator roller and protective goggles inside; roller with long pile sleeve for matt paint; paint kettle; masking tape; wide paintbrush for large areas and narrow one for small ones or for edges; protective dust sheet.

▼ **Pretty in pink**
The mellow colours of a quilted bedspread have been used as the basis of this colour scheme. The walls and picture rail pick out the two pinks in the fabric, while the cream colour is used above the picture rail.

PREPARING SURFACES

For a good-looking, long-lasting finish, careful preparation is essential. Do not be tempted to skip this stage or you may have to re-paint sooner than you expect.

1 Fill cracks and holes Use a multi-purpose filler to fill holes caused by hooks, nails or screws and sand smooth when set.

2 Wash all surfaces Use sugar soap to wash the surface, then rinse off with clean water.

3 Flaking or powdery walls should be rubbed down and treated with stabilising solution. Treat newly plastered walls with emulsion thinned with water or an appropriate primer.

Painting with roller and tray or brush

Walls and ceilings can be painted rapidly with a roller which gives good, smooth results. However because it splatters a lot, you should cover carpets and any furniture nearby, and put on overalls or old clothes. The edges and small or awkward areas, such as above a curtain rail should be painted with a brush.

Materials

Paint roller Choose a medium size, 17.5-20cm (7-7³⁄₄in) wide, for ease of use, with a hollow handle into which you can insert a pole to extend its reach. The sleeves are made in either lamb's wool or a cheaper synthetic equivalent. Choose one with the right pile depth – long pile for matt or on textured sur-faces, short pile for silk finish or solid emulsion paint.

Roller tray These are usually plastic, but you can get metal ones for really heavy use. They have a well at one end into which paint is poured, and a sloping, ribbed surface to remove excess paint from the roller sleeve.

Brushes If you don't want to bother with a roller and tray and don't mind taking longer with a large job, a 10cm (4in) brush is ideal for walls with a 2.5cm (1in) brush for the awkward bits.

Dust sheets Plastic dust sheets can be bought quite cheaply. Otherwise use old sheets to cover carpets and any furniture that cannot be removed.

Other useful equipment:

Goggles to protect your eyes when sanding and painting. They are particularly handy when painting the ceiling.

Radiator roller This is a mini roller on a long, angled handle which is used for painting behind fittings, such as radiators and pipes.

Paint kettle for transferring smaller quantities of paint from a large, heavy tin when you're using a brush.

Masking tape for protecting carpet edges, light fittings, glass, etc. If using on windows, make sure it doesn't get wet, or it will become very difficult to remove.

Step ladders Ideally get a pair so that a plank of wood placed between them will make a working platform from which to reach ceilings and high walls.

PAINTING A ROOM

1 Start at the top
Prepare the surfaces for painting (see previous page). Work from the window end, starting with the ceiling.

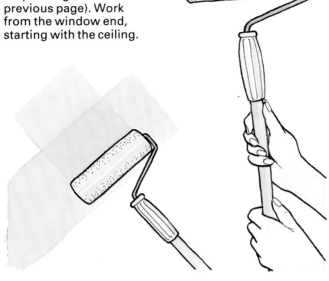

2 Painting with a roller Paint a narrow margin around the edges with a small brush. Load up with paint from the tray, running the roller back and forth over the ridges for even distribution. Wearing goggles to protect your eyes from splashes and with the roller fitted on an extension pole, roll the paint in criss-cross fashion across the ceiling, painting about 1m (1yd) wide strips at a time. Join up the strips quickly, before the wet edge dries, and aim to finish the ceiling in one go.

▲ **Come down**
A warm paint colour helps to bring down a high ceiling.

Successful storage
Sometimes, when you re-open a tin of paint you will find a thick skin has formed on the top which has to be cut out. Quickly inverting the tin before storing it seals the tin and prevents this skin forming.

3 Painting with a brush If you'd rather use a brush, you will probably need to make a platform with two ladders and a plank of wood to paint the ceiling. Start at the window and paint away from it, brushing in a criss-cross fashion.

4 Painting the walls Use a narrow brush to paint along the edges of skirtings, window frames, doors and light switches first. Then paint with a roller or large brush, aiming to complete one wall at a time. Start at the top right-hand corner and work across in horizontal bands from top to bottom. Allow to dry thoroughly before applying a second coat.

5 Cleaning up When you've finished work, wash the roller and brushes thoroughly, as instructed on the paint tin. The sleeves on rollers can be removed for easier cleaning. Store the brushes horizontally, and hang roller sleeves up.

Painting woodwork

Freshly painted woodwork gives a tired decorative scheme new life. Brilliant white is a traditional choice, but for a softer, country style, you could consider using one of the many tinted whites that are now available or a mellow pastel shade which compliments the other colours in the room.

Painting woodwork should be approached with care because the paint has a greater sheen than wall paint which means that irregularities show up more. For this reason surfaces should be very smooth and clean before you begin. Also paint splashes can be difficult to clean off because these paints are oil based, so you should avoid overloading the brush with paint as you work.

Having said all this, painting woodwork isn't difficult and it doesn't take long to paint a door, window frame or skirting. You don't need much in the way of materials either, which helps to keep costs down.

Paints for woodwork

Gloss with its highly polished finish stays looking clean and new for years. It is a very durable paint, making it ideal for windows and outside doors, and it is easy to clean and care for. It comes in liquid or non-drip form, although the slightly more expensive, non-drip gloss is best for the beginner. Liquid gloss needs an undercoat, whereas non-drip gloss can be used without one.

▲Blue link
Cornflower blue gloss, used to pick out door knobs and mouldings, acts as a link with the blue china and compliments the warm yellow walls.

Satin or **silk** paints designed especially for wood have the subtle sheen of an antique finish which is perfect for the cottage look.

Eggshell is an oil-based paint which, when dry, has a satin sheen similar to satin and silk finish paints. More commonly used for walls, it is not as durable as the other wood paints, but it is ideal for broken colour work on wooden surfaces – sponging, rag-rolling and dragging, for example.

Other materials required

Brushes Natural hog's hair bristles give the best finish, but nylon is cheaper and easy to clean. You will need different sizes depending on what you wish to paint: 75mm (3in) for doors, 50mm (2in) for skirtings and 25mm (1in) for window frames. An angled, cutting-in brush is best for windows.

Glasspaper, **paint stripper** and **scraper** to remove old paint as necessary.

Masking tape to protect window panes and other surfaces from paint. Remove before the paint is fully dry.

Cleaning solution to clean brushes afterwards. Check the manufacturer's instructions on the tin – some paints can be cleaned off with washing-up liquid and warm water, while for others white spirit is required.

Protective clothing including overalls and gloves.

PREPARING WOODWORK

Good paintwork If the existing paintwork is in good condition, prepare it by sanding with glasspaper. Alternatively apply liquid sandpaper, which roughs up the surface enough to make a key for the new paint.

Flaking paint If the existing paintwork is basically in good condition, but with some flaking in one or two small areas, you may find it is sufficient just to scrape off the flaking paint and then sand down so that the surface blends into the remaining paintwork.

Rough surface If the existing paint is pitted from layer upon layer of old paint, or if it is split or flaking badly, it is necessary to strip off and start again. Use a hot air or chemical paint stripper, following the instructions carefully and using a scraper to get off the melted paint.

Wear protective clothing including leather gloves if using a hot air stripper, or rubber gloves if using a chemical one. Treat the stripped wood as bare wood, sanding until smooth and then using primer.

Bare wood New wood or wood that has been exposed by stripping or sanding should be sanded smooth, starting with a rough glasspaper to remove the remains of any old paint, and finally smoothing with a fine grade glasspaper. Apply a coat of wood primer before painting.

◀ *Moody blue*
A pale colour paint, such as this moody blue, produces a very restful effect which is particularly suitable for bedrooms. The low sheen paint used here also adds to the mellow, low-key effect.

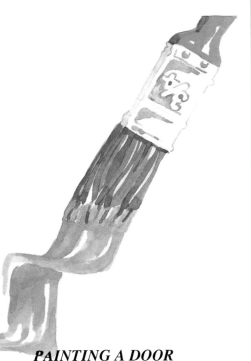

PAINTING A DOOR

Preparation Remove any door furniture and prepare the surface as described on the previous page. Wipe with a damp cloth to remove dust and wedge the door open while you paint. Bare wood should be given a coat of primer before it is painted. If using liquid gloss, you will also need an undercoat.

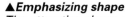

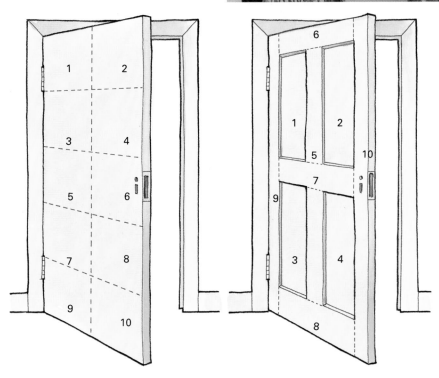

Flush doors Paint the edge of the door first, then starting from the top, make long, smooth strokes, brushing in one direction. Without re-loading the brush, lightly brush across the paint to prevent brush marks and to remove drips. Lightly brush from the bottom of the door up, to finish.

Panelled doors Paint the edge of the door first, then starting from the top, paint the panels first, applying the paint in the same way as for a flush door. Then paint the vertical, centre bar, followed by the horizontal bars above, between and below the panels. Finally, finish with the side vertical strips.

▲Emphasizing shape
The attractive shape of a panelled door is emphasized by using a darker colour – in this case a warm yellow – to pick out the panels and door frame. A pretty stencil is the finishing touch.

The door frame *When the door is dry, paint the frame. If the door fits snugly do not build up too many layers on the inner edge of the frame or the door may not close. Do not paint the door hinges.*

WIPING UP

The oil-based paints which are used for painting woodwork are more difficult to remove than the water-based emulsions used on walls. Splashes should be wiped up immediately, so keep a rag or cloth soaked in cleaning solution to wipe up splashes as they occur. Do not use tissue or kitchen paper for wiping, since these can leave fibres behind which may spoil the smooth look of the finished paintwork.

When you need to take a short break, there is no need to clean the brushes completely. Seal paint-laden brushes in air-tight polythene bags to keep them moist and ready for use.

PAINTING MOULDINGS

Narrow mouldings, such as picture rails or panelling, should be painted with a small brush, preferably a cutting-in brush which has an angled edge. For wide mouldings, such as skirtings or architrave, paint the edge with a small brush first, then fill in with a larger brush.

For skirtings, use a paint shield which not only keeps the floor clean, but prevents the dust under the skirting from getting on to the newly

painted wood. A piece of clean, stiff card can be used as an improvised paint shield.

PAINTING WINDOWS

Preparation Prepare the wood for painting, then, unless you have a very steady hand, mask off the edge of the glass with masking tape. When painting the outside of a window, make sure the tape does not get wet from rain, or it may be difficult to remove later.

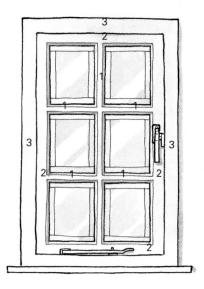

Order of work Using a narrow brush, or preferably a cutting-in brush which is angled for narrow areas, paint the horizontal and vertical glazing bars first. Then paint the rest of the window from the top down, and end with the frame. Remove any splashes from the glass while still wet, or use a razor blade to scrape away dry paint.

tip

Paint seal
To seal any cracks between the wood and glass, place the masking tape 3mm (1/8in) away from the wood. This means that the paint will just overlap the glass, forming a seal. Do not paint primer or undercoat on glass as this will not hold.

◀ **Pretty and practical**
Banisters and skirtings should be painted in gloss since this is the most durable of the woodwork paints, and stands up well to knocks. A cutting-in brush will make painting the spindles a lot easier.

Stencilled borders

A stencilled room has a memorable 'handmade' charm of its own. In addition to the special decorative qualities of the actual painted motifs, continuous stencil designs – stencilled borders and friezes – can work 'architecturally', just like wallpaper borders. They can, for example, be used to enhance existing features such as fireplaces and arches, or they can make featureless interiors more interesting. In a room with expanses of plain wall, a stencilled frieze or panel can add character as well as subtly altering the space's proportions, making it feel cosier.

Borders can be continuous or non-continuous – either the stencil is designed to be repeated or one or more motif stencils are arranged as a border.

Continuous stencilled borders can be used as substitutes for absent picture and dado rails, helping to 'lower' the ceilings. Around doors and windows, a stencilled border frames and decorates in the same way as a wallpaper border

▲ Fresh and fanciful
The clean white paintwork and clear light shining through this casement window are underlined by a lightly stencilled two-colour floral border. In a small room, details such as these bring a pretty and individual touch to the room's decoration.

but with more subtlety. Any part of the stencil can be picked out and used as a motif on furniture or accessories.

Planning and measuring

Any large, repeat stencil design needs to be accurately measured and marked out. If you are stencilling a border all around a room, first decide on its position: for example, above or below a dado rail, at ceiling level or above a skirting board. These are useful linear features against which you can line up the top or bottom edge of the stencil.

If you have chosen a mid-way point, use a plumb line to find the vertical (see page 59), and a set square or a batten and spirit level to find the horizontal. Make your marks lightly in pencil or chalk along the length of the wall to provide a guideline. Calculate how many times you will need to repeat the stencil to reach each corner, not forgetting to include in your calculation any spaces between motifs.

To avoid an unnatural break in the stencil pattern at corners, you may need to alter the length of the spaces between repeat sections. This only works if the design is flowing and isn't meant to join up precisely.

Some stencils are made from plastic which is flexible and can be bent around the corner. You will need to hold the stencil firmly in your hand while you apply the paint – it will spring back if it is only secured with tape.

Because walls are rarely absolutely straight and the corners are hardly ever at true angles – even after the most painstaking planning – you often need to make final adjustments by eye.

WHERE TO START

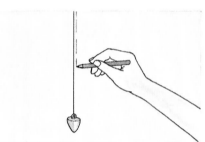 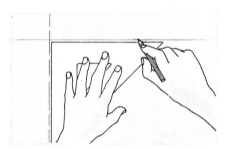

1 Marking the vertical Use a plumb line to find the true vertical and mark with chalk or pencil, which can be rubbed out after stencilling.

2 Marking the horizontal Using a set square, mark a horizontal line at right angles to the vertical line.

STENCILLING A CONTINUOUS BORDER

1 Preparation First assemble all the tools and materials you need and make sure the wall surface is clean, smooth and dry.

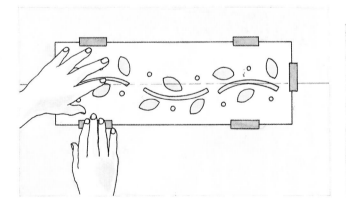

2 Positioning the stencil Mark the centre point of the wall, at the required height, lightly in pencil. Place the centre of the stencil on this mark and secure all round the outer edges with masking tape.

3 Preparing to paint Stir the paint and pour a small amount into a foil or plastic tray. Dampen sponge and wring dry before dipping it lightly into the paint and then dabbing against kitchen paper until the sponge seems virtually dry.

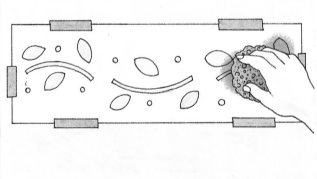

4 Applying paint Work from the outer edges inwards, pressing lightly. Don't worry if the impression seems very faint. It is better to build up colour gradually than all at one go. Too much paint on the sponge will only lead to smudging around the cut edges and seeping through on the underside.

◀ ▼ ▶Positioning a stencil
To break up an expanse of plain
wall, stencil a charming border at
dado level (left) – about 90cm (3ft)
from the floor.

The blue and green floral garland
(below) is stencilled in place of a
skirting board on this rough, white
plaster wall.

A trailing design is used to give
some definition to the plain
plastered walls (right). This sort of
ceiling-height stencil is perfect for
bedrooms and bathrooms, giving
intimacy and warmth.

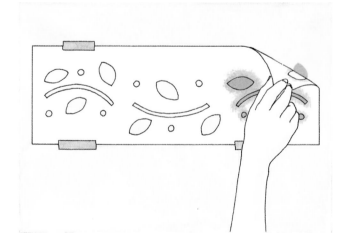

5 Monitoring progress Carefully lift up the stencil at
one corner to check the results, and, when you are
satisfied, peel it off, keeping the tape intact. There is no
need to re-apply it as you move around the room.

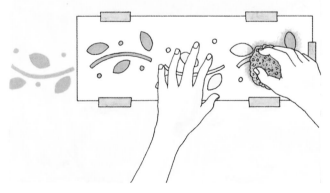

6 Continuing the design Re-align the stencil for the
next position. Work away from the centre of the
design towards the corners. If using one colour only,
continue all round the room.

Multi-colour stencils Where two or more colours are
involved, complete the first and allow it to dry before
returning to the starting point to stencil the next colour.
Some stencils offer one sheet for each colour. For
others you will need to mask out the areas already
painted in, with masking tape.

A NON-CONTINUOUS BORDER

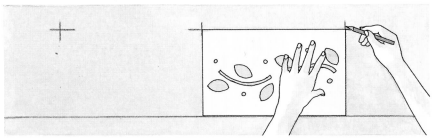

Organizing the repeats Take each wall separately and calculate how many times the stencil will fit into the space. The spacing between the motifs should be consistent.

▼ **Decorative arch** Floral motifs have been carefully planned to create a border around this hall arch. In the hall beyond, a border stencil has been used at ceiling level.

tip

Variations in colour Experiment with different applicators to vary the appearance of the colour. Natural sponges give a stippled effect, paint pads a more matt base colour, while small rags, crumpled up into a ball and dipped in paint create a water-marked look.

STENCILLING RIGHT ANGLES

For a stencilled border around a door or window you will need to pivot the design at the corners.

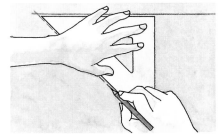

1 **Mitring geometric designs** To give a professional finish corners have to be mitred. Mark a horizontal line as before. Using a set square, draw a line at a 45° angle to cross it. Place masking tape along this line.

2 **Applying the paint** Stencil along the horizontal line, taking the paint over the edge of the masking tape. Remove the stencil and the tape and leave the motif until dry.

3 **The vertical stencil** Re-position the tape along the other side of the diagonal line, over the completed dry paint. Repeat as before. When dry, rub out the pencilled line.

Butting corners With simple, evenly-spaced designs, simply work out the best point to break off at a corner and start the vertical section directly beneath it.

Trailing corners With a flowing, floral type of design, it is possible to make it curve gently around a corner. Try a few experiments on test paper first. Start by printing the horizontal section, making sure it ends at a point where it looks complete. Turn the stencil at right angles and make the link with the vertical border by omitting or adding a few design elements.

Tongue-and-groove panelling

Lining the walls of a room with wooden panelling adds an old-fashioned warmth and character to more modern country-style decorations. You don't need to clad complete rooms, or even complete walls. If you cut the boards to just below an imaginary picture rail level, tongue and groove panels provide an excellent background for kitchen or alcove shelving or a facing for a redundant chimney breast.

However, panelling the dado or the sides of a bath are the most manageable projects to start on since you will be working with shorter lengths of timber in easily accessible areas. Tongue-and-groove panelling is available in easily assembled kit form for dados from major decorating supply stores; a kit for panelling a dado area generally comes complete with a dado rail and replacement skirting.

The benefits of panelling

Cut short, vertical boards fitted just to dado height and topped with a timber moulding provide a tough, attractive lower surface to the wall area. This is especially advantageous in areas such as halls and stairways which can suffer from rough treatment.

Apart from looking good, panelling has other benefits. It is an excellent way of concealing numerous shortcomings on the surface of the walls, covering old,

▼ Barely clad
Teaming simple tongue-and-groove panelling on the side of the bath and the low walls with limed floor boards embodies the spartan approach to a real country feeling.

crumbling or patched plaster and hiding unsightly pipes or cables. Cladding also provides both heat and sound insulation, especially if you place an insulating material like rigid polystyrene or a mineral wool blanket between the battens before you fix the boards in position. Because of the cavity behind the boards, cladding is good at cutting down on condensation, which makes it an excellent wall covering for steamy bathrooms and kitchens.

Choosing materials

In tongue-and-groove boards, one edge of each board has a groove machined along it, while the other has a matching tongue which slots into an adjacent groove when the boards are fixed to the wall. They are available from timber yards and decorating supply superstores.

When estimating quantities of timber required for battens and panelling, sketch a plan of each wall. Take the plan with you to the supplier. Remember each board overlaps along both edges so make allowances for this. Most boards come in 75-100mm (3-4in) widths.

In order to acclimatize the timber to its surroundings and reduce the risk of subsequent warping, store it in the room where you intend to hang it.

Preparing the walls

Cladding can be fixed over any wall surface, so no elaborate preparation is required. But covering the wall with panelling will not cure dampness; it merely hides any sign of damp that may occur, allowing it to spread without your knowledge. It is important, therefore, to solve any possible problems and allow the wall to dry before you start. To stop

condensation forming on the inside, you can fix a sheet of polythene to the wall before you fit the battens.

Starting with the battens

The tongue-and-groove boards are usually fixed to the walls by nailing them to a network of timber battens. First decide whether you want to fix the panelling vertically or horizontally; this will determine the alignment of the battens – along the wall for vertical boards, up the wall for horizontal ones.

It is usually simplest to treat shallow skirtings and architraves around doorways and window frames as pre-set battens and fix the boards over them. You can then either leave a gap at the bottom, trim the edges with some beading or fix new mouldings to the panelling. Heavier skirtings and frames which stand proud of the battens must be prised off.

Use lengths of 50 x 25mm (2 x 1in) timber, fixed to the wall at the top and bottom of the planned panelling and at intervals of 400-600mm (16-24in).

On a good wall you should be able to fix the timber to the wall with masonry nails; on crumbling plaster you will need to drill holes and use wall plugs with screws. **Take great care not to drill into cables or pipes buried in the wall, especially around electrical fittings. Check first.**

When fixing battens along the edges of walls, leave about a 12mm (½in) gap. This way you won't have to pin the boards too close to the edge.

Materials

Lengths of 50 x 25mm (2 x 1in) **batten**
Hand drill with no. 8 **wood bit**, no. 12 **masonry bit**, **wallplugs**, no. 8 (2½in) **countersunk wood screws** and **screwdriver**
Tongue-and-groove boards – with special clips in kit form
25mm (1in) **panel pins** or thin **lost head nails** and **hammer**
Chisel and **saw**

FIXING THE BATTENS

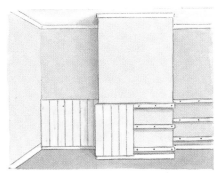

For vertical boards fit rows of horizontal battens to the wall. Drill holes in the battens at 45cm (18in) intervals. Fix the top batten flush with the top of the panelling, the bottom one about 12mm (½in) above the skirting and the middle one between the two. Make sure each batten is straight.

FIXING WITH CLIPS

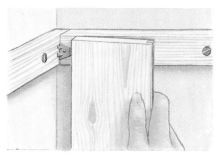

1 Fixing the first board Use starter clips, if available, to fix the first board in a corner of the room. Pin a clip to each batten close to the corner. Use a spirit level to check that the board will be truly vertical when fixed in position. Trim the tongue from the board and push the cut edge into the starter clips.

FIXING WITH PINS

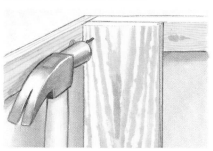

1 Placing the first panel Begin in a corner and place the first panel with the groove towards the corner. Check that the board is vertical with a spirit level, then pin it to each batten, carefully hammering the panel pins through the board about 12mm (½in) in from the groove.

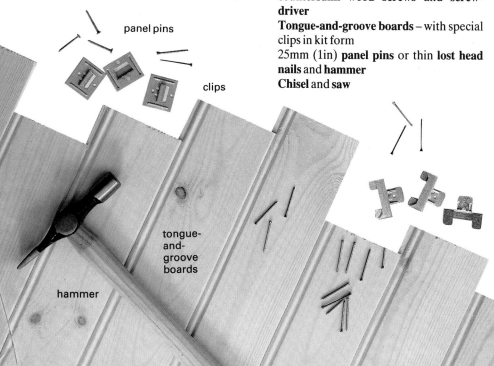

panel pins

clips

tongue-and-groove boards

hammer

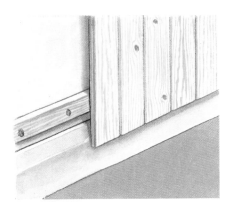

Add extra battens just above skirtings and around door frames and windows to support the edges of the cladding.

On an uneven surface, cladding is more tricky to install. Hold a length of batten against the wall to check for bumps and hollows. Fix to the highest point and pad out behind the battens where dips occur with scraps of plywood. Check the face is even with a spirit level.

Around sockets and switches cut short lengths of batten to butt up as closely as possible to the fitting and use panel adhesive to fix them.

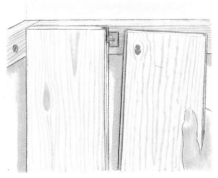

2 Using standard clips Fit standard clips into the groove in the board at each batten position and pin to the batten to secure. Slot the tongue of the next board into the groove.

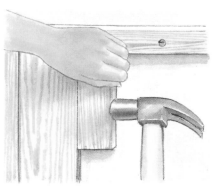

3 Fitting firmly Knock home securely with a hammer using a spare piece of board as a tamping block. Then fix the clips as before and continue fitting the remaining boards in the same way until you come to the final board in the run.

tip

Truly straight
Always make sure the first board is precisely vertical or horizontal with the aid of a spirit level before securing in place, rather than following the edge of a wall which might well be out of true. Any gap in the corner can be covered with beading.

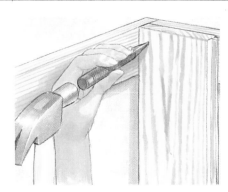

2 Hiding the pins Use a nail punch to drive each head just below the surface. If pin positions show when the panelling is finished fill holes with wood filler.

3 Angling the pins Fix a second pin through the board into each batten. Position it at the point where the tongue meets the board and angle it at 45° into the full-width board so that the tongue is left free for the next board to slot over it.

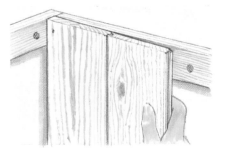

4 Fixing subsequent lengths Push the next board in so that the tongue on the first board is hidden in the new groove. Fix this second board with one pin in each batten as in step 3.

5 Fitting the final board The last board on any wall will have to be face nailed like the first.

FITTING ROUND CORNERS

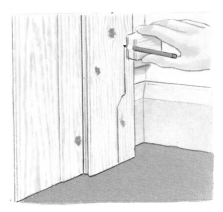

Fitting internal corners When you reach the first corner, scribe and cut the last board to fit the space left as tightly as possible. Then butt the first board on the adjacent wall up to cover the cut edge.

Fitting external corners Where possible, work away from an external corner. Fix the boards with grooves towards the corner and so that they just touch, then fill the angled space with beading.

FIT AROUND OBSTACLES

Fitting around doors Secure the last board to the batten adjacent to the architrave. Then fill the board and architrave junction with beading.

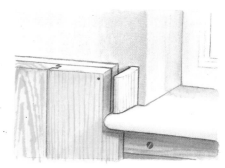

Fitting around windows Finish the panelling just short of the reveal and cover the batten and board edges with beading. If you want to take the panelling into the reveal, then stick a board, cut to fit, to the reveal wall. Finish in the same way as an external corner.

Fitting over sockets and switches Cut the boards so that the switch and socket plate will just cover the cut edges. Pin the boards to the glued battens around the socket or switch.

Before dealing with sockets and light switches, be sure **to turn off the power at the mains box**. Then loosen off the switch or socket faceplate and check there is enough slack in the circuit cables to pull the unit forward to the boards. If you don't fully understand electric circuits, it is probably wise to call in an electrician to advise you.

Finishing the panelling
Tidying up the corners However carefully you work, the cut edges of the boards in the corners always look a little uneven. Neaten them off by adding a length of quadrant or scotia beading.

Replacing or re-newing skirting boards Although the tongue-and-groove boards can be left plain, pin a strip of new skirting board at the base of the panelling for a trim finish.

Trimming with a dado rail A wooden moulding adds a perfect finish to the top of the dado panelling. Pin and glue with pva glue into position, or use special clips provided in some kits. Either spread a neatening skim of plaster filler along the shallow ledge of batten, board and dado rail, or fix a length of beading along the top of the dado rail to fill the gap between the wall and the wood and give it a neat finish.

▲ Colourful gutters
A faint shadow of blue-grey stain accenting the between-board channels looks effective when repeated on the brackets and shelves.

Finishing the timber
Apply a finish to the panelling as soon as possible to prevent damage or marking and avoid boards absorbing moisture.

The timber can be stained darker, to mimic more valuable hardwood, or left natural and polished or varnished. Alternatively, take advantage of the new pastel and bright colour wood finishes that add paint colour but still allow the grain of the wood to show through.

For a subtle effect, consider painting a row of boards in gradually deepening tones of one colour or using a range of pastels to form stripes in pale shades.

Wooden floors

Choosing the right floor surface or floor covering for the rooms in your home is important as it can often be a major investment. The flooring should take into account the kind of activities which take place in a room, as well as complement the style of furnishing and the colour scheme. Above all, most floors need to be practical surfaces.

An entrance hall which gets a lot of wear needs a hardwearing surface in a colour which will not show the dirt; a kitchen floor which is liable to be splashed with grease needs a surface which can be cleaned easily. A bath-room needs a surface which resists wa-ter, while a bedroom floor should be soft underfoot and does not need to be as hardwearing as the floor covering in a room used by all the family.

Country style floors
When considering flooring with a coun-try look, natural materials immediately come to mind. Traditionally, polished wood has been used, with rush matting and rugs to soften the hard surfaces and add warmth and colour. Styles and build-ing methods change and new materials are used in construction, so today's

▲ *A polished surface*
Rich dark wood which has been cared for and polished over the years has a wonderful warm glow. The furniture in the room has been chosen to match the floor – a rag rug at the side of the bed would be a welcome addition.

modern homes do not often have hard-wood floorboards. If your house does not have the kind of flooring you ideally want there are ways of changing the existing floor using modern equivalents which are relatively easy to lay.

▲ A varnished finish
This modern woodstrip floor has been finished with a coloured satin varnish to protect the surface and make it easy to clean and maintain. Once varnished, the surface will withstand a reasonable amount of wear and tear and retain its shine with an occasional polish.

◄ Herringbone style
Woodstrip flooring can be laid in decorative patterns such as this popular herringbone design which is quite easy to do. In this hallway the pattern is laid down the centre, with a straight strip edging.

The warmth of wood

Old polished wooden floorboards which have been cared for develop a rich shine but few of us are lucky enough to live in a house with such natural beauty. In some older houses, if you take up the carpet, you may find that the floorboards are in a good enough condition to consider sanding and polishing them and then leaving them uncovered. Hiring a sander to smooth the surface and remove any paint or stain is a possibility but before you start take a really good look at the floor to see if it really is worth all the effort. If one or two boards are very worn but the rest of the floor is in a good condition, consider taking them up and re-laying them the other way up rather than replacing them altogether. Remember to punch in all the nails before you start sanding.

If the floor is very uneven you could consider laying one of the wood strip floorings available from do-it-yourself stores. You will need to prepare the surface by laying down sheets of hardboard first.

In modern houses the floors are likely to be made of concrete on the ground floor and chipboard sheets on the upper floors. If floorboards are used they are probably made from pine and of a quality which is not suitable for staining or polishing. If you wish to lay a wood floor then modern wood strips or wood mosaic floor tiles are easily laid over these surfaces.

▲ Bleached out
While most varnishes and stains darken the original colour of the wood, bleaching can do the opposite. These floorboards have been lightened to match the furniture and sealed for protection.

◄ A lighter touch
These old floorboards have been sanded and varnished, keeping the original light oak colour. To have stained them to match the door and skirting board would make the hallway very dark. A bright rug adds a welcoming touch.

Where to use them

Wood floors are commonly found in sitting rooms, dining rooms or hallways and although there is nothing to prevent you having them elsewhere in the house you should consider the following points before making a decision.

Unless they are really well sealed, wood floors are best avoided in bathrooms and kitchens as the wood will absorb water and spills.

A wooden floor in a bedroom could be a little cold to walk on in bare feet so you will need to have a cosy bedside rug to avoid getting out of bed on to a bare floor in the morning.

Walking about on a wooden floor can be noisy, particularly for anyone in the room below, so they are not ideal for use in upstairs rooms or in flats. If you are considering a wooden floor upstairs, consider taking up the floorboards to add some sound insulation underneath.

Types of wooden flooring

Woodstrip flooring is available in two main types – solid planks or laminated strips with a decorative surface veneer. The length of the strips can vary from as little as 40cm (16in) to 180cm (70in) and widths range from 7cm (2 ³/₄in) up to 20cm (8in). Both types are usually made up from strips of wood which are shorter and narrower than the finished panel and the veneered type may resemble one continuous plank or have a basketweave effect.

Both types are generally tongued and grooved on both long and short edges for easy fitting but some are designed to be fixed to a timber sub-floor by secret nailing while others can be loose-laid using ingenious metal clips to hold them together. If you are likely to need access to underfloor services such as wiring or piping choose the type which is not nailed to the floor.

Another alternative is wood mosaic floor tiles. These are square tiles made up from a number of small fingers of wood. The fingers themselves may be solid hardwood or veneer on a cheaper soft-wood backing and are usually laid in a basketweave pattern, although other arrangements are also available.

Laminated veneers are generally pre-finished while solid strips may be finished or need sealing once they have been laid.

Types of wood

A wide range is available including elm, oak, ash, beech and maple. When choosing the kind of wood bear in mind the colour scheme of the room. Some woods have a warm reddish tone, others are very pale with an almost pastel look. If there will be any wooden furniture in the room choose a floor to match.

The following chapter describes how to lay modern woodstrip flooring. There's guidance on sanding floorboards on pages 91–94; pages 95–98 present ways of decorating a wooden floor.

▲Subtle variations of colour
Parquet flooring combines strips of wood, often in different shades, which are made up into tiles. Traditionally the strips are set at right angles to each other to create a basketweave effect. The tiles are usually made up in groups of four or sixteen, ready to be laid.

Laying a woodstrip floor

W ooden floors are among the most naturally attractive forms of flooring. Unfortunately, if you long for rooms with 'bare board' floors, you may be disappointed when you lift your carpet and discover what defects it has kept hidden. Sadly, not all old floorboards are worth the effort of sanding and polishing, particularly if they are littered with unsightly nail heads and have large draughty gaps between them. And if the sub-floor is concrete, laying a wooden floor on top would appear to be an extremely costly job best left to the professionals.

To meet the growing trend towards natural finishes in the home, however, there is a perfectly practical solution – long narrow strips of wood, about 1cm (⅜in) thick, in kit form which are easy to lay on any sub-floor. Whilst woodstrip is certainly not cheap to put down in the first place, it is very durable. Many manufacturers claim a life of at least 10 years for the original finish, after which the surface can be sanded down and re-sealed.

Made from solid wood or with a beech, pine or oak veneer on a particle board core, the strips are tongued-and-grooved on their edges so they simply slot together. They can be secured by nailing to a wooden sub-floor, fixed with clips set in a groove on the underside of the boards or glued firmly with PVA or wood glue where the floor is concrete. Consult the manufacturer's instructions for the particular boards you buy.

Measuring up

Wood strips are sold in a variety of lengths and widths – 200 x 20cm (78¾ x 7⅞in) is the average size, which is enough to cover 3.2 sq m (3½ sq yd). Most manufacturers of kits give guides on average coverage per pack of boards together with recommendations about suitable sub-floors on the packaging.

▲ All the comforts of wood
Knotty woodstrip flooring enhances the rustic charm of a cottage living-room. The floor feels warm and comfortable to walk on; a gay rug simply breaks up the expanse of bare boards for a cosier look.

Work out how much you need by measuring the dimensions of the room and drawing an accurate plan on a piece of graph paper to calculate the total floor area. Add an extra five per cent for cutting and wastage.

You can also use your plan to work out the best method for laying the flooring; strip flooring must be laid across existing floorboards or parallel to a light source coming through the window. Pay special attention to planning doorways, alcoves and bays, trying to fit in whole boards where unsightly cutting would show.

Good groundwork
Check the condition of the sub-floor.

On wooden floorboards If the existing floorboards are sound, you may only need to hammer home projecting nail heads and sand smooth any raised areas; if it is poor, the floor should be first covered with a layer of 3mm (⅛in) plywood to create a smooth level surface. PVC or linoleum floor coverings can remain in place.

On a concrete sub-floor you must be perfectly sure there's no suggestion of damp; check it out by taping a piece of glass to the floor for several days. If moisture collects on the underside, you have a problem which may need specialist attention. Any irregularities should be filled and the floor surface thoroughly cleaned. Then give it a continuous waterproof coating either with a polyurethane sealing compound or sheets of 0.2mm (0.008in) thick plastic foil.

Before you lay strip flooring on any surface, it makes sense to place a layer of insulating material in between.

Points to watch
Doors Remember that the new flooring will raise the original floor level significantly. If this is likely to impede the opening and closing of any doors, you will have to take them off their hinges before you lay the new floor – otherwise you could be trapped in the room behind an unopenable door! Before re-hanging the door, plane or saw off the bottom edge.

Matching edges Work out how many boards are needed across the room. If the last board is less than 5cm (2in) wide, then cut the first to an equal width so they match up at either side.

Expansion gap Wood expands and contracts, almost imperceptibly, with changes in temperature and humidity. It will eventually warp unless you allow an expansion gap all around the edges of the room. About 1cm (⅜in) is adequate and you can conceal it with the existing skirting boards, if you are prepared to remove them before starting work. You will have to lever them off carefully against a wooden block to minimize any damage to the wall.

Alternatively you can fill the gap with quadrant or scotia beading pinned to the skirting itself. It will be simpler if, before fixing, you paint the beading to match the skirting boards or stain it to match the floor. Then touch up or fill the pin heads once the beading is secured in place.

Acclimatization Allow wood strips to acclimatize in the room in which they will be laid. Store in unopened packages at room temperature for at least 48 hours before laying.

Materials
Hammer, chisel and a **small crowbar**
Fine-toothed saw and **fretsaw**
A **tamping block** made from a piece of softwood
Spacer blocks of wood about 1cm (⅜in) thick
Pencil, ruler and **adjustable template**
PVA or **wood glue, clips** or **nails**, depending on the fixing method

LAYING WOODSTRIP FLOORING

1 Laying the first board Place the first board with the grooved edge to the wall. Place spacer blocks, cut to the size of the expansion gap required, between the board and the wall.

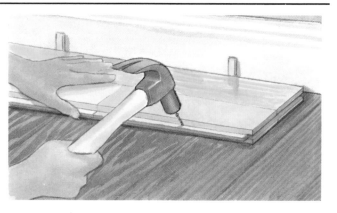

3a If using secret nailing, drive the fixing pins at an angle of 45° down through the tongues into the wooden sub-floor, punching the heads into the angle but taking care not to over drive them or the tongue will split. Nails should be spaced about 30cm (12in) apart. Punch heads below the surface; they will be covered by the next strip of board.

2 Laying the second board Lay further boards, end to end, to complete the first row. Fit them dry first and trim the end plank so that it falls 1cm (⅜in) from the wall. To do this, place the last board so that tongue lies next to tongue, with the end butted to the wall and a spacer block in position. Mark where to saw and cut to length.

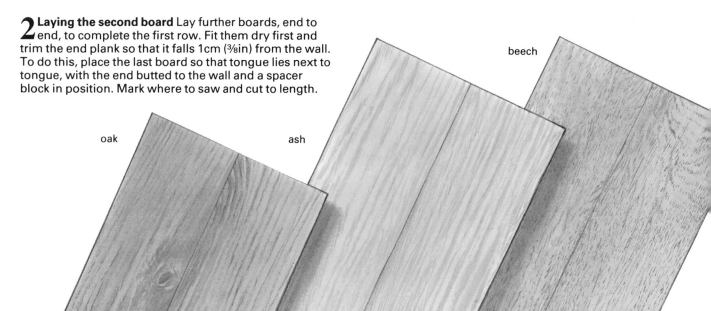

oak

ash

beech

3b If using fixing clips, the method of fixing depends on the system. The type shown here, you just tap the clips into the grooves in the underside of the boards, at the recommended intervals, and lay them against the spacer blocks. When you come to fix subsequent boards make sure you stagger the positions of the fixing clips.

3c If gluing the ends as they butt together, most systems recommend PVA adhesive. Apply a little adhesive to each plank and tap into position, wiping away any surplus adhesive with a damp cloth. Use a string line to check the boards are straight; if they need adjusting, remove, or add, spacer blocks accordingly.

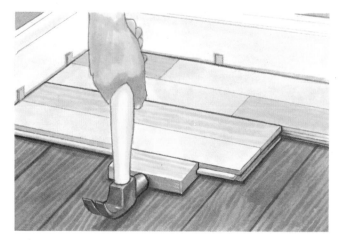

4 Fitting the next row Lay subsequent rows, with the joints staggered – they should not be closer than 30cm (12in) – by offering their grooved edges up to the tongued edges. Start the second row with the piece of board left over from the first. Tap into place with hammer and tamping block and secure as before.

5 Fixing the last strip When you get to the last row, measure the plank of woodstrip to fill the remaining gap by placing one board on top of the previous one and another with the tongue butting against the wall.

6 Easing into place Rule in pencil along the cutting line, saw to size and then ease into place using the bolster and hammer to press the boards home tight.

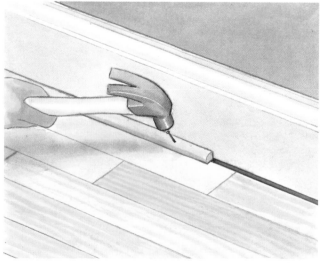

7 Replacing the skirting board Remove spacer blocks, replace skirting or fit beading strip to cover the gap.

FITTING AROUND AWKWARD SHAPES

Measure and mark the position of the pipe on the board. Saw two parallel cuts in from the edge for the required distance using a fretsaw, carefully sawing in a circle at the inner end to fit around the pipe. Slide in place up to the pipe. Trim to fit if necessary, leaving a 1cm (⅜in) gap between the edge and the wall.

Where planks meet awkward obstacles like door frames, use an adjustable metal template with movable rods or a paper pattern to transfer the outline of the obstacle to the board, ready for cutting. You may need a fine fretsaw to make all the intricate cut-outs necessary for a precise fit.

Finishing at a doorway Lay the appropriate threshold strip to provide a neat ramp from one room to the next.

tip

Caring for wood floors
Keep clean Sweep or vacuum regularly and clean with a mild cleaning agent and damp cloth. Never use abrasive materials.
Keep dry Avoid over-wetting. Wooden floors are unsuitable for shower areas and utility rooms.
Protection Stop dirt at the entrance with a door mat and deal with accidental spillages and stains immediately they occur. Take care when moving furniture; always lift rather than drag it across the floor.

◀ Wood sense
Natural wood proves to be a practical and good-looking choice of flooring in the kitchen. For a start, woodstrip is easy to clean, which makes it very hygienic. At the same time the hardwearing finish is robust enough to stand up to non-stop household traffic. But notice how the wooden flooring is not carried through into the utility room next door where it would not benefit from a regular soaking. When the floor is teamed up with matching beech units and worktops, it creates a smart working area.

Sanding a wooden floor

The natural good looks of bare floorboards fit perfectly into a country design scheme. Their rugged simplicity can either be used to set off a slightly rustic type of decoration or provide a moderating, plainer contrast to a more flamboyant style.

Most homes are fitted with pine floorboards but a few lucky houses have oak boards. Although plain wooden boards provide hardwearing and attractive flooring, in time they inevitably become dirty and dented and then get covered with carpet or lino tiles. Lifting an existing floor covering may well reveal that the floorboards underneath are unfit for immediate display. However, a thorough sanding will remove the old surface and expose fresh,

clean wood, which can then be protected by a sealer to give an inexpensive, durable and very beautiful floor.

Hiring the equipment

Preparing the floor involves sanding the floorboards, first with a powered drum sander and then with a small edging sander, which gets into areas the larger one cannot reach. You can hire these from your local tool rental centre.

Ask for a demonstration of the machines so that you know how to operate them and be sure to take plenty of abrasive sheets and belts of all grades away with you. Also buy or hire a face mask and safety goggles at the same time, so that you aren't choked or blinded by the fine sawdust. Change the

▲ Baring the boards
Brilliant sunshine streaming through the window throws a spotlight across bare floorboards and highlights the natural beauty of well-waxed wood.

filter in your face mask regularly to prevent it getting clogged. Ear protectors to muffle the noise are also a good idea, although not essential.

Ensure that the sander picks up as much dust as possible by emptying the collecting bag frequently into heavy duty plastic rubbish bags; collecting bags have been known to catch fire spontaneously when overfull. Never throw the dust on a fire later; the fine particles can flash into fierce flames.

Preparing the floorboards

Lift the existing floor covering and inspect the boards underneath. Check for sagging boards, which are a sign of damaged joists; lever the floorboard up to examine the joists beneath. Rotten timber and boards may have to be treated or replaced professionally. Also look out for any tell-tale signs of wood-worm which you can treat with an insecticide.

Using a claw hammer, remove the tacks or nails that were used to hold the old floor covering in place and watch out for protruding floorboard nail heads as well. Knock these back into the boards using a hammer and nail punch. If the abrasive sheet on a sanding machine catches on a nail during use, it can rip with a shocking bang.

Regular wide gaps between the floorboards become dust traps and an annoying source of cold draughts. They are most easily remedied by lifting the boards and re-laying them. The occasional unsightly split between two boards can be filled with strips of wood or papier-mâché. Creaking floorboards are often loose; knocking in extra flooring nails will stop any movement.

Materials

Overalls or old clothes
Face mask with spare filters
Goggles and **ear defenders**
Masking tape
Claw hammer, nail punch and **floor nails**
Drum and **small belt edging sander**
Coarse, medium and **fine abrasive strips**
Vacuum cleaner, white spirit and **rags**
Sealant and **brushes.**

A range of strips

Sealant

Face mask and ear defenders

SANDING A WOOD FLOOR

1 Cleaning the floor Preliminary cleaning exposes the true condition of the boards before you start sanding. Vacuum away any dirt and, if necessary, scrub the floor using the minimum of hot, soapy water. Wetting the floor will raise the grain which will need sanding off when it is dry. Where there is a heavy build up of wax, remove some of it by rubbing with wire wool soaked in white spirit.

2 Blocking the big gaps Plug any odd large gaps between the floor boards with thin strips of timber tapered into a slight wedge. Spread both sides with glue before knocking them down between the boards with a hammer. Use a wooden block to protect the floorboards. Then plane them level with the floor.

3 Filling the narrow gaps Mix some torn up newspaper, wallpaper paste and boiling water together in a bowl and add some wood stain to match the colour of the boards. Stuff this papier-mâché into the small gaps between the boards with a filling knife. Leave the filler slightly proud of the surface because it might shrink as it dries. Sand it smooth when hard.

Gloves

Goggles

4 Knocking in raised nails Go over the floor very carefully, punching down any protruding nail heads with a hammer and a nail punch. Fill any small hollows with wood filler later. Fix any loose boards with extra nails tapped in near the old ones to avoid pipes and electric cables.

5 Sealing the room The fine dust from sanding penetrates everywhere so clear the room completely of furnishings. Then, when you are ready to start sanding, and have all the equipment you need in the room close the door to the rest of the house. Seal around the frame with masking tape and open the windows for ventilation.

6 Starting the sander Fit a coarse abrasive sheet, making sure it is taut and firmly locked in place. Never start the machine while the drum is resting on the ground. Tilt the machine backwards, switch on and lower it gradually to the floor as it builds up speed. Be prepared to be tugged forwards as the drum contacts the floor.

8 Honing the finish Change to a medium abrasive strip and go on working diagonally across the floor. Next, sand the floor parallel to the floorboards, again going over each strip in both directions, minding the skirtings as you turn. Then switch to fine abrasive and repeat the whole process again. It's also a good idea to vacuum the floor from time to time to minimize the amount of fine dust flying around.

▼ In the wood
With their pronounced grain and warm honey colour, stripped pine floorboards supply the perfect complement to the light and airy atmosphere in this garden room. Sealed with a coat of varnish, they are able to withstand any hard wear from dirty shoes traipsing through.

7 Beginning to sand Start by working diagonally back and forth across the room at 45° to the boards. Avoid stopping while the machine is running as you risk gouging the boards; tip it back as you turn at the end of each run instead, avoiding the skirtings. Check the abrasive sheet occasionally to make sure it is not clogged; change to a fresh piece when it becomes worn. Continue with the coarse abrasive sheets until the worst of the marks have gone.

9 Going round the edges Now switch to the smaller edging sander to tackle the borders of the room. Work with coarse and medium abrasive sheets to clear the marks and fine ones for a smooth finish.

10 Cleaning up the dust After sanding, vacuum the floor thoroughly, along with the skirtings, door and window frames and mop up the last specks of dust with a dampened cloth. Leave for 24 hours to let the dust settle before vacuuming again. Finally, give the boards a wipe with white spirit to remove all dust before sealing.

tip

Safe sanding
Don't let children anywhere near the sanding machine; always unplug the machine when changing the sanding strips; keep the sander's flex out of harm's way during use by draping it over your shoulder.

Sealing the floor

Once the bare wood of the boards has been exposed it needs to be protected from staining and damage with some form of durable sealer.

Polyurethane varnish is the usual choice of sealer. It is easy to apply, using at least three, and preferably four, coats of cover. Thin the first coat of varnish with white spirit, following the maker's instructions, to encourage the sealant to permeate into the wood. Apply the varnish with a 100mm (4in) brush, working along the grain. After each coat is dry, sand the surface lightly using fine glasspaper on a block or a wad of medium grade steel wool. Vacuum again and wipe over with the white-spirit-soaked cloth before applying the next coat of varnish.

Solvent-free varnishes are more user and environmentally friendly. They combine all the traditional benefits of a tough, scratch-resistant surface with a low level of odour and a rapid drying time. Each coat is 'touch' dry in only 20 minutes and you can apply another coat after two hours. Best of all, when you have finished the job, you can simply wash out your brushes in water.

Stain and varnish stain The natural tones of the wood can be altered by staining, or by using a coloured polyurethane varnish. Stain on its own is applied before sealing: use a spirit-based stain, and apply it with a cloth pad, not a brush.

This gives a more even coverage over the wooden boards.

When using varnish stain, apply a thinned coat of clear varnish first. This lightly seals the surface so that it will absorb the colour evenly. Follow that with two or more coloured coats. Finish with another clear coat of gloss, matt or silk, according to your choice.

▲ *A warm footing*
Lovely old floorboards are the ideal surface to enhance the country mood of a cottage-style bedroom.

▼ *Immaculate planking*
Expanses of brand new boards provide a fresh, easy-to-clean floor that suits open layouts.

Decorated wooden floors

Once you decide to opt for a wooden floor, rather than for tiles, vinyl flooring or carpet, you have many options on how to treat it. Those lucky enough to have a house with very high quality floorboards, mellowed with age to a rich attractive shade, will probably neither want nor need to do anything to enhance the beauty of the wood. Simple varnishing or waxing will be enough.

If, however, your floorboards leave something to be desired, you have a good choice of decorative finishes: dyeing, staining, painting, and stencilling being the most popular. You can treat large areas like the hall, stairs and landings, living rooms, kitchens and bathrooms in

this way. If you prepare the wood properly and apply several coats of varnish over your work, the finish will last for ages, and the mellowing effect of time and sunlight will make your efforts prettier as the years go by.

Decorating your wooden floor is an infinitely cheaper option than carpeting, but it is very time consuming, and the floor you are working on will be out of commission for a couple of weeks while you first prepare it, then paint it, then finally treat it with several coats of varnish. It is really important that all decorative finishes are applied on clean, bare wood, sanded, filled where necessary, scrubbed and rubbed with white spirit.

▲ **A stencilled rug**
A stencilled border with a circular central motif gives the effect of a carpet on this wooden kitchen floor. Only three colours have been used in the design but each colour has been shaded from dark to light to vary the intensity.

Base coats

Lightening and bleaching At this stage you may decide that the basic colour of your floorboards is too dark, or has yellowed over the years. To lighten it apply a lavish coat of white, oil-based paint. Wait a few minutes, then rub the paint off with a rag. White residues will remain in the cracks and pores. This forms a good base for colourless varnish. Alternatively you can bleach the floor by scrubbing it with household bleach and then rinsing off with clean water, but varnishing over bleach you may still end up with a yellowish cast, so lightening with paint may be a better option for a really pale floor.

Dyeing and staining When you dye or stain floorboards you will still be able to see the grain and notches in the wood as these finishes are transparent. Take the natural warm colour of most woods into account when choosing a colour. When using dyes and stains, build up the colour gradually to get the effect you want.

Dyeing You can use ordinary fabric, leather or carpet dyes, but make up the solution with half the specified amount of water and apply two or three coats, according to how intense a colour you want, before varnishing.

Staining With the staining process the colour goes deeper into the wood. There is a good range of traditional wood colours to choose from, from palest ash blond to the colour of darkest oak. You can also buy bright stains in reds, blues and greens. There are various different kinds of wood stains on the market, but for floors, you will find that an oil-based stain produces the best and most even finish.

Staining suggestions Untreated floorboards tend to be very pale, and you can keep this look by simply sealing them. However, if you want to make them look warmer and more distinguished you can stain them in the light honey shade that we associate with polished pine, or a deeper, richer, reddy-orange colour for a much warmer look. If you plan to stencil or paint designs on to your floor, you will still probably want to stain the boards first.

Both dyes and stains can be used to create a lively effect in which each individual floorboard is stained in a different shade. Try a combination of reds, oranges and light browns for a warm feel; use blues, greens and chalky whites for a cool effect.

Staining works very well with stencils; try a design in various woody shades such as chestnut, spicy brown and mahogany on light, honey-stained floorboards to create a marvellous marquetry effect that will mellow beautifully.

Painting With floorboards that do not bear close inspection, a coat or two of paint on a prepared surface will work wonders.

A floor painted in a single colour can provide the perfect background for several brightly coloured rugs or a larger carpet. Make sure the colour tones with the rugs you plan to use or the furnishings in the room.

Using the same technique as for staining, paint each board in a different colour. A child's bedroom or playroom would look very jolly and be very hardwearing with floorboards painted in bright primary colours and sealed with multiple layers of varnish.

For the more ambitious, the possibilities with paint are endless. Once you have applied your basic colour (two coats of flat, oil-based paint is best, as you can

▲ Painted to match
If your floorboards are not good enough quality to paint or stain you could lay sheets of hardboard, nailing them to the boards, and then prime and paint the surface. A stencil was made from the boldly patterned fabric for use on the floor.

make the final effect as glossy as you like with varnish) you can give your imagination free rein. Many floor paint effects imitate other floor coverings – one simple but very dramatic effect is to paint a chequer board arranged in a diamond pattern to look like tiles. Traditionally this is done in black and white, but if your floor area is small, it could look better in subtler shades, in soft grey and white, for instance, or sepia and ivory.

▲ A hint of a colour
The blue theme has been carried through on to the floor of this pretty bedroom. The floorboards have been sanded and then stained a pale bluish-grey to match the painted and stained furniture. The wood takes up the stain unevenly which gives a textured feel to the surface.

◄ A stained pattern
This simple diamond pattern is achieved by drawing a squared grid pattern on the floor and then using masking tape to outline the areas of the floor to be stained. A geometric pattern like this looks effective used in a hall or lobby.

Stencilling Using stencils, you can create painted rugs or carpets, repeating the same design again and again, and surrounding the whole with a stencilled border. This looks especially good on a floor stained in a light colour, with the stencilled motifs in shades of dark red, brown and russet, or in transparent jewel-like reds, blues and greens. On a bedroom floor, a really pale wood base could be stencilled in transparent pastel shades.

To keep your stencilling simple, you can stick to just doing a decorative border around the walls, leaving the centre of the floor free for a rug or carpet; alternatively you could just do one large stencil in the centre, and leave the rest of the floor plain. If you live in a self-contained house and can cope with the noise, a decorated wooden staircase can be immensely attractive; leave the treads plain, but stencil motifs on to the risers, or simply stencil borders all the way up on both sides of the stairs.

Polishing off

Varnish The hardest wearing finish for a wooden floor is polyurethane varnish, which is heat and stain resistant, easy to apply and easy to clean afterwards. It comes in matt, semi-gloss or gloss finishes, and you can get it in a clear or a tinted finish. When you apply it the floor must be clean and dust free and you must wait for each coat to dry completely before you apply the next. You will need at least three coats in a room with light wear, and at least five in a hall or kitchen or living room. Renew the varnish every couple of years.

Sealing Floor seal is easy to apply, as you can simply swab it on with cloth, working first across the grain, and then with the grain for subsequent coats. Sand the floor lightly between coats. Like varnish, you should re-apply it when it wears thin, first removing all dirt and grease with a sugar soap solution.

Waxing There is nothing quite like the shine and wonderful smell of a floor that has been polished with beeswax, but achieving this finish requires hard work and lots of elbow grease, starting with making the polish. Modern wax polishes are easier to apply and tougher wearing, but waxing is still not an easy option.

You must first seal the floor with a coat of floor seal, allow it to dry and then sand it down. Then apply the beeswax polish or modern commercial wax polish with a soft brush. Leave it to dry, and shine it with first a soft shoe brush, and then a soft cloth.

▲ Beautiful borders
A simple border stencil worked in two colours around the edge of a room. Mark the stencil positions carefully so that the effect is visually satisfying. Here the motif is centred

◄ Zigzag effects
The strip floor laid in a herringbone pattern has been stained in three different colours, the colour changing with each board. Use masking tape and stain all the boards in one colour before moving on to the next.

Staining wood

S taining timber is a way of changing the wood's colour without sacrificing the character of the grain and knots. This can be done discreetly using wood tones to improve the natural shade or imitate a more expensive timber. Or you can completely transform the appearance of the wood with a whole spectrum of un-wood-like rainbow colours. Brilliant patterns and motifs can be developed from a widely varied palette of colours to pick out moulded details in carved wood and cheer up timber.

In contrast, modern pastel, semi-translucent, grain-displaying paints mimic the soft, faded appeal and weathered finish of old country cottage joinery and furniture. By reproducing the muted colours and distressed finish of genuinely matured rustic features, they can blend new timber articles with old or bring recently stripped older pieces back to life. The effect works equally well on floorboards and panelling, giving the timber an instantly seasoned quality and the room a peaceful atmosphere.

▲ In the pink
The warm tones of a pastel pink paint stain successfully soften and meld bare floorboards into a comfortable bedroom decor. The same stain is used again on the bedhead and skirting boards to complete the picture.

Objects for staining

Wooden furniture responds well to staining, either to restore its original hue or mellow new pieces to blend in with older ones. Old pine pieces that have been stripped can often look slightly grey and bleached; a coat or two of a golden stain re-develops its former warmth.

For pine, avoid red tones of stain, like mahogany, which are better for close-grained woods. Antique pine tones are available, but test them first. If necessary, mix different tones until you achieve the desired effect.

Skirtings and doors Staining rather than painting woodwork around the house makes a pleasant change, presenting a more natural or delicate look than conventional gloss and eggshell finishes. Slightly subdued, worn shades integrate beautifully with muted pastels and sheer fabrics, creating a soft focus in the room.

Timber floorboards or panelling offer a broad surface for colour treatment. Decorating a wooden floor is infinitely cheaper than laying carpet or tiles. Already divided into parallel strips, the boards can be stained in stripes, panels, zigzags or mosaics of different shades.

Staining a chequerboard layout simulates the crisp, clean lines of a tiled floor very realistically. Mark out the grid carefully on the floor before you start working in the stains, using masking tape to define the margins. As an extra precaution to prevent the stain bleeding from one area to another, score the borders of the pattern elements lightly with a sharp knife.

Household equipment Plain wooden items around the house gain individuality when stained, particularly if you add a special pattern or motif of your own for extra distinction. In the kitchen a bread bin or paper roll dispenser can be picked out in a rustic stain. In the bathroom, towel rails and accessories retain a naturally grained appearance while adopting a colour that ties in with the rest of the design scheme.

Types of stain

Stains for wood fall into two main types: those, usually put on with a cloth, that sink into the wood but give no surface protection, and those which are incorporated in a varnish so that colour and protection are imparted at the same time (see page 106).

Stain on its own comes in a range of wood and primary colours. They can be water or oil-based. Many stains tend to soak in quickly which can make it difficult to apply evenly, especially with a brush. If you brush on the dye, more tends to soak into the wood where you first touch it with the bristles. When the wood does take up the stain unevenly the surface acquires an interesting blotchy, textured feel which can be appealing in its own right.

A clean, lint-free cloth often proves a more satisfactory means of applying a smooth coat of stain. The pad absorbs the runny stain and distributes it evenly, especially into the crevices of carved and turned wood. Alternatively, a sponge paint pad is a good way of getting consistent cover, except in tight corners.

The wood itself has to be protected by wax polish, oil or clear varnish after using this type of stain. When you prepare the wood thoroughly in the first place and apply several coats of varnish over the stained timbers, the finish should be robust enough to withstand wear-and-tear for many years.

Semi-translucent paint displays the grain like a stain, allowing the natural beauty of the timber to show through, but instead of wood tones it comes in a range of pale pastel colours. A combination of chalky green, blue and white produces a cool, refreshing impression; misty pink and peach add a warmer, comforting touch.

The paint is easy to apply and protects woodwork with a tough, low-sheen coating that is quick to clean and resistant to damage. Brush it on evenly in the direction of the grain and leave to dry for at least six hours before re-applying; two coats are recommended. For good results, this paint needs to be applied to a new light-coloured or stripped wood in which a strong fingerprint of the grain is evident.

Exterior stains Special microporous sealers or stains must be used on external woodwork.

▲ Emerging shadows
Even after staining in pale grey, the grain in the wood of these display units and drawers is clearly visible. Fascinating shadows in the timber emerge from the stain, conveying a worn look that is totally compatible with a matured country kitchen.

Applying wood stains

Whatever type of stain you decide to use it is important to do a test first on an inconspicuous spot to check the colour. The result depends on the colour and grain of the original wood and how much of the stain it absorbs. Remember also that further coats of stain will deepen the colour. So let the first coat be absorbed and test a smaller area with another coat on top. You can mix stain colours of the same type to achieve the shade you prefer.

You should also test the effect of the final finish you intend to use over the stain; most waxes and oils tend to darken surfaces while even clear varnish contributes a yellowish hue.

Quick dyes
Cold water fabric dye powders diluted in water are fine for staining small areas and even better if you want a faded, worn look. Since they are not specifically designed for use on wood they tend to fade further in direct sunlight.

▼ Accumulating colour
The gradation of shades in these panelled shutters is achieved by working down the panels, giving each board one more coat of the same coloured wood stain than its neighbour above.

◄ Grizzled grain
Staining small wooden items of furniture like this free-standing towel rail grants them a peculiar distinction. The mottled effect of colour-stained wood blends particularly effectively with the blotchiness on colour-washed walls.

◄ Outdoor shades
These lovely bright stain colours pick out the decorative details of an unusual plant trough for the garden. It's a good idea to choose your flowers to complement the colour scheme.

► Step by step
Alternating bands of natural and colour stained boards in a random fashion creates an intriguing individual pattern on the floor.

Preparing the surface

Untreated, light wood shows off the colours best. Previously painted or varnished wood should be stripped thoroughly before applying a fresh finish. Fill any blemishes with wood filler. Make sure all surfaces are sanded to a nearly smooth finish, dry and free from dust and wax.

The same goes for wood floors as well. Usually you will need to hire a sander to smooth the surface and remove any old paint and stain. Rub down the surface with white spirit.

Materials
Rubber gloves
Old saucer or **shallow container**
Clean, lint-free cloths
Fine glasspaper

USING WOOD STAIN

1 Taking care Wear rubber gloves to avoid staining your fingers. Decant some of the stain from the can into an old saucer or shallow container, so that you can judge how much the cloth soaks up each time it is dipped into the dye.

2 Putting on the stain Take a clean, lint-free rag folded into a pad and dip it into the stain. Pressing lightly and evenly, apply a thin coat of stain to the wood, working with the grain. Work swiftly without a pause to avoid patchiness. Then quickly wipe over with a clean cloth to pick up any excess.

3 Completing the finish Allow to dry – a couple of hours for a water-based stain, at least 6 hours for an oil-based one. If the finish is too light apply a second coat in the same way; if the finish is too dark lightly sand the surface.

Stencilling with wood stains

After staining a surface in one colour to serve as a base coat, you can use wood stains in other shades to stencil a pattern on to it. Carefully done in various woody tones, this creates a convincing marquetry-like result which can look very mellow and individual. Worked out in brighter colours, you can stencil a rug on the floor or a cloth on a table; patterns picked out in pastel shade look good on bedroom floors and furniture. Running a stencilled border around the fringes of the floor clearly defines its boundaries, especially when teamed with a co-ordinated skirting and a central rug in toning colours.

Quick brush patterns Using a thin paint brush dipped in stain of a darker tone you can casually apply lines and squiggles of pattern to stained timber for an impromptu design.

◄ Stain stencils
Executing an ambitious stencilled pattern in coloured stains on plain door panels produces a magnificent result and transforms ordinary pine dresser and cupboard units into a treasured family heirloom.

Stripping wood

Old timber furniture, varnished, polished or oiled to a soft sheen, is very much part of the traditional country look. But all too often the beauty of the wood has been lost under layers of scuffed paint or hard, darkened varnish. These need to be stripped away before the wood beneath is exposed in its original glory. The time and trouble spent resurrecting an immaculate piece of furniture from behind a dilapidated exterior can be tremendously fulfilling.

Checking the finish

It is important to know what the finish is before you start to sand, clean or chemically strip it, since methods vary.

Painted finish Usually a glance at the back, underneath or inside of the drawers or doors reveals the nature and quality of the timber beneath. Old pine furniture has often been painted in the past. You need to remove the paint with a chemical stripper.

Doors and less valuable pine furniture can be commercially stripped in baths of caustic soda, which saves time and effort but has disadvantages. Old glues are dissolved by the process so that the sections of the furniture can come apart. Also, the grain of the wood is raised when the caustic soda is washed off and careful sanding is necessary to restore the surface. Remember to remove fittings before immersion.

▼▶ From ugly duckling to swan
All the effort and attention lavished on this chair is rewarded when a delightfully mellow wood hatches from beneath the scruffy surface.

Blow lamps and hot air strippers are best avoided as there is a danger of scorching the wood.

Varnish Old varnishes are usually very dark in colour; alternatively a modern clear polyurethane varnish may have been used. If you are not sure whether a piece of furniture has been varnished do a quick test to check. Clean the surface with reviving fluid. If the surface does not respond to this treatment, then it has probably been varnished. Varnish has to be removed with chemical stripper or a hard surface remover.

Veneered furniture Wood veneer is a fine layer of a quality wood such as walnut or maple which has been glued to the surfaces of a cheaper wood like pine. It is important to check if an item is veneered, as it can be easily damaged or partially removed if handled roughly. The bottom edges of drawers and doors will often provide the necessary information but if these are covered with paint you will need to scrape away a section so that you can study the wood more closely.

It is best to hand-sand a finish gently on veneered furniture but this is hard and very time consuming if the furniture has been painted or varnished. In this case, use chemical stripper gel or paste and remove the paint in thin layers, taking great care not to scratch the surface as you peel the stripper away.

Waxed or oiled furniture This usually responds to cleaning with a reviving fluid but if you wish to change the colour of the wood or the finish you will need to remove it completely. Sanding is the best method. First use a medium then a fine glasspaper and work with the grain of the wood. When you are back to bare wood give the surface a final rub with very fine 000 grade wire wool. On very large surfaces you can use an orbital sander to do most of the work but the final rubbing down should always be done by hand.

Types of chemical stripper

Liquid, gel or paste strippers react with paint and varnish, softening it so that the paint becomes easy to scrape off. In all cases, test a little of the paint stripper on a concealed patch of the furniture to check how long you will need to leave the stripper to work and if it causes any unwanted discolouration in the wood.

Remember to remove any metal or ceramic knobs or hinges before you use the chemical stripper as these can be damaged by the chemicals in the stripper. Wooden handles are also best removed and stripped separately.

Liquid or gel strippers may be water or spirit based. On furniture it is best to use a spirit-based stripper as this will not raise the grain of the wood as water does, so you won't have to sand the surface smooth again.

Check the manufacturer's advice. As a guideline, if water is recommended for washing down the wood after stripping then the stripper is water based; if however white spirit or methylated spirits is used to wash down the wood instead, the stripper is spirit based.

Paste stripper is ideal for use on carved or turned wood like chair backs and banisters.

Materials
Rubber gloves
Old paint brush for applying the liquid or gel
Trowel or **old palette knife** for spreading the paste
Liquid, gel or **paste stripper**
Flat scraper and **shave hook** for smoothly paring away the softened paint
White spirit or **water** and a clean **cloth** for rinsing off the stripper
Fine grade glasspaper and **fine wire wool, 000 grade,** for rubbing and buffing down

USING CHEMICAL STRIPPER

Liquid and gel strippers It is best to apply gel strippers with a paint brush. When blisters appear on the surface, strip off the softened finish with a scraper, using a shave hook or old nail file for crevices and carvings. You may need to apply several coats of stripper if there are a number of layers of paint to remove.

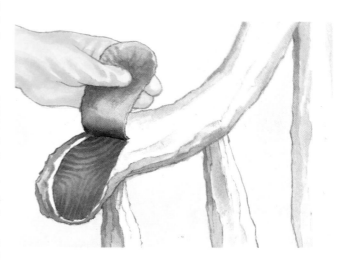

Paste stripper Mix the powder with water to form a thick paste according to the manufacturer's instructions. Apply thickly with a trowel and leave for about 30 minutes. Then peel away in strips. Rinse with a damp cloth to neutralize.

If there are several layers of paint you may need to leave the paste on longer. To prevent the paste stripper drying out, cover and bind the pasted areas with sheets or strips of polythene; you could use old polythene bags for this. The paste will liquefy the paint and sometimes this will run down on to the floor.

Always stand the furniture on several thicknesses of newspaper covered with a dust sheet or, if stripping items like banisters, remove carpeting or other floor coverings as it can work out expensive if you have to buy new carpets too.

Re-finishing
Once the old finish has been removed the surface will probably need sanding smooth and then bleaching and filling if necessary before the final protective surface is applied to the wood.

Wood bleaches

Sometimes stripping off the existing finish reveals stains in the wood which can be removed with a proprietary wood bleach. This is useful, too, for lightening the natural colour of the wood so you can apply a lighter coloured stain. After bleaching you will need to sand down the surface since the process usually raises the grain of the wood.

You can either use oxalic acid crystals or a proprietary solution, which comes in two bottles that are applied separately but work in conjunction when used according to the manufacturer's instructions.

Materials
Proprietary wood bleach, 2 glass jars and an **old paint brush**
White vinegar and a **bucket** and **cloth**

BLEACHING WOOD

1 **Priming the surface** Pour the first solution into a clean, empty jam jar. Apply generously to the surface with an old paint brush and leave for 10 minutes. The wood may darken slightly as it soaks in.

2 **Mixing on the surface** Brush on the second solution and leave it for several hours or overnight. Remove any scum that appears with a scrubbing brush and clean water.

3 **Rinsing off the bleach** Wipe over the surface with a half-and-half mixture of white vinegar and water. This treatment raises the grain which will need sanding to smoothness again.

Grain filling

Even the most finely planed and sanded wood is full of minute cracks and pores which deflect the light in different directions, dulling the surface. Using a grain filler makes the surface more reflective and therefore glossier.

Materials
Very fine glasspaper, grain filler and **white spirit**
2 lint-free cloths and **wood dye**

FILLING THE GRAIN

1 **Rubbing down** Sand the surface in the direction of the grain with very fine glasspaper.

2 **Mixing the filler** Dilute the grain filler to a thin paste with white spirit.

3 **Smoothing a loose grain** Apply the filler to the surface with a cloth, rubbing in across the grain. Remove excess filler using a clean cloth. Leave overnight to harden.

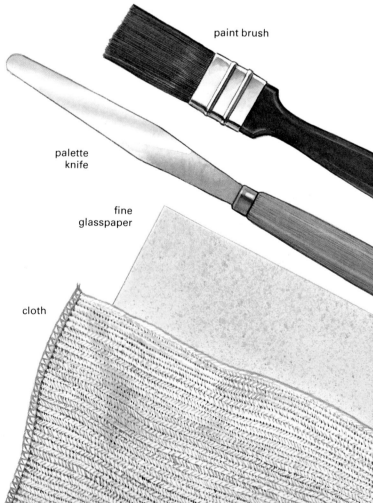

paint brush

palette knife

fine glasspaper

cloth

Varnishing wood

As one of the most hardwearing and easy-to-apply finishes, polyurethane varnish can be clear or tinted to simulate real wood colours, with a gloss, silk or matt look. Modern varnishes must only be applied to surfaces which are free from dirt, grease, oil and wax.

Coloured varnish or varnish stains are varnishes which have been coloured with dyes or translucent pigments. They are easier to put on than stain on its own and provides protection at the same time. As the colour is brushed on with the varnish each coat slightly deepens the tone.

When using polyurethane varnish on bare wood, it is usually advisable to thin the first coat so that it soaks in quickly and seals the grain. Solvent-based polyurethanes are thinned with white spirit, according to the manufacturer's instructions, and generally applied with a cloth to avoid minute bubbles forming in the surface. Afterwards, the sealed wood can be sanded and finished with further coats of full strength varnish or wax polished for a more natural finish.

Wash the brushes in white spirits and set them aside specifically for varnishing in the future.

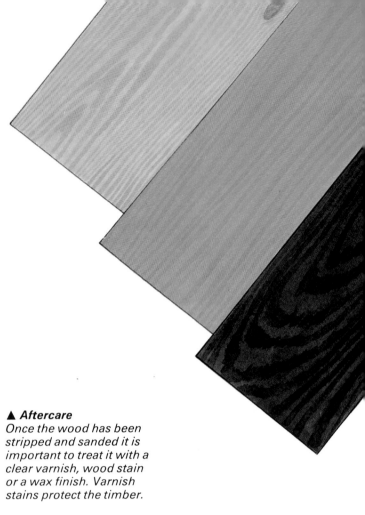

APPLYING VARNISH

1 **Wiping on the first coat** Using a diluted varnish and a clean cloth, wipe over the surface to seal it.

2 **Varnishing** Apply the varnish along the grain first, drawing the brush backwards and forwards. Don't overload the brush. Dip it in the varnish and touch the ends of the bristles against the side of the tin; don't scrape the bristles across the lip as this tends to create bubbles in the finished work.

▲ *Aftercare*
Once the wood has been stripped and sanded it is important to treat it with a clear varnish, wood stain or a wax finish. Varnish stains protect the timber.

3 **Brushing on the final coat** Using light pressure, brush at right angles across the grain. Then finish off along the grain as lightly as possible using the tip of the brush.

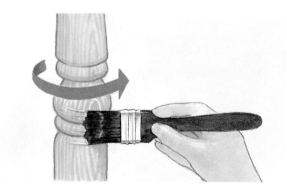

4 **Working on turned wood** When varnishing stair or chair spindles work round the pattern this will keep the effect even. On mouldings, work only along the grain to avoid major drips and runs.

Applying varnish stain
Apply a first thin coat with a cloth so that it seals the wood's surface. When this is dry lightly sand to remove any bubbles or brush bristles in the finish. Then apply further coats with a brush. Remember that the colour will deepen slightly when each coat is applied.

Tile style

An imaginative use of tiling in your kitchen or bathroom can cleverly combine sensible practicality with design flair. From a functional point of view, ceramic tiles are tough, resistant to water, steam, heat and staining and make an ideal covering in any location where a wipeable surface is desirable.

The tiles may be glazed or unglazed, patterned or plain, and vary greatly in size, shape and thickness. For the adventurous and creative, there is a huge range of vibrant colours; plus decorative patterns and textures in period, regional or contemporary styles. In addition there are narrow borders and richly decorated mural and panel effects, from which to choose. You will find good selections in home decorating stores, builder's and plumber's merchants, supermarkets, department stores and from specialist tile centres

Costings

Tiles do vary in price, but tiling is not necessarily the most expensive method of covering any surface. You will need to balance the initial outlay against their practical advantages, decorative effect and subsequent low redecorating costs.

Ordinary white and neutral tiles are generally less expensive than ones in vivid hues, original patterns or hand-made tiles. If you are tempted by anything particularly vibrant or unusual, be sure you won't tire of the finished result, as a mistake will be costly to rectify. Try to be open-ended in your original selection, so that the tiles will adapt readily when it comes to refurbishing.

Plain and patterned

If you want to keep costs down, stylish design effects can be produced by an

▲ Spoilt for choice
As this dazzling array of tiles demonstrates, tiling can be a very creative experience. Such a welter of sizes, exciting patterns and lively colours can be very inspiring, although maybe initially a little daunting, too, when it comes to deciding on the final selection.

enterprising use of plain tiles. On their own, a wall of cleverly positioned plain tiles can be subtly pleasing. Square and rectangular tiles can be laid stepped, in bricklaying fashion, while square tiles laid diagonally make a considerable design impact.

Plain tiles can also be combined with decorative ones, run as borders or interspersed as single motif tiles, panels or a tiled mural. Remember, if you use tiles from different ranges, check that they are of equal thickness.

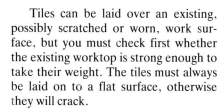

Tiles in kitchens

Ceramic tiles are an ideal covering for worktops and splashbacks because they are robust and durable enough to withstand the brunt of most cooking activities and be quickly wiped clean again to prevent them becoming shabby or grubby.

While most ordinary ceramic tiles can be used as work surfaces, tiles manufactured especially for this purpose will last longer. Quarry tiles, designed as a floorcovering, are not suitable, unless they are sealed. Even though worktop and quarry tiles are thicker than ordinary ceramic wall tiles, they can be fixed to a wall to create a co-ordinated splashback. Thick, hand-finished ceramic tiles, with their pleasing individual variations of colour and pattern, look very attractive with pale or dark wood fitted units and give the kitchen a suitably country feel.

Tiles can be laid over an existing, possibly scratched or worn, work surface, but you must check first whether the existing worktop is strong enough to take their weight. The tiles must always be laid on to a flat surface, otherwise they will crack.

On the down side, tiled work surfaces can be noisy to work on, and individual tiles can be chipped or cracked if something heavy is accidentally dropped on it. But generally, when treated with respect, a tiled worktop is hard-wearing and long lasting.

Visually, a colourful or highly patterned tiled splashback can become the focus of the kitchen. Either the splashback or the worktop should dominate the scene, without fighting each other for prominence. So a bright splashback is best set against a plain or pale worktop, and vice versa, to avoid creating a working area that is too loud.

▲ White out
A wall-full of easy-to-clean white tiles is a good way of ensuring a fresh, bright look in a kitchen.

▼ Two by two
A splashback made of odd pairs of hand-finished tiles is delightfully sympathetic to the old-fashioned character of this kitchen.

► Farmyard characters
A tiled wall, decorated with charming little farm animals, dictates the fresh colour scheme of this country-style kitchen. You could give a plain white tiled wall a similar and completely new look by painting ducks, hens, cockerels, goats, dogs and horses on to the tiles with stencils and ceramic paints.

Fitting tiles

Before you let your imagination run away with you, however, you should sort out the practicalities. Start by examining the shape and size of your room, work out a design scheme in some detail and assess how many plain or patterned tiles you will need.

Look out for ranges which include curved edging tiles for a neat finish. Some manufacturers produce mitred edging for the corners. Alternatively, a wooden edging strip will frame worktop tiling. You can also find right-angle tiles to continue the work surface smoothly up the wall behind. Failing that, you can buy quadrant-shaped tiles to fill the angle between the wall and worktop.

Tiling can be a satisfying activity. However, if you have any doubts about your tiling prowess, you would be well advised to employ an expert, because bad tiling looks dreadful.

▲ **Display panels**
Two posturing cockerels boldly face up to each other behind the hob. In this case, rather than using individual motifs, each image is assembled by matching up six separate tiles in jigsaw fashion. Positioned prominently like this, tiled panels become quite an eye-catching feature of the room. When selecting the plain tiles to go with the patterned ones, make sure they are of a compatible size and the same thickness.

Tiles in bathrooms

Ceramic tiles have long been recognized as one of the most practical surfaces for a bathroom. Being non-absorbent, they help to contend with the problems caused by condensation. Steam billowing from a running hot-water tap creates a high humidity that can eventually make the wallpaper peel and paint flake. In fact, a mixer tap that runs hot and cold water together, prevents clouds of steam forming in the first place.

In recent years, the options for the creative use of tiles have expanded rapidly with the burgeoning choice of styles. Some manufacturers produce tiles that match the colours of standard bathroom ware which allows you to create a co-ordinated scheme; this is useful in small spaces where a unified colour scheme is desirable. These co-ordinating ranges are often plain but can be marbled, speckled or textured. They also provide a neutral background for inserting patterned or relief tiles.

◄ Out of the blue
In this bathroom, a three tile system of one heavily and one lightly patterned tile with a matching half-tile has been laid to produce an all-over, co-ordinated effect.

► Dado designs
Inserting a dado band of narrow coloured tiles is an excellent way of jazzing up a bland expanse of plain tiling. Dividing the wall up like this gives the room a definite structure. Here, motif tiles are alternated with all-white ones below the dado level to create a regular pattern. The design could easily be made more haphazard by interspersing the patterned tiles irregularly.

◄ Patchwork of tiles
Instead of opting for a ready made, cohesive look, shop around for individual tiles that catch your eye. Working to a colour scheme creates a unified theme, but is not essential. When you have a good collection, including a few plain tiles, arrange them like a patchwork until you are happy with the design and then fix them to the wall.

▼ Bathtime classics
It only takes a few large tiles, embossed with scenes from Greek mythology and slotted into a room-full of marbled tiles, to bring a glamorous touch of luxury to this bathroom. Note how the band of narrow tiles under the rim of the tiled bathside is carried on at the same level around the wall.

Border lines

A narrow border strip is one of the most attractive ways of giving a smart finish to tiling. This can range from a delicate band of fine pattern to a bold, wide frieze. Borders can be added at ceiling or dado level or to round off a partly tiled surface. Running a border or frieze round the room at dado height can help draw together aspects of an awkwardly shaped room, and may give an impression of more pleasing proportions. Tile strips can also be used very effectively to frame attractive features like a pretty mirror or a small window.

Tiles specifically designed as borders are frequently made to complement a whole tiling range. They are usually narrow rectangular half-tiles with flat or raised surfaces. Dado tiles with a raised sill are also available. You could create your own border effects by laying single rows of coloured or patterned tiles round plain ones.

Grouting

For good looks at low cost, consider using coloured grouting with in-expensive plain tiles, to give a very striking fine grid of colour. Grouting can be bought in a range of colours, or you can buy pigment to colour it yourself.

Water is liable to collect on a horizontal worktop, particularly in the grouted strips. Always use waterproof grouting to stop water seeping under the tiles. Also ensure that the grouting fills the gaps between the tiles, to stop crumbs accumulating in crevices.

In time, grouting can get very dirty and needs to be cleaned regularly with a stiff brush and domestic bleach. It may occasionally be necessary to rake out the existing grout and replace it.

Tiling options

Tiles are far too decorative to be restricted to worktops and walls. They can be laid as a waterproof, wipeable lining on kitchen or bathroom shelves and windowsills, or to brighten up window reveals. A series of tiles intended as a mural or wall panel can look equally striking when fixed horizontally on a table-top, a kitchen work surface or beside a wash basin.

As the existing focus of a room, the fireplace is one of the very best places to display beautiful tiles. Use them as panels on either side of the grate and to line the hearth.

Disguising poor tiling

Sometimes when you move house, you inherit a hideous tiled bathroom or kitchen. Unfortunately, tiles can be tricky and costly to remove. A more immediate remedy is to paint over them, using a coat of metal primer before covering them with gloss or eggshell paint in your preferred colour. Another

▲ A grate idea
Decorative tiled panels flanking the grate can turn a fireplace into a stylish showpiece. Here, the Art Nouveau style of the tiles and the fireplace complement each other perfectly. Plain heat-resistant glazed tiles in the hearth are easy to keep spotlessly clean.

way of disguising unwanted tiles is to stick tile effect panels on top of the original tiles until you can get round to fitting new ones.

Tiling a splashback

Ceramic tiles provide a decorative and practical finish to walls, worktops and fireplaces. The choice is enormous, with a splendid array of colours, shapes and surface textures available – from plain tiles with clear or mottled colours, to charming rustic designs or bold, multi-coloured motifs.

With the ever-increasing range of equipment for home decoration, tiling is now well within most people's capabilities. Careful planning and the use of the right tools will reward you with a highly professional finish.

Choosing the tiles

Tiles are one of the most long-lasting surfaces in the home, so make your choice carefully. Catalogues, magazines and shop displays give ideas on colours and designs. Decide whether you want plain or patterned tiles, or a combination of both. Plain tiles are cheapest, but you can liven them up by adding a few patterned tiles in groups or at random. Border designs and contrast edgings will also add interest to plain tiling, and can be used to pick out the main colours of the room.

The size of tile and its surface texture should also be considered. Most tiles are square, either 110mm (4$\frac{1}{4}$in), 150mm (6in) or 200mm (8in), but the larger 'continental' size of 150 x 200mm (6 x 8in), is being used more and more. Many-sided tiles, curved tiles and mosaics are also available.

Tiles usually have smooth, glossy surface finishes, but for rustic appeal, tiles with an uneven or embossed surface, make unusual alternatives.

▼ *Combining colour and patterns*
White tiles with blue corner details are combined in different ways for a variety of effects. They make a chequerboard when used with plain blue tiles. Used with each other, the corner patterns combine to form circles. The single motifs and border tiles add extra interest.

Measuring up

As ceramic tiles are expensive, it makes sense to measure up accurately. Multiply the height by the width of the area to be covered to find the number of square metres (yards) and divide by the area of one tile to find out how many you need – add at least 10 per cent for breakages.

If combining different tiles or using a border pattern, make sure you buy all the tiles in either metric or imperial measures. Metric and imperial measures will not convert exactly, so if you try to mix them, the tiles will not line up.

Layout

It is usually necessary to cut some of the tiles in order to fit an area exactly. These cut tiles should always be placed at the edges of the tiling, and never in the middle. Since it is difficult to cut thin strips of tile, try to arrange the tiles so that those at the edge are not too narrow.

Preparation

Careful preparation of the walls makes it easier to fix the tiles and prevents problems later on. Strip off any wallpaper, fill cracks and holes with interior filler and remove flaking paint. Sand smooth, then follow up with a coat of stabilizing solution to provide a good surface for the adhesive.

If necessary, it is possible to tile over old tiles provided that they are securely fixed. Clean the old tiles and use a tile cutter to score the surface to give a key for the adhesive. Don't lay individual tiles directly over the old tiles; stagger the starting level so that grout points don't coincide anywhere along the lines of tiling.

Tools

adhesive Choose the right one for the job: thin bed adhesive for smooth, level surfaces; waterproof for bathrooms and showers; heat-resistant for use around cookers and fireplaces; flexible on wooden surfaces that have a tendency towards movement. Five litres (1 gallon) of thin bed adhesive will cover approximately 4.16 sq m (5 sq yd).

trowel or spreader The notched edges apply the adhesive in even ridges. A plastic or metal spreader is often supplied free with the adhesive.

grout As with adhesives, different types are available – buy the waterproof type for showers and splashbacks. There is a special non-toxic version, with added fungicide, which should be used for kitchen worktops. Normally white, grout also comes in several colours. 500g (1 lb) of grout will cover approximately 1.65 sq m (2 sq yd).

grout finisher A special tool or piece of dowel used to press grout firmly into place and give a neat, regular finish.

measuring rod Make your own from a long piece of batten, and mark it off at intervals by the tile depth, allowing for the thickness of the grout between each one.

spirit level Used to ensure a straight line and a **plumb line and bob** to measure the true vertical (see page 59). A spirit level which measures vertical as well as horizontal lines can be used instead, if preferred.

marking tools Chalk, felt pen and ruler.

sponge Use a damp sponge to spread grout over the tiles and into the joints. Quicker for large jobs, is a thin rubber squeegee, with a handle, like the ones used to clean windows.

tile spacers These ensure a regular gap is left between tiles. Accuracy is easier to achieve with 'universal' tiles, made with specially angled edges which, when butted together, leave a gap the correct size for the grout.

batten Use for larger jobs to position and support the tiles on the wall.

hammer and masonry nails To secure the battens to the wall.

tile cutter There are several types, ranging from a simple tile spike to a tool resembling a pair of pliers with a wheel used to score the tile, and jaws that snap the tile on the scored line. For more ambitious projects, it might be worth investing in (or hiring) one of the combination tools, which will measure, score, cut and snap.

tile file To smooth over cut edges; a carborundum stone, file or abrasive strip is the most effective.

tile nibblers These pincers are used to break off small pieces of tile to fit them round awkward shapes.

frame saw Useful for cutting tiles to fit around pipes and switches.

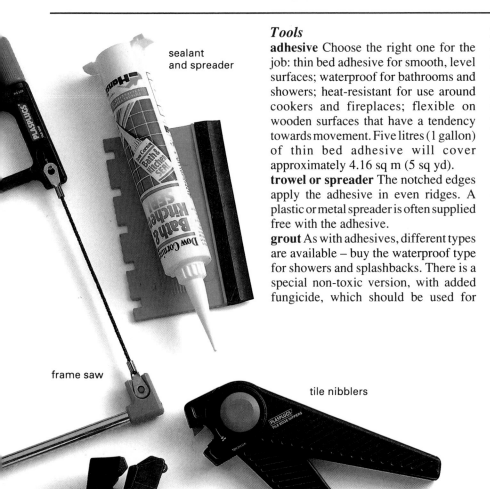

sealant and spreader

frame saw

tile nibblers

tile spacers

tile cutter

tip

Professional touch
To ensure the tiles are level and to prevent them from slipping down the wall on to the sink, basin or bath, professionals fix a wooden batten to the wall just below the position of the second row of tiles.

It isn't difficult to do this – a few masonry nails or panel pins will secure a thin batten to a plaster wall. The bottom row of tiles is fixed to the wall last, after the batten has been removed.

▶ *Bath surround*
Two rows of tiles round a bath are easy to tile yourself, and provide an attractive and practical finish.

STARTING TO TILE

1 Planning tile positions Place a row of tiles in front of the wall to find the best arrangement. A symmetrical arrangement usually looks best, with cut tiles at each end. However, if tiling round three sides, as round a bath, place a whole tile at each front end, and cut tiles at the back corners.

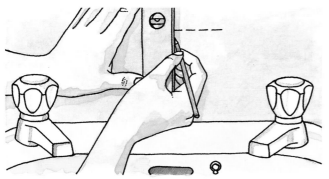

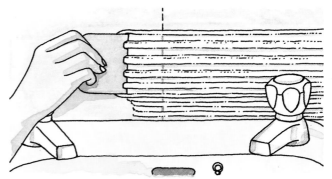

2 Marking the wall Using a plumb line or spirit level, draw a vertical line in the centre of the area to be tiled. Mark where the top of each tile will be to check finished positioning of rows.

For a professional finish, fix a batten below the level of the second row of tiles, using a spirit level to get it straight. Leave the nails sticking out of the batten to make them easier to remove later.

3 Apply the adhesive Using the notched spreader, apply adhesive, working on an area the size of six tiles at a time. Draw the spreader firmly across the wall to get the adhesive even. Do not apply adhesive at the ends of rows where cut tiles will go, and avoid getting any on the batten, if you're using one.

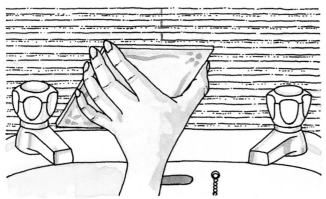

4 Position the first tile Using the basin, bath or batten for support, position the bottom edge of the tile against the wall first, and then press flat. Use the spirit level to check that the tile is horizontal, and adjust slightly if not.

5 Tile the first row Continue laying tiles along the first row. Universal tiles with curved edges can be butted together, but for standard tiles, position tile spacers at upper corners, bedding them down below the level of the tiles so that the grout will cover them. Leave gaps at the ends where tiles need to be cut.

6 Finishing the whole tiles Cover the remaining area with tiles, row by row. Use a spirit level at regular intervals to ensure that the tiles are straight. With a clean sponge, wipe off any excess adhesive from the surface of the tiles.

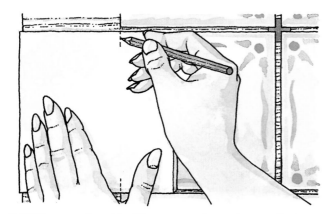

7 Tiling at edges To fill gaps at edges, place a tile in each gap, glazed side down, and mark it at top and bottom with a marker pen; allow space for grouting. On the glazed side, join the marks with the pen and a ruler. Check the tile fits the gap before cutting.

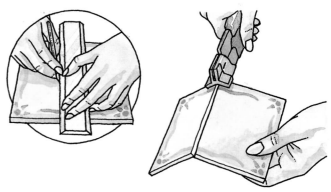

8 Cutting tiles Firmly score once along the marked line using a ruler to guide the blade. Position the jaws of the snapping tool on either side of the marked line and squeeze to make a clean break. Smooth down cut edges with a file before fixing. If a tile only needs to be trimmed, score the tile, then use pliers or nibblers to remove the excess.

9 Leave to set When all the tiles have been laid, wipe them clean and allow 24 hours for the adhesive to set completely. If using a batten, wait until the tiles above it are firmly fixed and the adhesive has set. Then remove the batten and tile the last row. Leave to set.

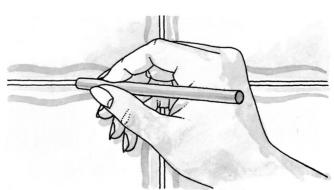

10 Apply grout Mix the grout, according to the instructions and, using a slightly damp sponge or squeegee, spread liberally over the joins between the tiles, forcing the grout into the gaps as you go. Wipe off any excess before it sets. Smooth down the surface with a bit of dowelling or the blunt end of a pencil. Polish with a soft cloth.

11 Apply sealant Use a proprietary sealant or sealing strip instead of grouting where the splashback meets the sink or bath to prevent water penetration. Apply sealant directly from the nozzle of the tube, then smooth with the back of a spoon dipped in water. Remove excess immediately with a damp cloth.

PART THREE

WINDOW TREATMENTS

Basics of curtain making

Curtains, pelmets and valances transform a room. To be really effective, they need to be planned carefully. Even using curtains on their own gives a variety of different effects, depending on the fullness and length of the curtains, the heading tape used, and the type of pole or track.

Choosing curtain track

Pick a strong enough track, lightweight for sheers and unlined cottons; medium weight for standard sill-length curtains; and heavyweight for floor-length or heavy, interlined curtains.

If the track has to go round corners, as in a bay or bow window, choose a flexible plastic track or a metal track fitted with sections which can be easily slotted together as required.

If the track is covered by a valance or pelmet, it doesn't need to be elaborate, but if the track is on display, pick one that will fit the decor and the style of the curtains.

For maximum light and to reveal the shape of the window, allow extra track at each side so the curtains can be pulled back. The amount of extra track will depend on the thickness of the curtain and the space available. Generally 15-46cm (6-18in) at each side will be sufficient.

Check that you have everything you need. Tracks are usually bought as a complete kit with screws, brackets, overlapping arms (where necessary) curtain hooks and gliders. However, there may be optional extras.

Always follow the fixing instructions supplied with the track, making sure that the end fixings are strong and that there are sufficient holding brackets in between to prevent the track from sagging. To save time, check through all the fittings first, so that you are familiar with them. If there is a concrete lintel above the window or the wall is badly plastered, the track will have to be mounted on a wooden batten fixed above the window for a level result.

◀ *Elegant window dressing*
These blue and white chintz, tailored floor-length curtains have been partnered with the full range of window dressing – boxed pelmet with a pleated valance, sheer curtains and tailored tie-backs. Piping adds a crisp finish to tie-backs and pelmet.

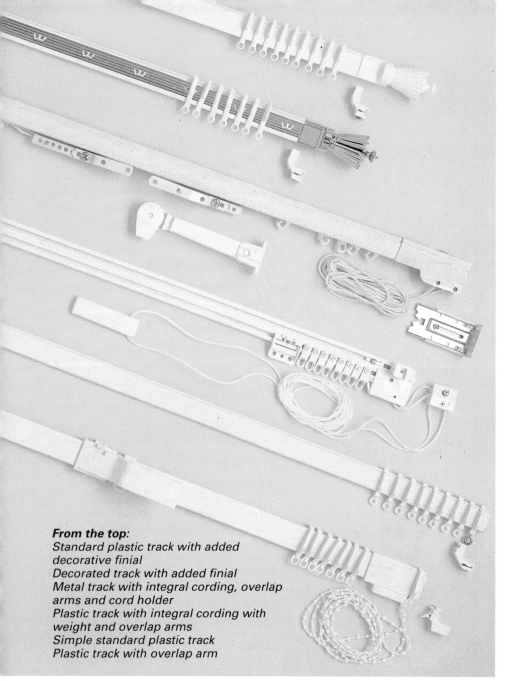

Track additions

There are several tracks available with useful extras. To hang curtains with detachable linings, you can buy a track with hooks which make it possible to remove the lining without taking down the whole curtain. For heavy curtains choose a track with integral cording, or add a cording set to it. Easier to fit are draw rods that hook into the leading runner and hang behind the curtains.

If you wish to have a valance above the curtains, consider getting a valance rail which is slotted on to the front of curtain track. There are also triple tracks to hold a blind behind the curtains, as well as a valance in front.

Heading tapes

If the length of the curtains is correct and the seams and hems are straight, the only addition needed for a beautifully tailored result is an attractive heading. With the advent of commercially made heading tapes this part of curtain making is easy. If you like, you can make beautiful pleats by hand, but for most windows an evenly pleated pencil or triple pleat gathered by heading tape is all you need.

Choosing heading tapes

Choose a type of heading tape which suits the style of the curtains and flatters the fabric. Decorative headings add interest to plain fabrics, while plainer ones with shallow pleats will show off fabrics with large prints.

From the top:
Standard plastic track with added decorative finial
Decorated track with added finial
Metal track with integral cording, overlap arms and cord holder
Plastic track with integral cording with weight and overlap arms
Simple standard plastic track
Plastic track with overlap arm

Box pleat A formal heading tape, this will emphasize the length of the curtains. The tape automatically makes equally spaced pleats which show up best on plain fabrics. You will need fabric twice the finished curtain width.

Cartridge pleat A good choice for curtains in heavier fabrics or interlined curtains. Hooks should be placed at each end and behind each pleat. Match the pleats across the centre opening unless curtains overlap. You will need fabric twice the finished curtain width.

POSITIONING THE TRACK

You can create illusions with the window proportions by positioning the track at different levels.

The tracks can be fixed either to the wall, the window frame or, if necessary, to the ceiling. If you wish to have a pelmet, you must leave space between the track and the ceiling for the brackets to be fixed.

To make a window seem longer, hang track high above the frame without much extra each side.

To give extra width, increase the space at each side.

To make a window seem larger all round, increase space at the sides and above.

Pencil pleat *Ideal for most settings, this heading tape gives an elegant look to curtains. It comes in different widths to match the curtain lengths – deeper headings to give a better proportion on longer curtains. When buying fabric you will need 2¹/₂ times the finished curtain width.*

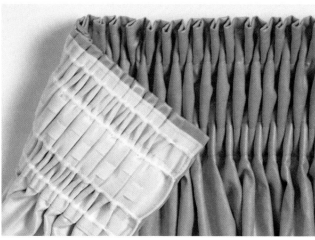

Tudor ruff *This type of heading is a decorative alternative to the pencil pleat and is ideal for jazzing up plain fabrics. You will need fabric twice the finished curtain width.*

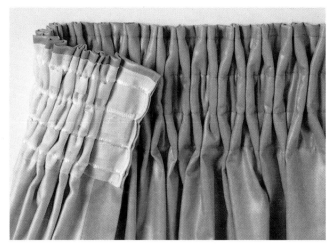

Smocked *This is extremely decorative and looks good on both plain and patterned fabrics. You will need fabric no more than twice the finished curtain width.*

Triple pleat *This heading tape drapes the fabric beautifully for a tailored look. Position the tape so that the pleats fall evenly across the curtains with equal space at each end and match pleats across the centre opening, unless curtains overlap. As for cartridge pleats, hooks should be placed behind each pleat. You will need fabric twice the finished curtain width.*

▶ Dormer delight
In an upstairs or attic bedroom with sloping ceilings, the wide windowsill dictates the window dressing. The curtain track has been placed in the window recess, on the wall above the frame, and the curtains made to sill length. If there is no room for a track in this position use a track that can be mounted on the ceiling of the recess.

Measuring up

Before measuring up for curtains, fix the track in place so that the exact height and width can be measured. The track placement will depend on the window – its shape, whether it has a recess or not or if it is a bay.

Calculating the curtain length

Once the track is in place, decide on the curtain length. Curtains usually look best reaching to the floor or sill. They can hang between sill and floor, but check the proportion in relation to the height of the ceiling first as this length can give the impression that it was a mistake.

For a really luxurious look, curtains can look effective cut extra long to drape over the floor.

Measure from the top of the track to the chosen length, using an expandable metal ruler for accuracy. For floor or sill-length curtains, deduct 1cm ($^3/_8$in) so the curtains will sit just above the floor or sill. Then add the allowances for hems and heading.

Calculating the width

The curtain width is dictated by the length of the track and the chosen heading. Each type of heading requires a certain amount of fabric to achieve the chosen result.

Calculate fabric requirements

Measure the required length of the curtain, including allowances for hems and headings.

Measure the length of track; decide on the type of heading and how many curtain widths you need to gain this effect.

Multiply the curtain length by the number of fabric widths to find out how much fabric you need. You must allow extra for pattern matching – one pattern repeat for each fabric width other than the first one. The shop assistant will be able to give you the measurement for the pattern repeat of the fabric.

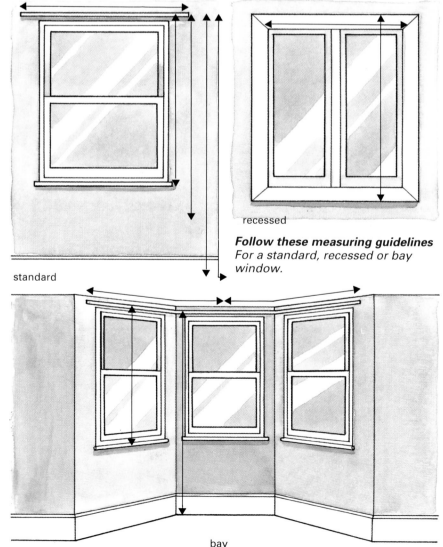

standard

recessed

Follow these measuring guidelines
For a standard, recessed or bay window.

bay

Stylish curtains

Hanging curtains at the window will instantly make a room look and feel warmer. In fact, windows without some form of dressing can look unfinished. In a plainly decorated room curtains give you the opportunity to add a splash of colour or to introduce pattern and texture. Simple, unlined curtains are no more complicated than sheers or nets, and although they look impressive, even heavy, lined curtains are not difficult to make although they do, of course, take a little longer. This chapter gives the basic techniques used in curtain making; later chapters will cover a variety of decorative treatments.

▲ A well-dressed window

These sewn-in linings are made in a colour taken from the pattern on the curtains and are displayed when the curtains are held back. The same fabric is used to add box pleated frills to the valance and tie-backs, completing the co-ordinated effect.

Whether to add lining

For summer use or in kitchens, bathrooms and stairways, simple unlined curtains are all you need. They provide some privacy without obscuring all the natural light. The finer and lighter in colour the fabric, the more light will be able to pass through.

However, if using an expensive fabric, or when making curtains for warmth or privacy, it is important to add a lining. This increases the insulation, cuts out light and protects the fabric from the damaging effects of dust and sunlight. It also improves the hang of the curtains by adding body and weight, giving them a more tailored look, which is ideal for bedrooms and living rooms.

For best results the lining should be of good quality and suitable for the fabric weight, so that it wears as well as the curtain. Choose a lining in a matching or toning colour, or go for traditional white or beige. If choosing a darker or contrasting colour, take a scrap of the main fabric with you when you buy, since coloured linings can show through paler curtain fabrics.

Lining methods

Detachable lining A detachable lining is attached to the curtain with curtain hooks, and can easily be removed for washing or during the summer months. It can be added to an existing unlined curtain, and is an ideal choice for difficult fabrics, since the lining and curtain can be cleaned separately. In addition, it does not need to be gathered as much as the main curtain, which means a saving on fabric.

Sewn-in lining This is literally sewn into the curtain while it is being made, and cannot be detached for washing. It gives good results quickly, and helps to support the main fabric. Unless the curtain and lining have the same care properties, the finished curtain must be dry cleaned or the fabrics may shrink at different rates.

Types of lining

Cotton sateen is a tightly woven, hard-wearing fabric, available in a variety of colours. It is the most readily available lining fabric and comes in two standard widths, 122cm (48in) and 138cm (54in).

Thermal sateen feels like standard cotton sateen, but has been coated to give it insulating properties. It contains a mixture of cotton and synthetic fibres.

Milium lining is a cotton sateen which has been coated on one side with a solution of aluminium particles giving it a silvery appearance. The silvery side should be placed up against the wrong side of the fabric to reflect heat back into the room. Its insulating qualities mean that in hot weather it will also help to keep heat out if the curtains are drawn during the day.

Blackout lining is thick, heavy and usually beige coloured. It has all the properties of thermal lining but will also keep out the light, making it ideal for people who are easily woken by light. It will also help to dampen noise from

▼ Simple but effective
These unlined curtains are hung on the pole using hooks threaded through ungathered standard heading tape.

UNLINED CURTAINS

1 Measuring up Measure the drop from the curtain rail to the finished curtain length and add extra for heading and hem allowances. Usually 20cm (8in) extra is sufficient. Calculate the number of fabric widths you need for each curtain – generally twice the finished curtain width. Then multiply the length by the number of widths. For each additional fabric width you will need to add one pattern repeat for pattern matching.

2 Cutting out For accuracy, straighten the fabric edge before cutting out as many fabric widths as required. Match patterns if necessary, then stitch together with French seams, positioning any cut edges at the outer edge of each curtain. If using the selvedges, snip into them at 10-15cm (4-6in) intervals, to prevent puckering.

3 Stitch side hems Turn under 5mm (¹/₄in) then 2cm (³/₄in) to wrong side along both sides. Slipstitch or machine stitch in place.

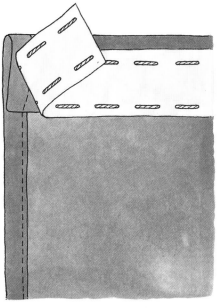

4 Fold top hem Turn down the top edge of the fabric by the depth of the tape plus 5mm (¹/₄in) for stand heading. Cut a length of heading tape the width of the curtain fabric plus 2cm (³/₄in). Place the heading tape, 1cm (³/₈in) from the folded edge, over the top raw edge of the fabric; trim fabric edge if necessary and pin.

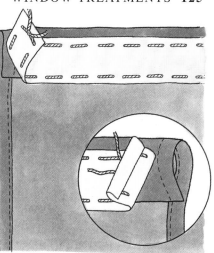

5 Neaten heading tape ends At the leading edge of the curtain (where the curtains meet), pull out the heading tape cords from the *wrong* side of the tape; knot. Turn under edge of tape by 1cm (³/₈in) and position against the edge of the curtain.

On the outer edge, pull out the heading tape cords from the *right* side of the tape. Turn under the edge of tape by 1cm (³/₈in) and place against the curtain edge.

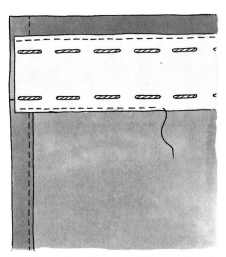

6 Stitch heading tape Pin, tack and stitch heading tape in place along the marked line on each long edge of the tape. Stitch both rows in the same direction to prevent puckering.

7 Gather the curtain Pull up the heading tape cords from the outer edge until the curtain is the correct width; knot and trim ends or wind surplus cords on to a cord tidy. Hook the tidy into the heading tape.

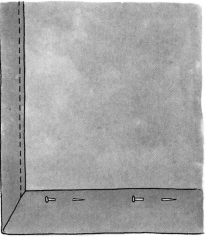

8 Stitch lower hem Hang the curtain to check its length. Remove and turn up a double hem along the lower edge. To mitre the corners, fold the bottom hem allowance under at an angle at the corner until its top edge touches the side hem allowance. Slipstitch corners and bottom hem.

 tip

Working with patterned fabric
If you find that a large pattern has been printed slightly off grain, cut out the fabric widths following the pattern and not the grain. When cutting out the fabric widths, always position the complete pattern along the base hem edge. Any cut pattern at the top will be lost in the gathers of the heading.

To join widths together, match the pattern on the right side and tack with ladder stitch. Work from the right side of the fabric as shown right. Machine stitch in the usual way close to the tacking. Remove tacking.

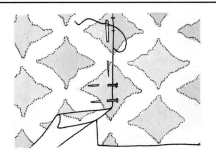

DETACHABLE LININGS

1 Making the curtain Make up the curtain in the same way as an unlined curtain, with 2cm (³/₄in) side hems and 8cm (3¹/₄in) base hems.

2 Making the lining Detachable linings only need to be one and a half to twice the track length. Make up the lining in the same way, but 2.5cm (1in) shorter than the curtain.

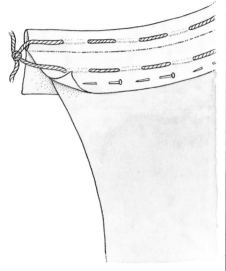

3 Apply lining tape Cut a length of lining tape the width of the lining, plus 2cm (³/₄in). Slot over the top of the fabric and pin. Tie the cords as for the main curtain. Fold under 5mm (¹/₄in) at each end of the tape and stitch. Stitch the tape to the lining along the lower edge of the tape.

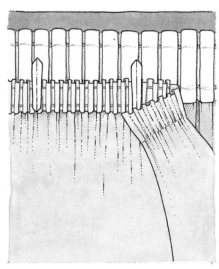

4 Hang the curtain Pull up both curtain and lining the required amount, so they match. Slot each hook through the lining tape, then the curtain tape and on to the track. Check the length of the lining, then remove and make a double hem.

SEWN-IN LININGS

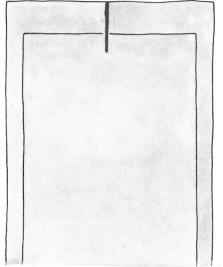

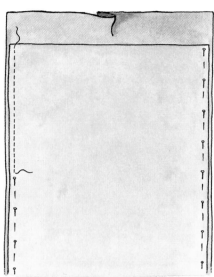

1 Cutting out Measure up and cut out the fabric for the curtain, joining widths together as necessary. Cut and stitch the lining in the same way to make a panel 8cm (3in) shorter and 4cm (1¹/₂in) narrower than the curtain. Do not tear lining fabrics, but use a T-square or set square and ruler to provide a straight edge. Mark the centre of both fabric and lining.

2 Stitch side edges Place the curtain to the lining, right sides together, matching side edges and with top edges level. Pin, tack and machine stitch side edges, taking 1.5cm (⁵/₈in) seam allowances and stitching from the top to within 18cm (7in) of the lower edge.

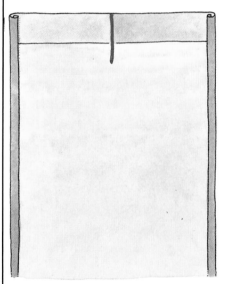

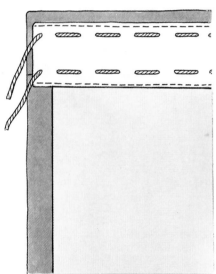

3 Turn right side out Turn curtain and lining through to the right side. Match the centre of the curtain to the centre of the lining and press. A 2cm (³/₄in) wide border of curtain fabric will form down the sides edges.

5 Hem the lining Hang the curtain at the window to check its length. Turn up a double 2.5cm (1in) hem along base edge of lining so that the lining will hang 2.5cm (1in) above the finished curtain; pin or tack and machine stitch.

4 Apply heading tape Treating the lining and fabric as one along the top, turn down the top edge of the curtain by the depth of the heading tape and stand. Apply heading tape in the same way as for an unlined curtain, above.

6 Hem the curtain Turn up a double 5cm (2in) hem along the lower edge of the curtain. Mitre the corners as in step 8 for an unlined curtain. At the lower side edges, slipstitch the lining to the curtains.

Curtains with a flourish

A frill is the final flourish which transforms a simple pair of curtains into something really special. It gives the curtains a freshness and softness which epitomises the country style, and provides that extra detail which is the mark of professionally made curtains.

The frill can be used to introduce a new colour into the room, as in the picture above, or perhaps to link in with the colours of other soft furnishings used. This is done by making the frill in a different colour, or by the use of an appropriate trimming. You can trim a single frill by binding the edge, or a double frill by separating it from the main curtain with a line of piping or a smaller, contrasting or toning frill. If using tiebacks, these should be trimmed to match.

▲ Prettily edged in pink
A frill edged with pink piping has a soft and warming effect on pale mint curtains chosen to blend in with the walls of the bathroom. Adding a clever touch, the binding has been stitched to the centre of the tie-backs to complete the look.

Adding a frill

A frill can be added to the leading edges (the centre edges of a pair of curtains), to the leading and lower edges, or to both the side and lower edges. Choose to add either a single or double frill, depending on the type of fabric you have and the style you wish to achieve.

Single frills These are mainly used on unlined curtains and are made from a single layer of fabric which gathers easily. The outside edge of the frill is finished neatly either with a double hem or pretty contrast binding. A single frill requires less fabric than a double frill, making it more economical. However, the light usually shows through a single frill, so where the main curtain is lined this may not look appropriate.

Double frills Mainly used on lined curtains, these are made from a wide strip of fabric, folded lengthways, so that the fold is on the outside edge. The fold gives a smooth, crisp finish, and the extra fabric gives the frill more body. If using very heavy fabrics, such as velvet or tapestry, use a lightweight lining fabric on the back of the frill instead of doubling the fabric to give less bulk.

Frill widths Depends on the weight of the fabric, the size of the curtain and whether it is double or single. As a guide the finished width should be between 5 and 10cm (2–4in).

UNLINED CURTAIN WITH SINGLE FRILL

1 Measure and cut out Decide on the finished width of the frill – 4-10cm (1½-4in) is usual. Add 3cm (1in) for seam allowances and cut out strips to this width across the fabric, from selvedge to selvedge. Trim off the selvedges, and using narrow French seams, join the strips to make one piece twice the length of all the edges to be frilled.

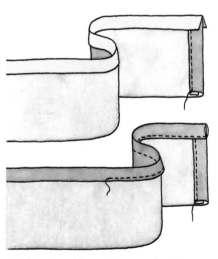

2 Neaten edges Turn under 1cm (³⁄₈in), then another 1cm (³⁄₈in) to make a narrow double hem at the two ends. Bind the long outside edge, or turn a double 1cm (³⁄₈in) hem.

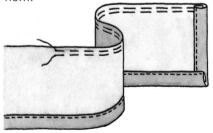

3 Gather up Sew two rows of gathering stitches along the raw edge of the frill, working in sections of up to about 80cm (31½in) to keep the thread a manageable length.

4 Cut out the curtain Cut out and join the curtain fabric widths to the required size, remembering to allow for the frill depth when calculating the finished dimensions.

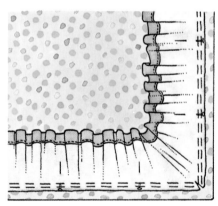

5 Pin frill to curtain Position the frill on the main fabric, right sides together. Match the hemmed ends of the frill to the position of the finished edges at the top of the curtain. Pull up gathers evenly to fit, allowing extra gathers at the corners for ease. Check the arrangement of gathers, pin and tack. Snip into seam allowance of frill at corner. Tack and stitch the frill to the curtain. Neaten seam allowances.

6 Finish curtain Fold over the top of the curtain and attach the heading tape of your choice in the usual way (see page 120).

▶ **The bottom line**
A frill along the bottom edge of the curtains adds length, allowing the curtains to billow on to the sill. The tie-backs, positioned high up, complete the illusion to make a fairly small window look longer.

LINED CURTAIN WITH DOUBLE FRILL

1 Measure and cut out Decide on the finished width of the frill, double it, and add 1.5cm ($^5/_8$in) for the seam allowance. Cut out and join strips as for a single frill to make up a strip twice the length of all the edges to be frilled.

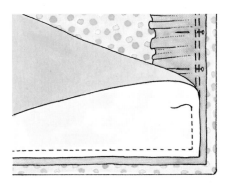

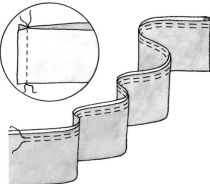

2 Prepare frill Fold the frill in half along its length, right sides together, and pin together at ends. Press and stitch a narrow seam at each end. Turn right side out, press and stitch two rows of gathering stitches along the raw edges, working in sections as for single frill.

3 Gather and attach Gather frill and pin to the right side of the curtain, allowing extra ease at the corner for turning, and tack in place. Place the lining on the main fabric, right sides together, matching all edges. Pin and stitch sides and bottom, taking a 1.5cm ($^5/_8$in) seam. Trim and turn through to the right side. Attach heading tape.

▼ Frills with everything
A frilled trio of curtains made from light and airy cotton fabric and lined to improve the hang. The double frill stands up crisply.

▲ New nets from old
Co-ordinate your
existing net curtains
with a new
bedspread or duvet
cover by attaching
matching fabric frills
to the curtains. The
curtains will look like
new.

▶ Lovely lace
A wide lace edging
makes an attractive
trimming on a set of
curtains, and is quick
to attach since both
edges of the lace are
already finished.
Piping is optional.

◀ Bound to succeed
A strip of fabric
bound on both edges
has been gathered in
the middle to make
an unusual curtain
frill. The tie-backs
and rosette are
bound to match, and
the wide, padded
binding on the top of
the curtain completes
the effect.

▶In contrast
A pale blue chintz
frill, used to trim a
patterned curtain
over an archway, is a
clever link with the
blue of the wallpaper
and the woodwork.

Elegant curtain tiebacks

B y catching the curtains back at just the right height, tiebacks pull the curtain fabric into an attractive sweep and allow natural light into the room. Wide, full curtains drape into deep scoops of fabric, while narrow drapes are given an elegant form when tied back against the frame. Don't feel that you are forced to choose one style or another by the width of the window – a large curtain swept to one side can be just as effective as the more usual set of curtains pulled back either side.

Easy to make and economical – you only need a small amount of the original curtain fabric or a remnant in a toning material – tiebacks can be made up in a variety of shapes and styles to suit any window in the home. Formal, curved tiebacks made from fabric and stiffened with heavyweight interfacing or buckram are the usual style, but softer shapes of plaited, frilled or ruched fabric are also attractive, particuarly where the tone of the room is softer.

▲ *Floral arrangement*
The large floral fabric used to make these summer curtains has been carefully positioned on the tieback so that the main floral motif is shown to best effect. On a pair of tiebacks, arrange the motifs so that the tiebacks make a symmetrical pair.

Positioning tiebacks

On sill-length curtains the tiebacks are usually positioned about two-thirds of the way down from the top of the curtain, but on longer curtains and floor-length curtains there is more scope for choosing your own position. Each position has its own effect on the look of the window, so choose carefully.

In general, the lower the tieback, the fuller the effect of the curtains but the more the view and the natural light are obscured. If the view is not particularly special or the window frame is unattractive or needs some work done on it, this can be an advantage. Try different positions, draping the fabric in a gentle curve or a fuller sweep.

Sill length tiebacks On long, floor-length curtains the sill can be about midway down the curtain. It allows the fabric to sweep into a generous curve above the tieback and drape elegantly below it.

Placed low Tiebacks set about two-thirds of the way down the curtain create a full effect that can make a narrow window seem wider. But the curtains cover more of the window, and this will obscure light.

Placed high Positioned one-third of the way down from the top of the curtain, the tiebacks will give the impression of length and will let in maximum light.

Selecting the fabric

Pick a mediumweight fabric, such as a closely-woven furnishing fabric for the tieback, using the same fabric on both sides, or selecting a matching or toning lining fabric for the back. If making them in the same fabric as the curtains, bind the edges with bias binding to give the tiebacks definition. Alternatively go for a contrast, to add a dash of colour to a plain window dressing or perhaps to pick up the colours of a rug, tablecloth or sofa.

When adding tiebacks to a pair of existing curtains you may not be able to find more of the original fabric, which may, in any case, have faded. In this situation it's best to go for a contrast which will look far better than a fabric that falls just short of matching the original window dressing.

Drape the fabric round the curtain to judge the effect, or if you only have a sample of fabric, pin it to the curtains and leave it there for a few days before you make your final choice. Check it in daylight as well as in the glow of artificial light.

Positioning the fabric

The tiebacks use only a small amount of fabric, but because they are an important element of the window decoration, and because they are often quite eye catching, it is important to arrange the fabric carefully. Move the pattern around on the fabric to see what sort of arrangement you can achieve.

If the fabric is patterned with separate motifs, look for a particularly attractive detail which would fit nicely into the tieback shape. If the motif faces in a particular direction, such as a bird or animal motif, try to get it facing towards the centre of the tieback, so that in the

Tieback tie in
When you wish to change a room's colour scheme, and the curtains don't quite tie in, make tiebacks in the new colour to act as a link. A simple trimming sewn to the leading edge of the curtains will complete the effect.

finished arrangement it will be facing the window, drawing the eye in this direction.

On a pair of curtains, a symmetrical arrangement looks best, rather than an identical pair.

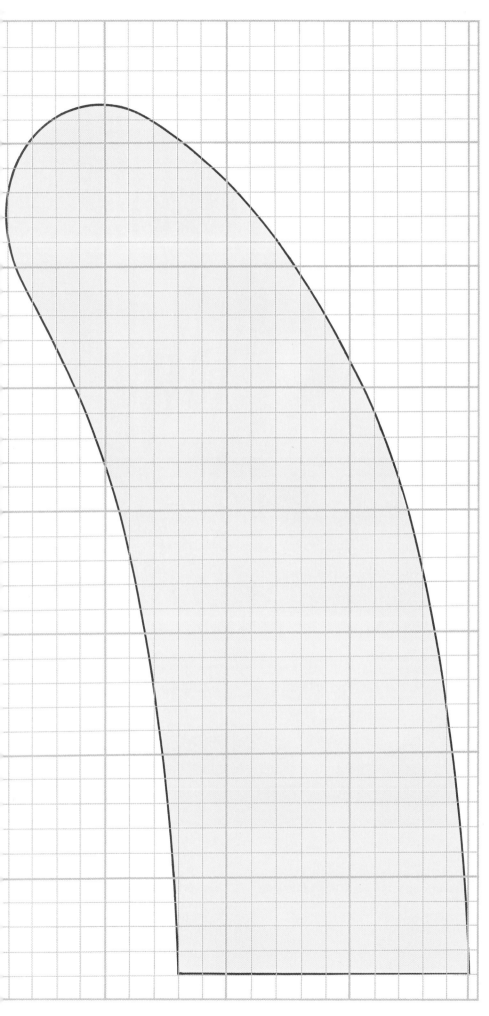

◀ *Tieback pattern*
On squared paper, draw up the pattern for the tieback from the grid so that each large square equals 5cm (2in). For quicker and more accurate results, use a photocopier to enlarge the pattern by 160% to full size.

A TAILORED TIEBACK

The pattern given here is for a standard tieback 10cm (4in) wide and 35.5cm (14in) long. Try out the effect by positioning your paper pattern on the curtain. On large curtains you may wish to widen or lengthen it.

Materials
Mediumweight fabric
Buckram or **heavyweight interfacing**
Two curtains rings per tieback
Matching thread

1 Positioning Hold a tape measure round the curtain, pulling it back, and sliding it up and down to find the best position for the tieback. Mark the wall where your head is. Ease out the fabric to create a draped effect, and read off the length on the tape measure; this will be the length of the finished tieback.

2 Making the pattern Fold a large sheet of paper or newspaper in half and draw up the tieback pattern from the diagram with the straight edge on the fold. If you wish to alter it, do so now, lengthening or shortening along the straight edge. Cut out the pattern and unfold the paper. Test the paper pattern by pinning it in place round the curtain.

3 Cutting out For each tieback cut out one piece of heavyweight interfacing or buckram to size. Cut out two pieces of fabric or one piece of fabric and one of lining, adding 1.5cm (⅝in) seam allowance all round the pattern.

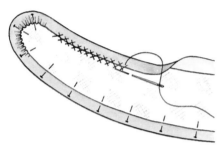

4 Attaching the front piece
Position the interfacing centrally on the wrong side of the front piece and pin. Fold the seam allowance over the interfacing, snipping so it lies flat. Pin and then stitch with herringbone stitch.

To sew herringbone stitch, take a small stitch in the fabric, cross to the interfacing and take a small backstitch, catching the interfacing, but not the fabric. Cross back to the fabric and take a small backstitch through fabric and interfacing. Keep stitching until you have gone all the way round. The stitches should be not show on the right side.

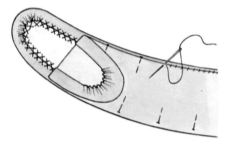

5 Attaching the back piece Turn the seam allowance of the lining to the wrong side. Place the back piece wrong side down on the interfacing and pin to hold. With small slipstitches, hand stitch all round to attach the back to the front.

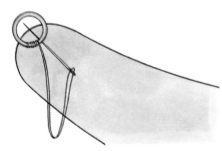

6 Attaching the rings Place a small curtain ring at each end of the tieback, so that it just overlaps the edge on the wrong side. Hand sew in place with a few straight stitches using double thread. Check the position of the tieback again by holding it in place. Then attach a small hook to the wall to hang the tiebacks from.

BOUND TIEBACK

Use the same pattern for a piped tieback as for a plain one. Bias binding is the only additional material required.

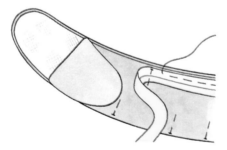

1 Cut out and pin Cut two pieces of fabric and one piece of interfacing for each tieback. Sandwich the interfacing between the fabric, wrong sides together, and pin. Tack the binding to the tieback, right sides together, with the join in the binding at one end. Snip into the seam allowance of the binding to ease round curves.

▲ Soft but stylish
A pale fabric used to bind this tieback softens the edges, giving the whole effect a look of comfortable luxury. For sharp definition use a darker colour from the fabric.

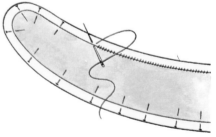

2 Stitch together Stitch the bias binding to the tieback, then press it over the edge of the tieback, and turn under the binding seam allowance level with the previous stitching line. Slipstitch the binding in place, then sew a ring to each end of the tieback as in step 6 for a tailored tieback, shown left.

Fancy curtain ties

Pretty or bold, subtle or elegant, flamboyant or formal, tiebacks can be used to enhance almost any curtain arrangement. Stiffened and tailored tiebacks are fine for formal effects, but for the softer look of the country style, why not opt for something really special. You will be surprised at the variety of attractive tieback effects you can achieve with a remnant of fabric and the minimum of sewing skills.

Soft tieback styles
There are many tieback styles to choose from, as simple or as complex as you like. Here is a selection to choose from.
Tieback bows can be made either from just one fabric, or with a backing or trimming in another colour – perhaps the colour of the curtain lining. For a soft effect the bows are unstiffened, but for a firmer, more structured look they can be stiffened with a light interfacing. The bows are attached in the desired position on a tailored or bound tieback.

Frilled tiebacks are a pretty idea for feminine room settings or for where the curtain or valance are also frilled.

Gathered tiebacks have the sophisticated look of a tailored tieback, but greater decorative interest. The tieback can be gathered or pleated by hand, but for quick results simply gather it up with curtain tape.

Plaited tiebacks can be made from just one fabric or up to three, depending on

▲ Frilled ensemble
Where the curtains and valance have a frilled edge, a frilled tieback is the final touch to complete the ensemble. The frill is narrower on the tieback than on the curtain since a wide frill would look too fussy on such a small item.

your colour scheme, and are much easier to make than they look. The secret is to pad the fabric strips which adds body and gives a more luxurious effect. This can be done by using kapok to stuff the fabric, but for a softer and more even effect you may find it easier to use a strip of lightweight wadding.

FRILLED TIEBACKS

1 Cutting out Cut out the tieback front and back pieces as for a tailored tieback, adding 1.5cm (⅝in) seem allowances all round (see page 101). Cut out a frill piece one and a half times the length of the front by 16cm (6¼in), joining pieces if necessary. Finally cut out a piece of heavy interfacing from the tieback pattern, omitting seam allowances

2 Making the frill Fold the frill in half lengthways with wrong sides together and pin and then stitch seams at each end. Trim seam allowances, turn right side out and press. Run a line of gathering threads 1 and 2cm (⅜ and ⅞in) from the raw edge through both layers along the length of the frill.

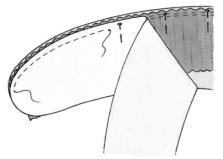

3 Attaching the frill Pull up the gathering threads on the frill so that it is the same length as the tieback piece. Tack to the lower edge of the front piece, right sides together. Place the back piece right side down on top, pin and then stitch the seam along the lower edge of the tieback, enclosing the frill. Remove the tacking threads.

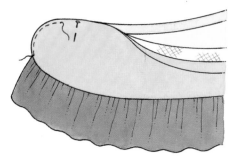

4 Finishing off Turn the tieback right side out and slip the interfacing inside. Fold the seam allowances of the front piece under, enclosing the interfacing and tack. Turn under the seam allowances of the back piece to match and tack. Working from the right side, topstitch close to the edge starting at the frill and going up one side, across the top and down to the frill on the other side. Attach a curtain ring to the wrong side at each end.

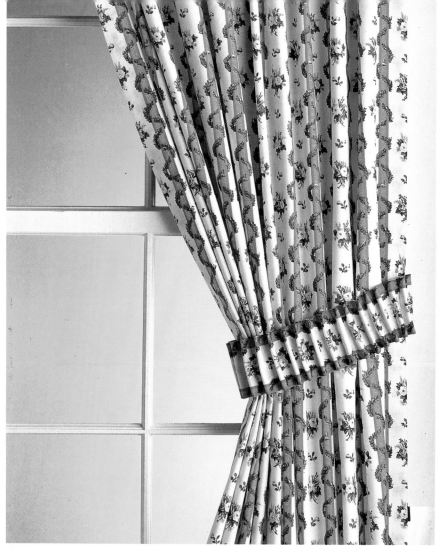

GATHERED TIEBACKS

1 Cutting out Calculate the finished length of the tieback as in step 1 above. The length of the front and back pieces depend on the type of heading tape you choose. If the tape requires twice the fabric length to gather correctly, cut out two pieces the width of the tape plus 2cm (¾in) x twice the finished length of the tieback plus 2cm (¾in). Cut the tape the same length.

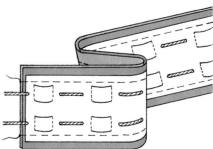

2 Stitching the seams Place the front and back together, right sides facing, and centre the tape on top. Pull out the cords from the tape at one end and fold under. Starting at the other end, stitch along one long edge, down the end, stitching across the cords, then stitch the other long edge, leaving one end free.

▲ Even results
This type of gathered tieback is perhaps the easiest of all to make. Curtain tape, the same width as the finished tieback, is used to achieve even gathers.

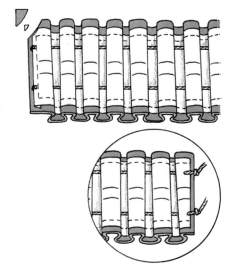

3 Completing the tiebacks Pull up the cord in the tape from the free end to gather and then knot to secure; snip off excess cord. Trim the corners and turn right side out. Tuck seam allowances inside at the free end, slipstitch closed and then attach a curtain ring at each end.

BOW TIEBACKS

1 Making the tieback Tie a measuring tape loosely around the curtain at the desired height to estimate the finished length of each tieback. Cut out and stitch the tieback, making it either tailored or with bound edges (see pages 131–134).

2 Cutting out the bows For each bow cut a rectangle twice the finished width plus 3cm (1¼in) for seam allowances x the full width of the fabric. If you wish to make the bow longer, join two strips of fabric with a seam at the centre.

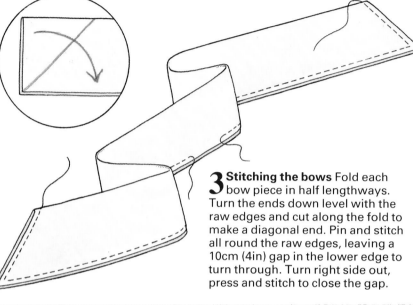

4 Finishing off Tie a bow, position the tieback at the window and arrange the bow in place in the most attractive position. Mark the tieback with tailor's chalk where the bow should go. Stitch the bow in position with a double thread in the same colour as the tieback.

3 Stitching the bows Fold each bow piece in half lengthways. Turn the ends down level with the raw edges and cut along the fold to make a diagonal end. Pin and stitch all round the raw edges, leaving a 10cm (4in) gap in the lower edge to turn through. Turn right side out, press and stitch to close the gap.

▼ *Bound effect*
These tieback bows look like they have a bound edge, but in fact this effect is achieved by cutting the back piece larger than the front. The seam allowances on both pieces are pressed to the wrong side, and then the pieces slipstitched together.

MAKING PLAITED TIEBACKS

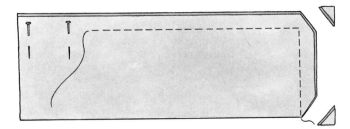

1 Making the tubes Decide on the required length of the tiebacks. For each tieback you will need three strips of fabric one and a half times the finished length x 9cm (3½in). Fold each strip in half lengthways with right sides together, pin and stitch a 1cm (⅜in) seam across one end and along the long edge to make a tube. Trim seam allowances at corners.

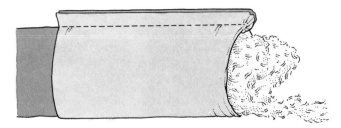

2 Stuffing the tubes Turn the tubes right side out little by little, starting at the stitched end and stuffing lightly with a strip of wadding or small amounts of kapok as you push the fabric through. When you reach the other end, pin closed.

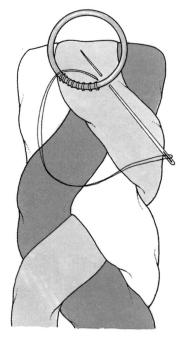

3 Checking the length Pin the three tubes together at the stitched ends and plait to check stuffing levels are correct. Check the length, and trim the tubes as necessary, remembering to add seam allowances to the trimmed ends. Separate the tubes and adjust the amount of stuffing in each one as required. Tuck seam allowances in and stitch the pinned ends closed.

4 Finishing off Pin the tubes together at one end and then stitch securely with small hand stitches. Plait the tubes and then stitch the other ends together. Sew a curtain ring on the wrong side at each end to finish.

▲ **Hand-crafted**
Plaited tiebacks, like wicker baskets and plaited rag rugs are very much in the country style because they look hand crafted. They work particularly well with wide curtains, such as those used over doors, since they look good even when very long.

tip

Covered cord
If you find it too fiddly to stuff the tubes with wadding or kapok, use covered cord for the plaits instead. Buy the thickest cord you can find, and cut the fabric strips 2cm (¾in) wider than the measurement round the cord. For quick coverage, cut the cord twice as long as the fabric. Wrap the fabric round it, right sides together, and stitch along the edge of the cord with a zip foot. Slide the fabric over itself on to the uncovered cord, turning it right side out. Trim off the excess cord.

Bordered curtains

A border, whether it is made from binding, lace, ribbon or fabric, can transform a simple curtain and take it above the ordinary look of standard, ready-made curtains. In a toning colour it has a subtle effect, adding definition to the shape of the curtains and, perhaps, linking in with a second colour used in the room. In a country pattern it will add decorative interest as well as definition, particularly where the main fabric is plain; while in a bold contrast colour it will add drama, drawing attention to the window.

Although borders can be added to finished or ready-made curtains, they should not be considered as a mere afterthought. When planning the whole style of the window dressing – the size of each curtain, the type of heading, and whether to have a valance, pelmet or tiebacks – the option of borders should also be considered.

By adding a wide border, you may be able to get away with using less of the main fabric, since the border can add valuable width to your curtains. This could mean the difference between using

▲ Bold border

A wide, black border adds drama to a pair of short kitchen curtains and forms a link with the new black kitchen chairs.

a favourite, but pricy fabric, and opting for a compromise from a cheaper price bracket.

The method for making this type of curtain can also be used to adapt existing curtains to fit larger windows when you move house.

Types of border

Double border for neat and professional results. This border is made from lengths of fabric, mitred at the corners and stitched to the main fabric so that the curtain sits neatly inside the border 'frame'.

Mock border for quick results. Ribbon or a strip of neatened fabric is stitched in place on the front of the curtain.

Lining border for curtains with attractive linings. The lining is cut larger than the curtain all round, and the excess fabric folded over to the right side of the main fabric to form the border.

There are several ways of positioning the border; it can go all round the curtain; down both sides and across the bottom, or only down the leading edge of the curtain and across the bottom. If the lower edge of the curtain is obscured by furniture or by items on the window sill, this edge can be left without a border.

◀ *Finishing line*
A three-sided border in a cheerful yellow fabric gives a neat and attractive finish to a very pretty bedroom curtain.

THREE-SIDED DOUBLE BORDER

A double border can be added to lined or unlined curtains, and is usually attached to both sides and the lower edge of the curtain. The border is cut in three sections, which are then stitched together to make the neat mitred corners, and attached to the curtain. The method requires very careful cutting and stitching and is more economical to make from plain fabrics because you don't need to worry about the direction of the pattern.

1 Assembling the curtain fabrics Cut and join the curtain fabric and lining (optional) to the required finished size plus the heading allowance. There is no need to add seam allowances to the edges where the border will go. Place the fabric on the lining, wrong sides together with all edges matching. Pin and tack together all round.

2 Cutting the border Decide on the finished width of the border – this will depend on the size of the curtain and the effect you want. Double this measurement and add 3cm (1¼in) for the seam allowances. Cut three strips this wide. Two of them, for the sides, should be the finished length of the curtain and heading plus 3cm (1¼in). The other, for the base edge, should be the finished width of the curtain plus 3cm (1¼in).

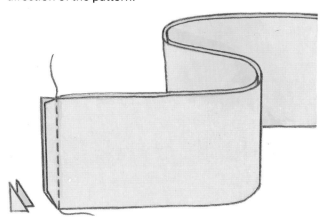

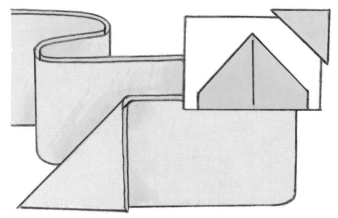

3 Preparing the side pieces Fold each side border piece in half lengthways, with right sides together. At the end which will be at the top of the curtain, stitch a 1.5cm (⅝in) seam. Trim the seam allowance at the corner and turn right side out. Press in half lengthways, this time with wrong sides together.

4 Cutting mitred corners Fold the base piece in half lengthways, wrong sides together, and press. At each end turn up the raw edges diagonally to match the fold and press. Unfold and cut along the diagonal foldlines. Repeat to cut the lower end of each of the two side border pieces.

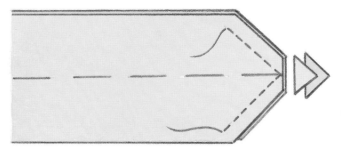

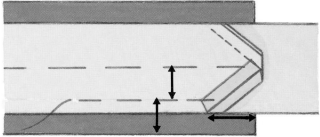

5 **Stitching the mitres** With right sides together, place one mitred end of the base piece to one of the side border pieces. Pin and stitch round the pointed edges, taking a 1.5cm (⅝in) seam and leaving 1.5cm (⅝in) free at each end of the seam. Trim off the point in the seam allowance and turn right sides out. Repeat to stitch a mitre at the other end of the base piece. Fold the fabric in half lengthways to form a frame and press along the fold.

6 **Attaching the lower border** Unfold the border and pin the lower edge of the bottom piece to the curtain with right sides together, the depth of the border minus the 1.5cm (⅝in) seam allowance from the lower edge. The arrows show the finished width of the border. Open out the seam allowances of the lower half of the mitre; tack and then stitch the border to the curtain, taking a 1.5cm (⅝in) seam allowance on the border, and stitching exactly to the mitre seam.

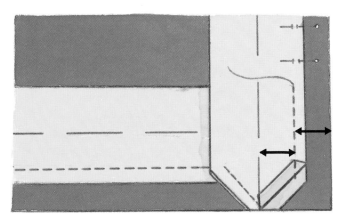

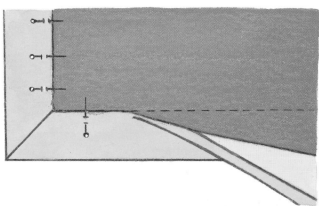

7 **Attaching the side borders** Turn each side border up, positioning it the depth of the border minus 1.5cm (⅝in) from the edge of the curtain (arrows show finished border width). The top of the border should be level with the position of the finished top edge of the curtain. Open out the seam allowance on the mitre, and taking a 1.5cm (⅝in) seam allowance on the border, pin, tack and then stitch from the top of the curtain to the mitre seam on one side of the curtain, and from the mitre seam to the top of the curtain on the other side.

8 **Finishing off** Turn the border over to the wrong/lining side of the curtain. Tuck the raw edge of the border under, and slipstitch to the curtain over the previous line of machine stitching. Turn down the top edge of the curtain, and attach the heading tape, rings or ribbons to fix the curtain to the pole or track.

SIMPLE APPLIED BORDER

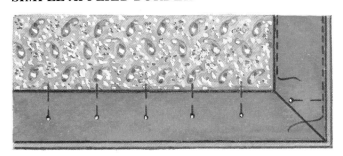

A quick way to achieve a bordered effect is to use wide ribbon or a strip of fabric hemmed on each long edge and then stitched to the curtain. If the curtain is unlined, press the raw edges of the curtain to the right side first, pin the border on top, close to the folded edge, and topstitch along both long edges of the border, enclosing the raw edges. At the corners, fold the ribbon diagonally to make a quick mitre, slipstitching across the mitred fold. If the curtain is lined, attach the border the width of the seam allowance from the edges on the right side of the main fabric, and then attach the lining in the usual way to complete the curtain.

tip

Adding width
Use a border to add width to a curtain, by stitching it to the curtain only a seam allowance away from the edge, instead of inserting the curtain fully into the border. Before cutting out, calculate the finished size of the curtain exactly, taking into account the extra added by the border; then cut out the border pieces as in step 1, of the three sided double border, and continue to make the curtain in the same way, stitching the border only 1.5cm (⅝in) from the fabric edge in steps 6 and 7.

MAKING A LINING BORDER

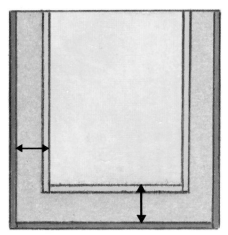

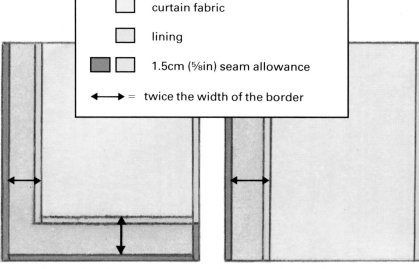

KEY

☐ curtain fabric

◤ lining

▨ ☐ 1.5cm (⅝in) seam allowance

◄——► = twice the width of the border

Three-sided border
Lining fabric:
width = finished curtain width
　　　　plus 2 x border width
　　　　plus 2 x seam allowance
length = finished curtain length
　　　　plus 1 x border width
　　　　plus heading allowance
　　　　plus 1 x seam allowance

Curtain fabric:
width = width of lining
　　　　minus 4 x border width
length = length of lining
　　　　minus 2 x border width

Side and lower border
Lining fabric:
width = finished curtain width
　　　　plus 1 x border width
　　　　plus 2 x seam allowance
length = finished curtain length
　　　　plus 1 x border width
　　　　plus heading allowance
　　　　plus 1 x seam allowance

Curtain fabric
width = width of lining
　　　　minus 2 x border width
length = length of lining
　　　　minus 2 x border width

Leading edge border
Lining fabric:
width = finished curtain width
　　　　plus 1 x border width
　　　　plus 2 x seam allowance
length = finished curtain length
　　　　plus heading allowance
　　　　plus hem allowance

Curtain fabric:
width = width of lining
　　　　minus 2 x border width
length = length of lining

1 Cutting out Cut out the main fabric and lining using one of the diagrams above, depending on where you wish to add the border.

2 Stitching the seams Matching raw edges and with right sides together, stitch the lining to the curtain along each side edge, taking a 1.5cm (⅝in) seam allowance; turn right side out and press in position, with centres matching. The extra width of the lining will form a border on the side edges.

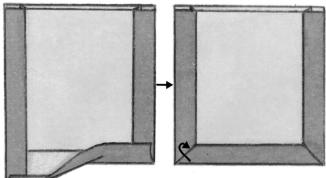

3 Lower border If there is a border on the bottom, turn the 1.5cm (⅝in) seam allowance to the right side, and then turn the fabric up again by the depth of the border; pin. At each corner, fold the fabric under at an angle to make a mock mitre, trimming off the excess fabric to reduce bulk. Stitch the hem, taking a few stitches into the mitred corner to secure. Attach the heading tape to complete.

◄**Taking a lead** The border down the leading edge is the same colour as the casing at the top used to hang these colourful curtains.

Tab headings for curtains

Traditional heading tapes are the most common means of hanging and displaying curtains, but they are not always the most effective. Some windows will really benefit from the freshness and individuality of an innovative curtain heading. Fabric tabs looped on to a thick wooden pole can look as formal or informal as you please, depending on the curtain style and the choice of fabric. Alternatively, you can create a more dramatic effect by using

▼ *Make a point*
This luxurious striped curtain is attached to the pole with matching tabs, each of which has been tailored to a point and carefully positioned to emphasize the fabric design.

luxurious tassel-trimmed cord or ribbon, threaded through eyelets in the curtain, to secure it to the pole.

The curtain ideas featured here all give full coverage of the window when drawn, but use far less fabric than a tape heading, even when extra widths are added for fullness. Hang heavy curtains from thick wooden poles with ornately carved finials, or from slimmer iron poles for a more authentic rustic feel. Though most of the styles shown here can be pulled back along the pole, they look best when drawn either partially or fully across the window, then secured at the sides with matching tiebacks.

The fabric tabs can be made in the same fabric as the curtain, or in a contrasting colour and pattern; you can even use two or more fabrics for the heading tabs, either in toning or contrasting shades, depending on how striking an effect is wanted.

Measuring up

When using a fabric tab or eyelet heading, the curtain is usually hung just below the pole, rather than on it. Ensure you have at least a 5cm (2in) gap between the pole and the top of the window to accommodate the tabs, otherwise the tab headings will allow light to filter through at the top of the window.

To calculate the length of the actual curtain, measure from a point 5cm (2in) below the base of the pole, to just below the window or to the floor, as preferred. Add 3cm (1¼in) to the length for heading and hem allowances.

The curtain width depends on how full an effect is wanted when the curtains are drawn. For curtains that lie flat against the window, you will only need fabric the width of the window, plus extra for side seams and joining fabric widths. For a fuller effect, add a half or a whole fabric width to each curtain.

Materials

Fabric for curtains (for quantities see *Measuring up*)
Lining or **contrast fabric** if required
Matching sewing threads
Tape measure
Tailor's chalk

SIMPLE TAB HEADING

The instructions given here are for lined curtains.

1 Making up the curtains Measure the window area as described, and cut out the curtain fabric and lining to the correct size, joining fabric widths where necessary. With right sides together and edges matching, pin, tack and stitch the lining to the main fabric down both sides and across the lower edge, taking a 1.5cm (⅝in) seam allowance. Turn right side out.

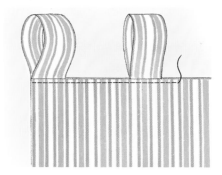

2 Spacing the tabs Decide how wide you would like the tabs to be – generally 5-7.5cm (2-3in). Then measure across the top of each curtain to see how many tabs you will need – you should begin and end with a tab, and allow approximately twice a tab's width for the spaces in-between. Use tailor's chalk to mark the position of each tab on the lining side of the curtain.

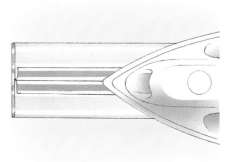

3 Stitching the tabs For each tab, cut one strip of your chosen fabric, 23cm (9in) long, and twice as wide as the finished tab plus 2cm (¾in). With right sides together, fold each tab in half lengthways and stitch down the long edges, taking a 1cm (⅜in) seam allowance. Centre the seam on the tab, open out the allowances and press. Turn the tabs right side out and press their edges into a sharp crease.

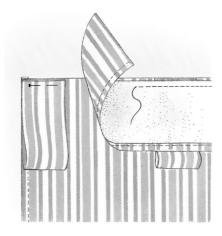

4 Attaching the tabs Lay out the curtain right side face up, and fold in 1.5cm (⅝in) of both the lining and the main fabric along the top edge. Fold each tab in half widthways, with the seam on the inside. Pin in place along the top of the curtain, slipping the raw ends of each tab in-between the lining and the main fabric, for 1.5cm (⅝in). Top stitch across top of curtain to attach both the lining and the tabs.

UNLINED CURTAINS

A tab heading can also be easily attached to unlined curtains, by means of a top facing.

1 Preparing the facing Hem the sides and bottom edge of the curtain, and make up the tabs as usual. Cut a facing 11cm (4¼in) deep and as wide as the curtain, plus 2cm (¾in), then cut and apply iron-on interfacing. Stitch a 1.5cm (⅝in) hem along the bottom edge of the facing.

2 Attaching the tabs Fold the tabs in half widthways and pin in place on the right side of the curtain, matching raw edges. Lie the facing over the tabs, wrong side up. Tack then stitch across the curtain top, through the facing, the tabs and the main fabric, taking a 1.5cm (⅝in) seam allowance. Flip the facing over to lie against the wrong side of the curtain, turn in 1cm (⅜in) of the facing at each side and slipstitch to the curtain's side hem to finish.

GATHERED TABS

A gathered tab heading will create a full curtain, which falls in soft folds when drawn across the pole. Make the tabs and their gathering bands in the same fabric as the main curtain, or use fabrics in toning or contrasting shades.

1 Marking up the tabs Make up the curtains as usual, leaving the top edges unstitched. In this design, each tab is double the usual width, so that it measures 11-15cm (4¼-6in); the space left in-between each tab is the same width as the finished tab. Mark the position of the tabs on the wrong side of each curtain.

2 Stitching the tabs For each tab, cut out a strip of your chosen fabric 23cm (9in) long and twice the width of the finished tab, plus 2cm (¾in). Stitch the tabs as before, and attach them to the curtain top.

◀ *Gathered for fullness*
Gathered tab headings are as simple to make as plain tabs, but create a far softer, fuller curtain.

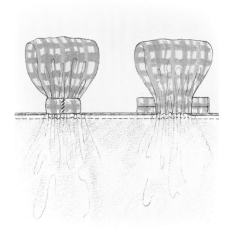

3 Gathering the tabs For each tab, cut a fabric strip 11 x 6cm (4¼ x 2¼in). Fold each strip in half and stitch, as for tabs, with a 5mm (¼in) seam allowance. Turn through to right side and place one over the base of each tab, with seam underneath. Draw the ends of the strip round to the back of the tab, gathering up the tab as you go, and slipstitch strip ends together, folding in the raw ends. Hold in place at the bottom of the tab with a few stitches.

SPLIT-LEVEL TABS

Here the curtains are made up from two panels, one slightly larger than the other, and matching tabs provide a decorative link over the top. For the best results, choose toning fabrics and use the lighter of the two for the back panel.

1 Cutting out Measure the window as before. For each curtain, cut a piece of the light coloured back panel fabric to the desired finished size, plus 11.5cm (4½in) all round, and one of the front panel fabric to the finished size, plus 1.5cm (⅝in) all round; join widths where necessary.

2 Hemming the panels On the back panel, turn and press an 11.5cm (4½in) hem to wrong side all round the curtain; tack in place, mitring the corners and slipstitching them together for a neat finish. Repeat on front panel, taking a 6.5cm (2½in) hem.

3 Stitching the tabs Calculate how many tabs are needed, and mark their positions; the first and last tabs are placed slightly in from the sides of the front panel, and the spaces are twice as wide as the finished tabs. For each tab, cut a strip from your main fabric, 44.5cm (17½in) long and twice as wide as the tab, plus 2cm (¾in). Stitch tabs as before.

4 Making up the curtain With wrong sides together, centre front panel over back panel and tack then topstitch together down sides and along the lower edge, 10cm (4in) in from the curtain edge to make a flap, but enclosing raw edges.

5 Attaching the tabs Turn in 1.5cm (⅝in) at one end of each tab and slipstitch to close. Pin tabs in place across curtain top, with neatened ends against right side of back panel, and raw ends slipped in-between back and front panels. Both tab ends must lie 11.5cm (4½in) in from the top edge. Top stitch across curtain top, 10cm (4in) from top edge, securing tabs as you join panels. Remove tacking stitches.

▲ *Colourful combination*
Depending on the fabrics used to make this unusual tabbed curtain, various effects can be achieved. Back the front panel with a wide lacy border to create a soft feminine look, or use plain or striped fabrics for more modern settings.

▲ Bound to impress
This heavy, textured kelim fabric is bound to its ornate gold-painted pole by a length of richly coloured cord. A pair of sumptuous wool tassels casually looped over the pole end hold it in place and complete the effect. To finish tie back the curtain with tassels.

Threaded eyelet headings

Striking headings can be created by inserting large eyelets into the top of the curtain, and threading these with lengths of cord or ribbon which are looped over the pole. Large eyelet kits can be bought from department stores and come complete with detailed fixing instructions. The eyelets are usually available in silver or bronze, so choose the colour that best complements your fabric.

Always insert the eyelets through a double layer of fabric and, unless your fabric is very thick, strengthen the top of the curtain with interfacing. These curtains cannot be drawn open, so use decorative tiebacks to fix them at the sides.

▲ Two-tone heading
Use a length of pretty ribbon or braid to bind a fresh, summery curtain to its pole. As both sides of the ribbon will be visible, either use a ribbon that is double-sided, or stick two lengths together using a fabric bonder, as here. To add interest and colour and to strengthen the curtain top, line the curtain with a contrast fabric, which will be visible when the curtain sides are tied back.

◄ Metallic effect
Rather than binding your curtains to the pole with lengths of cord or ribbon, use split metal curtain rings, which can be slipped through the eyelets and looped on to the pole. As well as cleverly extending the metal eyelet theme, the rings will also enable you to draw the curtain back and forth across the pole.

Valance variations

A valance, trimmed with frills, binding, braid or fringing, gives an attractive finish to the window dressing, and works particularly well when balanced with tiebacks trimmed to match. The softly flowing shape of a valance helps to relax the hard lines of the window, adding volume and movement. It is a soft style and should not be confused with the smooth, stiff and tailored style of a pelmet.

In addition to their decorative value, valances have a double function in concealing the curtain track and helping to enhance the proportions of the window. The standard valance is one sixth of the length of the main curtains, and extends about 6cm (2½in) on each side. A valance which is longer than usual helps to balance a tall window, while a very full valance can add width to windows of any height.

▲ Country co-ordination
This lovely, frilled valance, combined with matching curtains and a co-ordinating Austrian blind, gives this room a real country feel. The valance makes the window look shorter, but wider, like traditional cottage windows, and covers the curtain track for a neat finish.

Fitting a valance

A valance is basically just a short curtain, but it spans the full width of the window and is never drawn back. Like a curtain, it can be made using any number of curtain tapes, from simple gathers to triple or cartridge pleats, and like a curtain it can be hung at the window in a number of ways.

The easiest way to hang a valance is on a valance track, which runs in front of the main track and extends slightly on each side, covering the main track completely. A number of curtain track manufacturers produce these, usually as optional fittings which use standard curtain hooks and can be added to certain curtain tracks when required.

When the main curtain track is fixed inside a window recess, instead of using a valance track, a slightly longer curtain track, pole or rod can be fixed just in front of the recess, and the valance attached to this. Another option for attaching valances is to use a pelmet shelf, but this will be covered in a later chapter.

MAKING A SIMPLE VALANCE

1 Planning the effect A standard proportion for a valance is one sixth of the length of the main curtain. Cut a piece of paper this size and position it at the window to check the effect. If you wish to make a tall window seem shorter, make the valance longer, but to let in maximum light, make the valance shorter. Decide also on the heading tape you prefer – it doesn't have to be the same as the tape used for the curtains.

2 Cutting out Cut out strips of fabric the width of the fabric by the length of the finished valance plus 20cm (8in). The number of widths you need depends on the heading tape; cut out enough widths to make up a piece the required size, making sure the pattern will match across seams. Remember, the valance goes round both sides, so include these in your measurements.

Join the fabric widths together, taking 1.5cm (⅝in) seam allowances and stitching the fabric with right sides together: press seams open.

3 Adding a lining For a lined valance, cut out and join the lining fabric to make a piece 8cm (3in) shorter and 4cm (1½in) narrower than the main fabric. Lightly press the seams open.

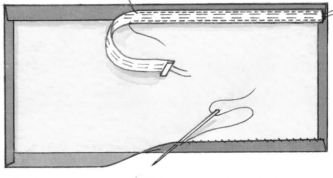

4 Stitching the valance Make up the valance in the same way as a curtain using a plain or decorative curtain tape. For a simple, unlined valance, follow the instructions on page 125. For a lined valance, follow the instructions for a curtain with sewn-in lining on page 126.

5 Hanging the valance Pull up the cords in the heading tape to fit the valance track and knot. Insert the appropriate curtain hooks into the tape and slip through the rings on the valance track to hang. If using a curtain pole or rod at a recessed window, attach the valance to this in the same way.

▶ *Valance elegance*
Even a simple valance with narrow heading can look smart. This lovely version, edged at top and bottom with pretty pink bias binding, adds width to this elegant landing window, and gives it a simple, but classic look.

tip

Depth gauge
Let the depth of the pattern repeat on the fabric dictate the exact depth of the valance – if one or more pattern repeats fit the depth, it gives the valance a professional finish.

A LINE AND FRILLED VALANCE

1 Cutting the fabric Cut out widths of fabric the finished length of the valance, with pattern repeats matching. Since the frill will add to the length, there is no need to add seam allowances at top and bottom. The width of the fabric depends on the heading tape – twice the finished width is average. Cut and join enough widths to make up a piece the required size, taking 1.5cm (⅝in) seam allowances. Cut and join the lining fabric to make a piece the same size.

2 Cutting the frill For a frill 6cm (2½in) deep, cut widths of fabric, with pattern repeats matching, 15cm (6in) deep to make up a piece two to two and a half times the measurement across the ungathered valance. Join the pieces together to make up one long strip, taking 1.5cm (⅝in) seam allowances and stitching with right sides together.

3 Making the frill Fold the strip of fabric in half lengthways, right sides together, and stitch across the ends, taking a 1.5cm (⅝in) seam allowance. Trim the seams and turn right side out, re-folding the fabric in half lengthways; press.

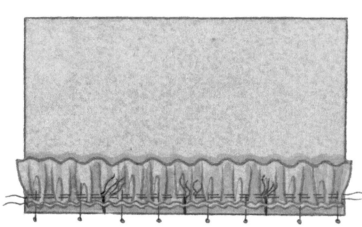

4 Attaching the frill Divide both the frill and lower edge of the valance into four and mark at the edges with tailor's chalk. Run two rows of gathering threads close to the raw edges of the frill, stopping and starting at marks. Pull up the threads to gather the frill to fit the valance, matching marks, but leaving 1.5cm (⅝in) free at each end for side seams. Pin and then tack 1cm (⅜in) from the raw edge.

▲ Short and sweet
A very attractive way of finishing a valance on a border fabric is to stitch round the design on the lower edge with narrow, close zigzag and then trim close to the stitching. This pretty effect looks particularly attractive when the fabric is only lightly gathered.

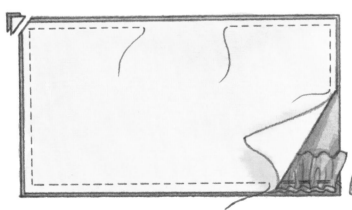

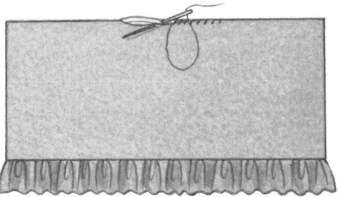

5 Attaching the lining Place the lining right side down on top of the valance and frill. Tack and then stitch together all round with raw edges level, taking a 1.5cm (⅝in) seam allowance and leaving a 20cm (8in) opening free on the top edge. Trim the seam allowances at the corners and then remove the tacking threads.

6 Finishing off Turn the valance right side out through the opening at the top edge and press. Oversew the opening closed with small stitches, then attach the heading tape to the lining side in the usual way (see page 125). Gather up and hang the valance on the track.

DECORATIVE OPTIONS

A curtain valance offers an excellent opportunity for using one of the many attractive trimmings on the market. Here are just a few to give you inspiration.

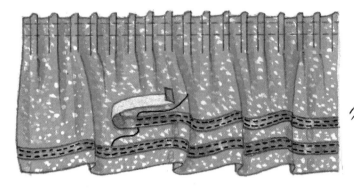

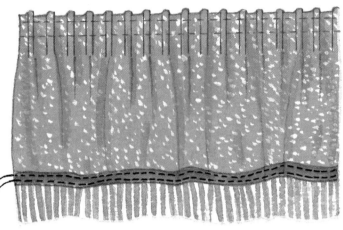

Ribbon trim Make a simple valance, and then purchase enough ribbon to go along the full width of the valance plus 3cm (1¼in). Turn the ends under, pin in position on the valance and then stitch in place along both long edges. Add a second row of ribbon if you like.

Fringing Cut out and make a simple valance. For a lined valance, follow the instructions for the frilled valance, but omit the frill. Cut a length of fringing long enough to go across the width of the ungathered valance plus 2cm (¾in). Turn each end under, pin to the valance and then stitch the fringing to the valance along each long edge.

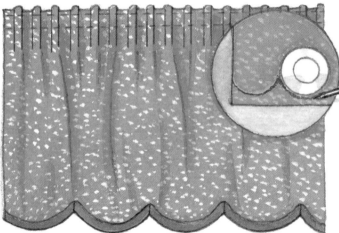

Bound edge Cut out and join the fabric to make up a valance the required width (depending on the tape used) by the finish length plus 4cm (1½in). Turn double 1cm (⅜in) hems to the wrong side along each side edge, then turn down 4cm (1½in) at the top and attach the heading tape. Attach bias binding to the lower edge (see *Decorative Soft Furnishings*, page 222).

   For a lined and bound valance, cut out the fabric and lining as for a frilled valance. Place the main fabric and lining right sides together, then stitch along both sides and the top edge, taking a 1.5cm (⅝in) seam. Turn right side out, pin the two fabrics together and then finish the lower edge with the binding.

Contrast trim Decide on the finished width of the trim, then make up a valance as for a bound edge, adding a 1.5cm (⅝in) seam allowance but deducting the depth of the trim from the length. Cut out and join fabric widths from the trimming fabric, twice the required finished depth plus 3cm (1¼in), matching the pattern repeats. Join to make up a piece the same width as the valance fabric. Fold both long edges 1.5cm (⅝in) to the wrong side, and attach like binding. Stitch the ends of the trim together with slipstitches, with seam allowances inside.

   For a lined, trimmed valance, make up like a lined, bound valance, adding a 1.5cm (⅝in) seam allowance and deducting the depth of the trim from the cut length. Attach the trimming like binding.

Scalloped edge Cut out and join the fabric as for a bound edge, then using a plate as a template, draw scallops on the wrong side at the lower edge of the main fabric; cut out. Turn double 1cm (⅜in) hems to the wrong side along each side edge, then turn 4cm (1½in) at the top and attach the heading tape. Attach binding to the lower edge, easing round curves and folding binding at the top of the scallops.

   For a lined, scalloped valance, cut out and make up as for a lined, bound valance, then cut the lower edge of fabric and lining into scallops before binding.

Formal fabric pelmets

Pelmets give windows an elegant, tailored look which is ideal for dining rooms and other formal areas of the home. Like valances, they are placed at the top of the window, defining the curtain arrangement and covering the curtain track, even when the curtains are drawn back. Unlike valances, which are soft and flowing, pelmets are made from wood or fabric stiffened with buckram or self-adhesive stiffener.

Wooden pelmets are usually fairly straight across the lower edge because it is difficult to cut complex patterns in the wood with accuracy, but with a fabric pelmet, you can make the shape as intricate as you like. Cut the edge into scallops, curves or waves for a soft, flowing effect, or shape it into turrets, like a castle, or ledges for a more formal effect. You can even cut round the shape of the design on the fabric for an unusual and really individual, tailor-made look.

Choosing a fabric

Most furnishing fabrics which are suitable for curtain-making can also be used for the pelmet. Cotton, chintz, ging-ham, brocade and even silk are suitable, but lightweight and loosely woven fabrics including sheers, lace and net are not – if you wish to use these, then choose a valance style instead.

▼ *Making waves*
The large, soft waves on this pelmet have been carefully cut out to complement the floral design of the fabric. Co-ordinated braid at the top and bottom of the pelmet give the whole thing a neat finish.

Choosing a stiffener

Buckram is traditionally used to stiffen the pelmet, and is combined with an additional layer of interlining to provide extra body and to make the finished pelmet look more luxurious. It has to be hand stitched in place, but the extra effort does mean that the finished pelmet will last well and can be washed or dry-cleaned as required.

Self-adhesive stiffener is the modern equivalent of buckram. It is made from strong, flexible pvc with a printed backing which contains several suggested designs already drawn to scale and full written instructions. It does not require interlining and is self-adhesive for quick results.

There are two types of self-adhesive stiffener to choose from – with an adhesive backing on one or both sides. Choose the type with one adhesive side for quick and economical results, or the type with adhesive on both sides if you wish to line the pelmet. Neither type can be washed or dry-cleaned, although some marks can be sponged off.

Using self-adhesive stiffener

Self-adhesive stiffener is easy to use, particularly if you wish to cut round one of the five pre-printed pelmet designs on the back. Even if you wish to make your own design, self-adhesive stiffener makes it easy by providing a grid to aid measurement and design. Choose one of three widths: 30cm (12in) for small windows, 40cm (16in) for standard windows, and 60cm (24in) for large windows, such as french windows.

▼ Pre-printed design shapes

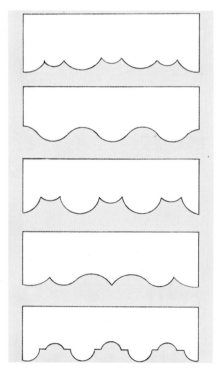

PRE-PRINTED DESIGNS

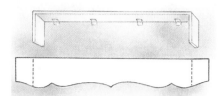

1 Measuring up Fix a pelmet box at the window. Measure the length of the pelmet front and sides for the total length of the pelmet. With the design on the self-adhesive stiffener centred, mark the required length. Mark where the pelmet turns the corner and check that the design looks good from the front. You may need to adjust the pattern at the sides for a neat effect. Cut to length, then cut along the lower edge, following the lines for your pattern.

2 Cutting the fabric Press the fabric to remove any wrinkles, then place the self-adhesive stiffener on the wrong side of the fabric with the pattern centred in the middle. Draw round the self-adhesive stiffener with tailor's chalk, then draw another line round this 2.5cm (1in) beyond. Check that the pattern works well with the shape of the self-adhesive stiffener, then cut out, following the outer chalk line.

On very wide windows it may be necessary to join fabric pieces together to make up the required width. If so, use a full fabric width in the middle with two smaller pieces at the sides. Join the fabric with right sides together and trim the allowances to 1cm (3/8in). Press seams open before cutting to shape.

3 Sticking on the backing Starting at the *centre* of the self-adhesive stiffener, lift and then cut through the centre of the backing. Peel back part of the backing, then place on the wrong side of the fabric with the adhesive backing face down. Smooth the exposed adhesive on to the fabric, making sure there are no wrinkles in the fabric. Peel away the rest of the backing a little at a time, smoothing the backing on to the fabric as you do so.

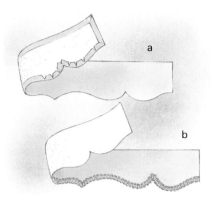

Single adhesive side Snip into the allowance all round 3mm (1/8in) from the self-adhesive stiffener and then turn the edges over to the wrong side. Carefully glue in place with fabric glue and leave to dry (a). Alternatively, trim the excess fabric close to the edge of the self-adhesive stiffener and stitch or glue braid along the bottom edge to finish (b). Attach the fixings to hang to the pelmet box above the window.

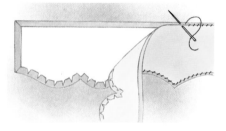

Both sides adhesive Snip into the fabric allowance all round 3mm (1/8in) from the self-adhesive stiffener. Peel the backing off the reverse of the self-adhesive stiffener and fold the excess fabric over, pressing on to the adhesive. Cut the lining the same size as the shaped self-adhesive stiffener. Press 1cm (3/8in) to the wrong side of the lining all round, then place wrong side down on top of the adhesive. Press in place carefully to avoid wrinkles. Slipstitch the lining to the fabric all round and attach the fixings to hang to the pelmet box.

---

tip

Easy-hang pelmet
The type of self-adhesive stiffener which has one adhesive side only, has a soft backing on the non-adhesive side which will stick to the hook side of velcro. Simply glue the hook side of the velcro along the top edge of the pelmet box and press the pelmet in place.

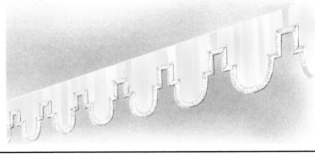

MAKING UP A DESIGN

1 Preparation. Fix a pelmet box at the window. Measure the length of the box and the depth of both sides. Add together, and cut a piece of self-adhesive stiffener this length. Mark the self-adhesive stiffener with the depth of the side at each end and mark the centre to ensure you obtain a symmetrical pattern.

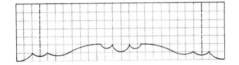

2 Making the design Draw your pattern on to the back of the self-adhesive stiffener so that it is centred across the pelmet front. Use the grid pattern on the self-adhesive stiffener to draw straight lines, and a french curve and circular object such as a cup to draw curves and scallops. When you are satisfied with the design, cut the self-adhesive stiffener to shape. Press the fabric, cut out and then make the pelmet, following the instructions for a pre-printed design.

USING THE PATTERN ON THE FABRIC

Border fabrics make attractive pelmets when the fabric is turned sideways to run across the top of the window. Use the width of the pattern repeat as a guide for the depth of the pelmet, using exactly one or more pattern repeats.

1 Applying the stiffener Fix a pelmet box at the window. Measure up and cut out the self-adhesive stiffener to the required length; do not trim the width. Cut out a strip of fabric 2.5cm (1in) larger than the self-adhesive stiffener all round, with the pattern centred widthways and with its lower edge 5cm (2in) above the lower edge of the fabric. Place the self-adhesive stiffener, backing side down, centred in the wrong side of the fabric. Peel away the backing from the centre of the self-adhesive stiffener and stick

to the fabric. Slowly peel back more of the backing until all the self-adhesive stiffener is firmly stuck to the fabric.

2 Making the pelmet Trim the excess fabric on the side edges flush with the self-adhesive stiffener. At the top edge, trim the fabric in a straight line just above the pattern, allowing sufficient depth beneath for the pelmet. Trim the lower edge in the same way and add a braid trim along each edge, if required.

▲ Inspired by design
This cleverly designed pelmet uses the pattern as a guide for its shape.

Shaped lower edge If preferred, neaten the top and side edges as in step 2 above, and then shape the lower edge round the pattern. To do this, carefully cut close to the pattern with sharp scissors or a craft knife. If the pattern is not too intricate, and you wish to trim it with a suitable braid, cut round the pattern the width of the trimming away from it. Glue or stitch the trimming in place (see page 150).

Buckram for pelmets

Buckram requires more hand stitching than self-adhesive stiffener, and you will have to make your own pattern before you start, but the end result has a softer look than one made with self-adhesive stiffener, and it should last longer because it can be cleaned. The pelmet should be about an eighth to a sixth of the length of the window, but standard depths are 30-40cm (12-16in) at the deepest points. It must also hide the track even at the highest points.

For your pattern, choose one of the designs given on the previous pages, or use the pattern of the fabric to provide inspiration for the shape.

USING BUCKRAM

1 Cutting out Cut a piece of dressmaker's squared paper or graph paper the required depth by the length of the pelmet box plus the sides. Mark the position of the side edges and centre. Design your pattern, then hold it up to the window to check the effect. Cut from buckram using the template as a guide. Cut again from fabric, adding 2.5cm (1in) all round; from interlining, adding 1.3cm (½in) all round; and from lining adding 1cm (⅜in) all round.

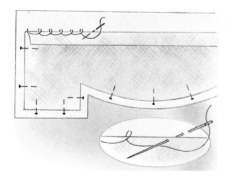

2 Attaching the interlining Centre the interlining on the wrong side of the main fabric and pin in the middle to hold. Lock stitch to the fabric by taking a small backstitch to pick up one thread from both the main fabric and interlining. Position the stitches 10cm (4in) apart and rows 30cm (12in) apart. This ensures the interlining will stay in place.

3 Attaching the buckram One side of the buckram is impregnated with glue. Dampen this side round the edges and then place on the interlining, this side up. Press the fabric allowances over the top all round, snipping into the allowances at corners and curves for ease.

4 Adding a trimming Stitch a trimming of braid or fringing to the pelmet before adding the lining to the back.

▲ *Trimming expertise*
A gathered trimming, is made into rosettes to emphasise the pelmet shape.

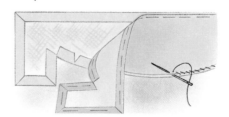

5 Attaching the lining Turn a 1.5cm (⅝in) seam allowance all round the lining so that it is slightly smaller than the main piece; tack. Pin centrally over the buckram and slipstitch together all round. Remove all the tacking stitches and attach the fixing to the back – the soft part of velcro, for example.

Swags and tails

Swags and tails are traditionally the reserve of grand houses and stately country homes, whose majestic windows demand lavish treatment. But although the style was devised with tall, slim windows in mind, it can very easily be adapted to suit all kinds of window shapes and sizes, whether tall or short, wide or narrow.

In a formal dining or living room where the windows are relatively large, swags and tails make an impressive crown for full-length curtains. To add definition and interest to an ornate arrangement, trim the swags and tails with a luxurious fringe, a full frill or decorative braid. For smaller windows and a less imposing effect, use swags and tails on their own to create a frame for the window and the view beyond it; if the window is overlooked, team them with a roller blind or sheer curtain.

Swags and tails are arranged to give the impression of a single length of fabric, draped across the window, but they are actually made up from three or more shaped pieces of fabric, assembled on a pelmet shelf above the window. The swag is cut on the bias so it forms natural, full folds when hung, and it can vary in depth depending on the window height and the desired effect. The tails which fall on each side of the swag can be spirals, flutes, asymmetrical (folding in from both tail sides) or the more common triangular cut, with staggered folds down one side only. To emphasize the folds and to give the tails a full, rounded appearance, they are usually lined with a contrasting fabric.

▼ Bedroom flair
In this stylish bedroom, swags and tails crown luxurious full-length curtains, to add emphasis and authority to the window. The arrangement adds a touch of grandeur, without being overly formal.

Proportioning the arrangement

There are no fixed rules for proportioning a swag and tail arrangement in relation to the window, but the following guidelines are worth bearing in mind. To avoid a top-heavy appearance, the swag should be no longer than about one-sixth of the window drop, particularly where the window is small and allows little light into the room.

The tails should fall halfway to two-thirds down the window, or even further where the arrangement is being used without curtains. The first pleat of each tail should lie at roughly the same level as the lowest point of the swag. Before you begin, take a look at several pictures to get an idea of the different effects that can be created for your shape and style of window.

Materials

Fabric for the swags and tails. (See instructions for quantities.)
Contrast lining to back swags and tails
Length of plywood 9mm (⅜in) thick, 10cm (4in) wide and slightly longer than your window, to make a pelmet shelf; the swags and tails are assembled on the shelf and attached to it
38mm (1½in) steel angle brackets, 1cm (⅜in) and 3.2cm (1¼in) woodscrews with wallplugs for fixing the brackets to the pelmet shelf and wall
Sew 'n' Stick Velcro one and a half times the length of the pelmet shelf
Tape measure
Matching sewing threads

▲ *Elegantly framed* Swags and tails need not always be teamed with curtains, but look just as stunning used alone or with a simple roller blind. This type of arrangement is ideal for the striking bathroom shown here, which calls for a lavish treatment, but where space around the window is too limited for curtains.

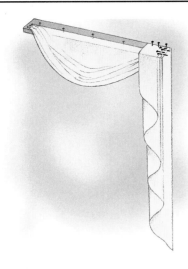

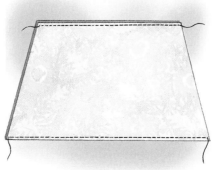

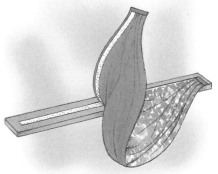

5 Shaping the tails Hang the tail in place over the pelmet shelf, covering one pleated end of the swag. Arrange the folds and pin them in place, adjusting the fabric and trimming it where necessary, until you are satisfied with the finished effect. Step back and check that the swag and tail arrangement works well as a whole, before taking down both pattern pieces.

6 Making up the swag The swag is often cut on the bias to create softer, more natural folds. Using your fabric pattern as a guide and adding a 1.5cm (⅝in) seam allowance all round, cut out the swag from your main fabric and lining. With right sides together and edges matching, pin and stitch the lining to the main fabric along the top and bottom edges, taking a 1.5cm (⅝in) seam allowance. Trim the seam allowances, turn the swag through to the right side and press.

7 Fixing the swag Gather or pleat up the ends of the swag on the pelmet shelf as you did before with the fabric pattern. Once satisfied with the effect, hold the folds in place with a few stitches at the sides; take down the swag and machine stitch the folds in place at the sides, trim and bind the raw edges for a neat finish. Stitch the stitching half of the Velcro along the top of the swag, and stick the other half to the top of the pelmet shelf. Fix the swag in place on the shelf.

SWAGS AND TAILS

The instructions given below are for a single swag and two triangular tails with three staggered pleats. Both the swag and the tails are lined with a contrast fabric to create a fuller effect and to emphasize the pleats on the tails.

1 **Fixing the pelmet shelf** Use the angle brackets to attach the pelmet shelf above the window, ready to carry the swag and tails. An arrangement of swags and tails on a small window can block out light, so fix the shelf well above it and make sure it extends beyond the window on both sides, this also makes the window look larger.

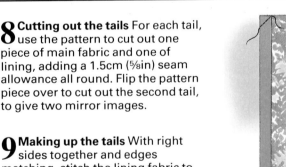

2 **Measuring up for the swag** First decide how far down the window you want the swag to hang. Using an old sheet to make a pattern, cut a rectangle from it 20cm (8in) longer than the shelf **(a)**, by 1½ times the depth of the finished swag, plus 5cm (2in) for attaching it to the top of the shelf **(b)**. Measure 20cm (8in) in from each side along one long edge, and mark. Join these points to the two corners on the other long edge and trim along the lines; the top edge of the pattern **(c)** will then be 20cm (8in) shorter than the shelf.

3 **Shaping the swag** Fix the swag pattern piece in place on the pelmet shelf, attaching it to the top of the shelf with a few temporary tacks; knock the tacks in halfway only, for easy removal. Pleat up the side ends of the swag pattern piece to form soft sweeping folds across the window; pin the folds in place slightly in from the ends of the shelf, where they will be covered by the tails. Adjust the arrangement until you are happy with it, and trim the fabric where necessary.

4 **Measuring up for the tails** Decide how long and wide the tails will be, and how many pleats they will have. Following our pattern for three 18cm (7in) pleats, cut a fabric pattern piece as follows: width across top **(d)** = 18cm (7in) x 7 (number of folds) + 10cm (4in) to wrap around the shelf ends; length of outer edge **(e)** = depth of tail + 7.5cm (3in) for fixing to shelf; length of inner edge **(f)** = depth of finished swag + 7.5cm (3in) for fixing to shelf. The tail's lower edge is cut diagonally to create the staggered pleats. Mark up the foldlines as shown.

8 **Cutting out the tails** For each tail, use the pattern to cut out one piece of main fabric and one of lining, adding a 1.5cm (⅝in) seam allowance all round. Flip the pattern piece over to cut out the second tail, to give two mirror images.

9 **Making up the tails** With right sides together and edges matching, stitch the lining fabric to the main fabric for each tail, down both sides and along the slanted lower edge, taking a 1.5cm (⅝in) seam allowance. Trim the seam allowances, clip the corners, turn through to the right side and press.

Alternative fixing

To save time, use staples and a staple gun rather than Velcro to fix the swags and tails in place on the pelmet shelf.

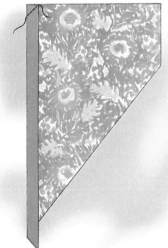

10 **A neat fit** Lay out one tail with right side face up, and fold in that part of the outer side edge which will extend around the side of the pelmet shelf. Make a dart by stitching through all layers of fabric, from the outer corner of the shelf to the top corner of the tail. The tail will then fit neatly around the corner. Repeat on the other tail.

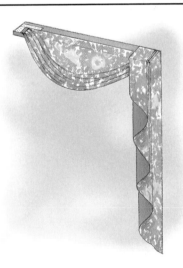

11 **Fixing the tails** Pleat up the tails on the pelmet shelf as before, checking the effect. Once satisfied, hold the pleats in place with a few stitches. Take down the tails and machine stitch folds in place along edge; trim top edge if necessary and bind or oversew raw edges. Attach Velcro to underside of the tails, and to the shelf, as for the swags, and fix tails in place.

Informal arrangements

In settings where swags and tails would be too formal, opt for an equally impressive but more casual approach, in which the window is framed by a single length of fabric draped to suit its style and shape. The finished effect can be as simple or elaborate as you please, from a single short fabric length used to crown a small picture window, to great swathes of fabric, draped around French windows and left to fall in abundant folds to the ground.

Like swags and tails, these types of arrangement can be used with or without curtains or a blind. On large windows, the fabric is generally draped over a decorative wooden pole, and fixed in place with tacks where necessary. Here, the pole should be extended beyond the window on each side, to avoid cutting out too much light, and to create the illusion of a larger window. Contrast line the fabric to give it volume and to emphasize its folds as it is twisted and draped around the pole.

On smaller windows which carry less lavish arrangements, the fabric can either be attached to a pelmet shelf as previously described, or alternative fixing techniques can be used, such as metal or plastic coils attached either side of the window.

▲ Swathed in fabric
This asymmetrical arrangement, teamed with matching full-length curtains, adds a touch of luxury to the modest surroundings. The fabric is lined, and the ends have been shaped to form the staggered pleats of a classic tail. The contrast lining also provides a decorative border for the main fabric.

◄ Crowning glory
This charming variation on a swag and tail arrangement is formed from a single long strip of unlined fabric. The fabric is simply pulled through metal or plastic coils fixed either side of the window, and then scrunched up to form full rosettes. The ends are left to hang in two short tails.

Lace panels

Until very recently sheer curtains were chiefly about privacy. They veiled a household from the prying eyes of passers-by, while allowing a diffused light to filter in through the window. To these traditional virtues, another security value can be added: the would-be burglar will find it difficult to survey the scene with screened windows.

Today, sheer curtains can be enjoyed for the range of interior light effects they provide. With an unparalleled choice of easy-care translucent fabrics on the market – from the most intricate laces to the lightest voiles – the choice is about sheer beauty as much as sheer practicality. You can use the fabrics' qualities of texture and drape for dramatic effects, to disguise an ugly window or glorify a pretty one.

Lace panels, like all sheers, tame the light and offer privacy and intimacy.

Unlike plain sheers such as voile and muslin, lace panels look their best hanging straight so that the pattern shows to best effect. However, by using metres of cheaper lace with a heading tape, you can create a window dressing that provides both atmosphere and privacy.

▼ **Graceful lace** Swathes of lace over and around the window and furniture impart serenity and lightness.

The range of panels

Now there are many cotton and synthetic mix laces available which offer the patterned charm and texture of antique lace, while being easier to care for. Again, with the country look in mind, it's best to stick to the traditional bridal colours of lace – white or cream.

Lace fabric with distinctive patterns can be bought as separate panels or by the metre. Sold as complete ready-made window coverings, these panels come in a range of set sizes and have the addition of integral eyelets or a casing along the top edge ready for slotting on to fine rods for instant window dressing.

If you prefer to make your own panels, or you have awkward shaped windows, lace can be bought by the metre in a range of different widths. Some narrow widths have integral eyelets or a casing running along one of the selvedge edges, the other edge decorated with a scallop. So buy the metre length to fit the width of your window. This is particularly suitable if you want to cover the lower half of the window, for example, in the kitchen or bathroom. For taller windows, buy the metre length to fit the length of the window and make your own choice of heading and hem.

Lace fabrics are also available with detachable edgings. These borders can be removed and added to hem and top edges to complete the decorative frame round a window covering.

Hanging panels

The quickest and easiest way to hang ready-made and homemade lace panels at a window is to use elasticated wire, a fine brass or wooden pole or one of the new fine plastic rods slotted through a casing at the top of the panel. This is particularly suitable for lightweight lace panels which are not to be drawn back and forth, but used as a permanent screen at the window.

If your homemade panel needs a hem or a casing, make sure that you turn under a double width allowance, which will hide the raw edge of the fabric.

Measure your window area and decide on the style first. Fix your rod or wire in place and plan what width of curtain panel you need. Do you want a fuller look or the lace flat across the window?

If your window is narrower than the fabric width, a cased heading will gather the lace gently on the fitment. In this case, choose an all-over pattern rather than a large motif design.

If you are covering large picture windows, lace panels can be either hung loosely side by side or stitched together.

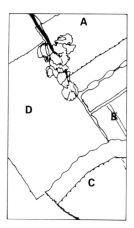

Different lace panels

A – Lace panel with a detachable border. The border simply peels away and can be used as a decorative edge on the hems.
B – Lace panel with an integral border. This can be used sideways across the window with the scallop at the top and base or lengthways.
C – Lace panel with eyelet holes. The lace is slotted over a slimline rod.
D – All-over lace patterns. This fabric is available by the metre in wide measures like furnishing fabrics. All the edges need to be finished.

TO MAKE A CASED HEADING

Decide where the rod or fitment is to be hung and then measure the depth of the window from the sill to the top of the rod. Measure the circumference of the rod, add between 1-3cm ($^3/_8$-1$^1/_4$in) for ease and double this measurement for the casing. This will be the cut length of the panel. Casings for elasticated wires need only be 3cm (1$^1/_4$in) deep.

1 As the hem edge of lace panels is usually decorative, measure the length up from the hem edge. Cut off the excess fabric from the top edge.

2 Turn under the casing allowance twice. Pin and topstitch across the casing close to the folded hem edge. Topstitch across the casing again against the top folded edge.

3 Slot the rod or wire through the casing and hang the lace panel in place.

TO MAKE A STAND HEADING

If you allow extra fabric above the casing this will form a short stand or, if the fabric is wider than the window, a slightly gathered frill. Add twice the stand depth to the casing measurement.

Form and stitch the casing along the panel, with the extra fabric between the top line of the casing stitching and the panel head.

◀ *Lace and wood Here lace has been used for a simple effect. The lace panel complements both the shape and the handsome wood of the window surround.*

COVERING A WIDE PICTURE WINDOW

To cover a wide window, lace panels can be placed side by side, with edges butting together. In this way the decorative side edges can be left free and visible.

With this method the casing is not made from the lace panels. You will need a length of sheer fabric in the same colour to form a casing. This should be as long as the panel widths and twice the width of the casing depth, plus seam allowances.

Stitching borders
If you prefer to join decorative panels together, instead of butting the edges together, overlay the two edges and machine zigzag stitch together with a wide stitch, following the line of the decorative edge.

1 Lay the lace panels, with edges butting, right side up. Measure up for the length of the finished panels and mark the position of the casing.

2 Fold the sheer fabric strip in half lengthways and pin the raw edges along the marked casing line on the right side of the lace. Stitch in place across the top edges of all the panels. Trim excess lace.

3 Turn the strip to the wrong side, with the seam to the top edge. Pin and zigzag stitch across the folded edge forming the casing. Stitch again close to top edge.

4 When placing two panels side by side, make sure that the design matches across the join.

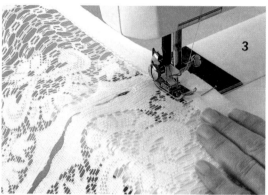

Looking after lace

Treat lace fabrics in the same way as you would other home furnishings by laundering according to fibre content. Most heavy lace fabrics are cotton or cotton based and substantial enough to withstand a delicate cycle wash in a machine. For preference, and to retain a bright white colour, use a biological detergent. If you are unsure, you can wash these fabrics by hand with a handwashing soap powder.

Allow the lace to dry naturally in an airy place away from direct sunlight.

Synthetic lace fabrics can be washed in the same way, but check their fibre content to choose the correct washing programme. If they become a bit dull and lifeless use a proprietary nylon whitener. If you prefer a warm natural shade for your cotton lace, dip it in cold tea. The longer the curtain is submerged the darker the shade of beige.

▶ *Pretty as a picture A pair of lace panels are tied back loosely enough to provide a generous sweep and to display the large floral motif. Used like this, lace curtains impart an immediate charm to the window, from without as well as from within. In spite of its delicate appearance, lace is relatively easy to keep fresh and clean.*

Sheer curtains

The simplest effect with nets and sheer curtains is a plain, translucent drop of white or off-white fabric. These curtains are usually hung from a lightweight track, pole or rod, using a heading tape or system specially designed for such lightweight fabrics.

Sheers are produced in every size and style, as well as an ever-increasing range of colours. Muslin, lawn, voile,

cheesecloth, flax and cotton mixes are all part of the rich sheer picture. Many manufacturers produce their sheer fabrics by the metre in the same standard widths as ordinary curtain fabric, with wider widths for extra large windows. Like lace panels, sheer fabrics can be bought with a casing along one edge and a scalloped or hemmed finish along the opposite edge.

▲ **Spotted charm** White spotted voile hung from a simple curtain track screens this small window. The curtains are swept back and held with ribbon-trimmed rosettes. For night time privacy this kind of curtain can be teamed with an opaque roller blind.

Fabric and effect

The diversity of the sheer fabrics available is equalled by the diversity of effects that can be achieved. By availing yourself of the special qualities of individual fabrics, you can achieve the most distinctive results.

Having selected the fabric, there are innumerable ways of treating it: jardinière styles where the central part of the curtain swoops up in the middle; café curtains that shield the lower part of the window; tiered effects where you can build up layers of curtain all on the same track system; or you can simply drape the fabric without doing any sewing at all. These different styles will be covered in later chapters.

Curtain fittings

Achieving the right sheer effect is not only a question of choosing fabric. The other major consideration is how that fabric is to be hung. Curtains with cased headings stay in position and either hang straight or tie back. If you want to draw the whole curtain back you will need a heading tape with hooks and rings. For example, an elegant white painted pole with curtain rings would be appropriate in a cool, quiet living room or bedroom. A brass rod might be better in the kitchen with its array of pots and pans, and a plastic track in the bathroom.

Covered wire

The simplest way to hang light net curtains is from a length of wire. The white plastic-covered wire is usually sold in packs in different lengths. Also included in each pack are two eyelet screws and two hooks. The eyelets screw into each end of the wire and the hooks into the window frame or surround. Their main drawback is length – a long length of covered wire can sag badly in the centre. To avoid this, cut the wire slightly shorter than the length required so that it is well stretched in position. The curtain is made up with a cased heading and the wire is slotted through and slipped over the hooks at either side of the window.

Some heading tapes incorporate loops along the tape to carry covered wire. With this method you can have the benefit of pleating with the simplicity of a wire hanging.

Telescopic rods

Slimline plastic and metal rods fit inside the window frame. Each rod has an internal spring which tensions the rod to hold it firmly in place. The curtain is finished with a cased heading used to thread it on to the rod before it is tensioned into position. If the curtain has a finished

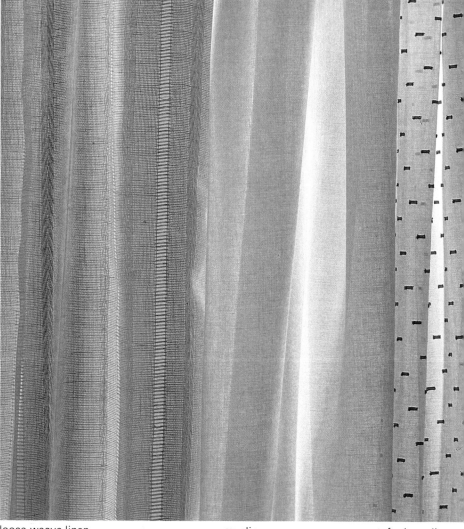

loose-weave linen — muslin — tufted muslin

covered wire

telescopic rod

clip-on telescopic rod

wooden pole

top edge, you can choose a rod that can be matched with clip-on rings. These hold the curtain top and slot on to a rod rather like a shower curtain.

Wooden or metal poles

For an emphatic country statement, fit wooden or brass-like poles. They come in a variety of wood shades, painted or stained, and in several metal finishes. Each pole can be purchased in a range of lengths complete with end finials, rings and supporting brackets. The curtain can be attached by rings combined with heading tape or with the pole through a deep casing, or simply throw the fabric over the fixed pole for a stylish effect.

Flexible tracks

Held on simple, easy-to-fit brackets, these white plastic tracks can be bent around curves, making them useful for bays and bow windows. The packs come with brackets and joints which secure the easily bent tracks at the bends of the bays. The curtains are finished with cased headings and slotted on to the track.

Curved steel rods

Available in single or double versions (the double rod allows you to hang cross-

spotted voile   sprigged polyester   printed voile

over nets and valances), these straight rods have curved ends that are held on either side of the window. The central span can be adjusted to length. The curved ends keep the curtain away from the window pane. This type of rod works well with a cased headed curtain.

Traditional curtain tracks

If you are hanging sheer curtains with a heading tape, choose a neat, slim track. Generally, these tracks can be wall or ceiling mounted – held in or outside the window reveal. The tracks can be bought in different lengths but are easy to cut down to size. Pliable enough to bend around bay windows, some tracks are also equipped to hold an additional valance track on the front.

Heading tapes

Sheer fabrics, because of their fineness, give you the opportunity to use some of the more decorative tapes. With the standard heading tapes, the curtains can be gently gathered with a barely visible lightweight tape or, if you prefer, into more elegant pencil pleats. With this type, there is a choice of depth from a neat mini pleat to a deep 10cm (4in) pleat.

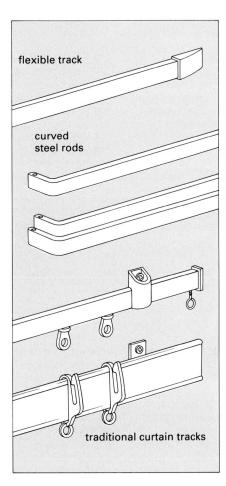

flexible track

curved
steel rods

traditional curtain tracks

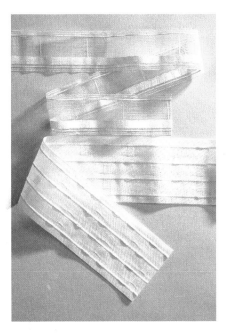

▲ **Heading tapes** *The translucent tape (top) forms a pencil pleat heading. The tape has pockets for curtain hooks and loops for curtain wire giving alternative methods for hanging. The wider tape (below) pulls up to give an attractive smocked heading which looks particularly effective when used with sheers.*

ESTIMATING FABRIC AMOUNTS

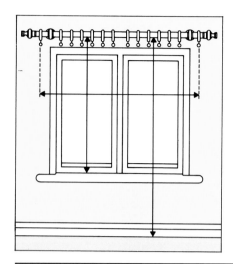

Fix the track Decide on your fitting and fix in place at the window, following the manufacturer's instructions. Covered wire and tension rods need to be positioned inside the window recess, while poles and tracks can be fitted outside.

If fitted inside the recess, check the depth of the curtain stand above the heading before fitting in place. Outside the window you have a free hand in positioning the fitment, but bear in mind the overall look.

Measure the track length
Depending on the heading tape, multiply by 1½ to 3 times the track length – check with the shop when you buy the tape. Divide this figure by the width of the fabric to find the number of fabric widths or drops needed for each curtain. If the figure falls between two widths, round up to the next full width.

Measure from the track to the desired length – to the sill or floor. Add the width of the heading tape and twice the hem depth.

To get the total amount of fabric
Multiply this figure by the number of fabric widths. Ask the shop to allow extra fabric to match patterns.

MAKING THE CURTAINS

1 Cutting the widths Make up each curtain in the same way. Straighten the fabric edge, then cut out as many widths of fabric as you need to cover the track, using the chosen heading tape. If there is a distinctive pattern or weave, this should be matched at each join.

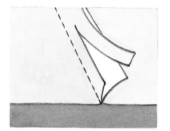
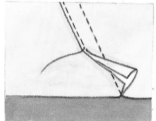

2 Joining widths If necessary, stitch the fabric widths together into one piece with flat fell seams. Place the two fabric widths with right sides together; pin and stitch 1.5cm (⅝in) from raw edges. Trim one seam allowance down to 6mm (¼in). Fold the wider seam allowance round the narrower allowance and flat against the fabric; press. Pin and stitch down the complete seam along the folded edge.

3 The double hem Turn in both side edges for 2cm (¾in); turn under again for 2cm (¾in) forming a double hem; press and tack. Turn up the lower hem edge in the same way to form a double 5cm (2in) deep hem; press. Check that the base corners look neat.

4 Finishing the hems Stitch the hems in place, by hand or machine, working round the curtain. Remove tacking.

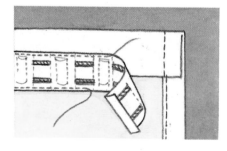

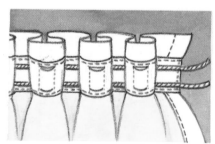

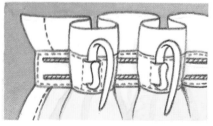

5 Positioning the heading tape Turn down the top edge for the width of the tape, plus the depth of the stand heading. Position the heading tape to the wrong side of the fabric, with base edge just covering the raw fabric edge; pin.

6 The cords At the inside edge of curtain, pull tape cords out from the tape and knot. Turn under tape end in line with curtain edge and trim to 1.5cm (⅝in); pin. At the outside edge, pull the cords out from the right side of the tape. Turn under the end in the same way as before; pin. Tack tape in place, hang on the track and check length.

7 The heading tape Stitch heading tape in place, stitching over the cords at the inner edge, but leaving them free at the outside edge.

8 Hanging the curtains Pull up the cords to fit window, then ease gathers evenly across the width. Tie the cords. Hang the curtain on the track with hooks provided, spacing them at about 20cm (8in) intervals.

Austrian blinds

Whether teamed with curtains or used on their own, elegant Austrian blinds are at home in many different types of surroundings, from the simplest country cottage to the grandest town house. Their soft folds and swooping scallops provide the luxurious fullness of curtains, but take up far less room, making them an ideal choice where space around the window is limited.

Like curtains, Austrian blinds are gathered across their width, giving them a full effect whether lowered or raised.

The scalloped effect across the bottom of the blind is created when the blind is pulled up, by means of cords threaded through vertical rows of ringed tape, attached to the blind at regular intervals. Always make the blind a bit longer than the window to retain the scallops even when the blind is lowered.

The choice of fabric will determine the effect created by the blind, whether grand and sophisticated or pretty and informal. Rich fabrics like moiré, slubbed satin or heavy silks will form deep, well-defined folds, and look

▲ Perfect combination
Striped or plain fabrics work well with Austrian blinds, giving a stylish simplicity to their exuberant folds and flounces.

elegant and luxurious, particularly if trimmed with braid or fringing. Crisp cotton chintz bunches up into casual, puffy folds for a fresh, cosy look, and looks smart trimmed with a frill.

If covering a wide window, use two Austrian blinds side by side, rather than a single one, which would sag.

Materials

Note: Austrian blind kits can be bought
from most department stores and include most items listed below, except
fabric and basic sewing equipment.

Austrian blind track available from
department stores

Fabric for the blind and frill trimmings
(for quantities, see *Calculating fabric
quantities* and step 1 of *Lined Austrian
blind*)

Lining fabric

Bias binding 1.5cm (⅝in) wide, in a
contrasting shade, to trim the frill

Fabric-covered piping to match binding

Pencil-pleat heading tape to fit across the
top of the blind; you will need a length
2½ times the length of the track

Austrian blind tape the length of the
blind by the number of tapes required

Non-stretch cord to draw up the blind

Cleat

Matching sewing threads

Tape measure and **tailor's chalk**

Calculating fabric quantities

To ensure accuracy when measuring up for the blind, fix the
blind track in place above the window before you begin, and
take your measurements from it. If the blind is to lie inside a
window recess, fix the track to the recess ceiling. Where it will
lie outside the reveal, fix the track 5-10cm (2-4in) above the
window, and extend it by this amount on each side to give full
coverage of the window.

To calculate the blind's width, multiply the track length by
2½ – this will give you a wonderfully full blind once gathered
up by the pencil pleat heading tape. Divide this figure by the
width of your fabric to determine how many fabric widths you
will need; round up if necessary. An additional width can be
split between a pair of blinds for extra fullness.

To calculate the drop, measure from the track down to the
windowsill, and add 45cm (18in) for turnings and to ensure that
the bottom edge of the blind remains prettily swagged, even
when lowered to fully cover the window. To calculate the total
amount of fabric needed, simply multiply the drop of the blind
by the number of fabric widths. Remember to add on a little
extra for pattern matching across the seams. (The fabric
quantities needed for making a frill trimming extending down
both sides and across the lower edge are given in step 1 of
Lined Austrian blind.)

tip

Invisible rings
Rather than using Austrian blind tapes, which can
sometimes show through the blind and which
require lines of stitching down the front, you can
thread the pulling cords through rows of clear
curtain rings stitched to the back of the blind.

LINED AUSTRIAN BLIND

These instructions are for a lined Austrian blind, trimmed
with contrast piping and a bound frill. Lining the blind
gives it fullness and creates more luxurious swags, as
well as making it more durable and giving a neater
appearance when viewed from outside.

1 Cutting out Cut out the main fabric to the correct size
(see *Calculating fabric quantities*), adding a 1.5cm
(⅝in) seam allowance all round; join fabric widths where
necessary, being sure to match the pattern across the
seams. Cut out the lining to the same size as the main
fabric, but deduct 2cm (¾in) from the length. For the
double-sided frill, join widths of the main fabric to make
up a strip, 17cm (6¾in) deep, and twice the length of the
blind plus its width, multiplied by 1½-2.

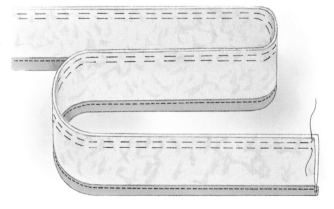

2 Making the bound frill Fold the fabric strip in half
lengthways with wrong sides together, and bind the
folded edge with the contrast binding. Run two rows of
gathering threads along the other long edge, 5mm (¼in)
and 1.5cm (⅝in) in from the edge. Draw up the frill to fit
round the two sides and lower edge of the blind.

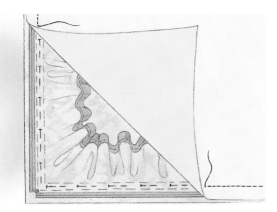

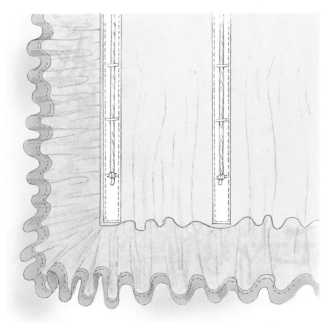

3 Attaching the lining Lay out the main fabric, right side up. Pin and tack the piping and then the frill along the blind's sides and lower edge, with their raw edges lying slightly inside the blind's edges. With side and lower edges matching and right side down, put lining on top. Taking a 1.5cm (⅝in) seam allowance, stitch through all layers down sides and along lower edge. Snip into corners and turn through to right side. Press to lie flat, then tack across top edge.

4 Marking the positions of the tapes Decide how many scallops you would like the blind to have: the vertical Austrian blind tapes are usually placed about 60-75cm (23-30in) apart, to give scallops of 24-30cm (9-12in) on the finished blind, once it has been gathered across its width. Choose a scallop size which divides evenly into the width of your blind. Use tailor's chalk to mark the positions of the tapes on the lining side of blind; the first and last tapes run down the blind's side edges.

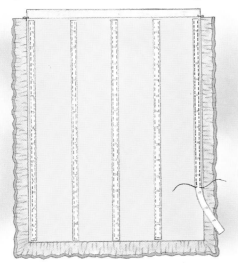

5 Attaching the vertical tapes Cut lengths of Austrian blind tape, the same length as the blind's lining plus 1cm (⅜in); when cutting the tapes, make sure that the bottom loop on each length lies 6cm (2¼in) from the end of the tape, so that the blind will pull up evenly across its width once the cords have been threaded and tied in place. Turn 1cm (⅜in) to the wrong side at the bottom of each tape, then pin, tack and stitch the tapes in position on the blind.

6 Attaching the heading tape Cut a length of pencil-pleat heading tape the width of the blind, plus a little extra for neatening the ends. At the top of the blind, fold the overlapping 2cm (¾in) of main fabric over the lining to enclose its raw edge. Place the pencil-pleat heading tape across the top of the blind on the lining side, enclosing the raw edges of the fabric and vertical tapes; stitch the heading tape in place. Draw up the heading tape to fit the window.

7 Threading the cords For each vertical tape, cut lengths of cord the finished width of the blind plus twice its length. Lay the blind out flat on the floor, with lining side up. Starting at the bottom left-hand corner of the blind, tie the end of one length of cord to the bottom loop on the vertical tape. Thread the cord up through all the loops on the tape. Repeat on all the other vertical tapes.

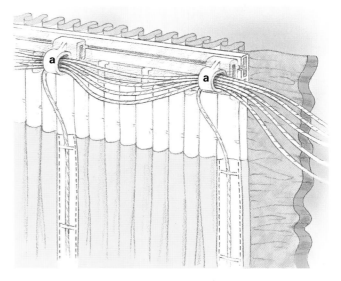

8 Mounting the blind Remove the track from its wall brackets and hook the blind on to the track, as for a curtain. Adjust the position of the track eyelets (**a**) so that there is one above each vertical blind tape. Thread the cords from each vertical tape through the eyelet above, and then through the other eyelets along the track, until all the cords are at one side of the window. The blind track is then replaced on its brackets. Fix the cleat to the wall or window frame next to the blind, about halfway down the window.

9 Checking the blind Pull the cords to check that the blind can be raised and lowered evenly, and adjust the cords where necessary. Once satisfied, lower the blind and double check that all the cords are straight, before tying them together in a knot at the end of the track. Plait the cords together to make a single pulley cord, and trim the ends with scissors to neaten. Pull the blind up to the desired position and secure the cords around the cleat at the side of the window.

Stylish variation

With a few minor alterations in the vertical cording and the addition of imaginative trimmings, Austrian blinds can be given a number of different looks. One popular variation is to shape the blind into a swag and tail arrangement, by simply omitting the vertical tapes at the side edges; this allows the sides of the blind to hang freely, while the centre is gathered up into sweeping swags. The arrangement makes a stunning crown for a window, and looks striking used alone or teamed with a sheer curtain for daytime privacy.

Alternatively, by drawing up the pull cords to different lengths, you can gently graduate the scallops so that they fall to the sides in progressively longer lengths from a high point at the centre of the blind. This type of arrangement can look stunning on a picture window, and creates an attractive frame for the view beyond.

All manner of trimmings can also be used to decorate the blinds and complete the effect. Trim rich fabrics with fringing, and emphasize their full scallops by hanging a tassel below each vertical tape. Frills and lace will further soften the effect, while piping in a contrasting shade gives a sharper outline and is ideal for blinds in a formal setting.

▲ **Crowning glory**
This striking Austrian blind, shaped into a swag and tail arrangement, makes a superb crown for the bedroom window, giving it height and linking it to other furnishings in the room. Rosettes fixed at each end of the blind and trimmed for a perfect match, make elegant finishing touches and add interest to the heading.

◄ **Take a bow**
In this carefully co-ordinated bathroom, the bows of the wallpaper border are carried on to the blind heading, which is decorated with fabric bows in a matching shade of pink. The ribbon theme is also reflected in the fabric of the blind and frill. Decorating the heading of the blind creates a pleasing balance between it and the full swags below.

Sheer festoon blinds

The most decorative of all blinds, a festoon is ruched into soft gathers even when lowered. When raised, the fabric is swept up into swathes of fabric. Festoon blinds look striking in sheer fabrics, as the material lends itself to the vertical and horizontal gathers. This style of blind offers privacy, but lets the light filter though – a perfect alternative to a plain net curtain. For a final flourish and

▲ *A festoon with a frill* The soft voile, delicately printed with flowers and butterflies, co-ordinates with the curtains. The gathers allow light to filter through but give more privacy than a sheer curtain.

to give the edge definition, add a frill to the base edge. You can make a bold statement with a deep one or choose a narrower edging.

Positioning the track

Festoon blinds are held at the window on either a special blind curtain track or on a standard track fixed to a length of wooden battening.

The blind track carries cord holders which can be moved to a position above each length of vertical tape. A cord lock fixed at one end of the track holds the cords neatly in position, so the blind can be raised and held at any height over the window.

The standard track mounted on battening will have to have small screw eyes added to the underside of the battening above each vertical tape to hold the pulley cords.

The track or battening can be wall or ceiling mounted. In a recessed window, the track will fit inside the recess, while on a flat window, the blind can extend beyond the surround on either side to suit the décor of the room.

Cut and fit the track or battening in place at the window before working out your fabric quantities.

Fabric quantities

For the length, measure from the track to the sill and allow for one and a half times this measurement. Measure the width of the track and double this measurement. Allow extra fabric for the base frill. For example, if the frill is 8cm (3in) deep, calculate the extra fabric for a strip 10cm (4in) deep (to allow for the seams and hem) and twice the width of the blind.

Constructing the blind

The blind is composed of vertical tapes which are evenly spaced across the back of the blind. The position of the tapes will depend on the blind width. When joining fabric widths together, position the seam centrally, then cover the raw edges of the seam with the festoon blind tape. Divide the area between the outer and central tapes into equal sections and place the remaining tapes at these points – the closer the tapes, the tighter the swags. If the tapes are up to 40cm (16in) apart, for example, they will produce a wide, full swag. Further apart, the swag will be shallower.

The tapes are pulled up to fit the window depth. The blind is lowered and raised by cords threaded through the vertical tapes. The complete blind then has the addition of a heading tape which gathers up the blind horizontally into regular pencil pleats.

Festoon blind kits are available. They contain everything you need (except the fabric, thread and track or track and batten) and are available from major department stores.

MAKING THE BLIND

1 Cutting out Straighten the edge of the fabric. Cut pieces of fabric to chosen size and join any widths. The width of the blind will depend on your choice of heading tape.

3 Placing the tapes Lay the fabric wrong side up on a flat surface. Mark the position of the tapes at either side and equally spaced in between. Cut a length of festoon blind tape for each position, the same length as the fabric, with the first loop of each tape 5cm (2in) up from the end. Pin the first two vertical tapes over the side hems with the inner edge just covering the raw edge of the fabric.

2 Hem the sides Turn under a 2.5cm (1in) hem down both side edges. Pin and tack hems in place.

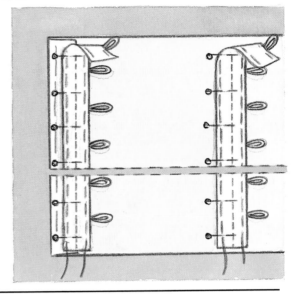

4 Stitching the tapes Draw out the ends of cords on the wrong side of the end of each tape, and knot. Place the loops towards the inside edge of the blind. Stitch in place down the centre of each tape, catching down side hems at the same time.

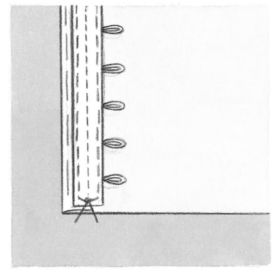

▼ *Festoon blind track* Seen from the back are the curtain hooks; cord tidys for vertical tape cords, with the cord holders on the track above taking vertical cords across to the cord lock, on the left.

Materials

Blind track or length of wooden battening, screw eyes and standard curtain track.

Sheer fabric, see above for how to work out quantities.

Festoon blind tape, the length of the blind times the number of tapes.

Matching thread

Plastic rings, small curtain rings, one for each length of vertical tape.

Transparent curtain heading tape, the width of the blind.

Fine nylon cord, for each vertical tape you need twice the length plus one width of the blind.

Cleat

◀ **Pretty pink swags** A festoon blind in glazed cotton hangs in more voluptuous folds than a sheer festoon which lies flatter against the window, making it simpler to draw the curtains. These patterned, frilled curtains are tied back and it is the festoon that is used to cover the window at night.

5 Making the frill
Measure the lower edge of the blind and double the measurement. For an 8cm (3in) deep frill, cut out 10cm (4in) wide strips from across the fabric width, until you have the correct length. Pin and stitch the strips together with narrow French seams into one long length.

6 Hemming the frill
Turn under a double 6mm (¼in) hem on lower and side edges of frill; pin and stitch in place. Work two rows of gathering stitches 6mm (¼in) and 1.5cm (⅝in) from the top raw edge.

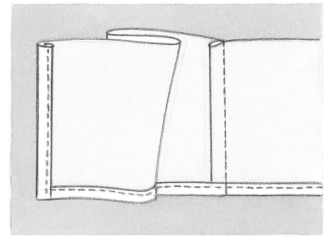

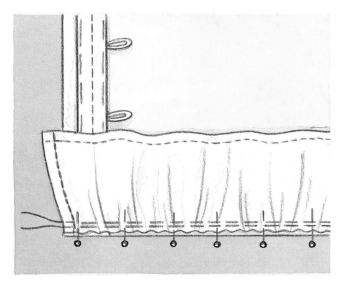

7 Stitching frill to blind Place the frill to blind with wrong sides together, pull up the gathering stitches evenly to fit the blind. Pin and stitch frill in place, 6mm (¼in) from the edge, catching in ends of vertical tapes.

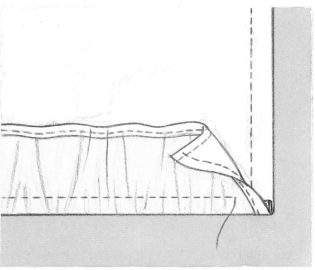

8 Completing French seam Re-fold with right sides together, then lightly press with seam to edge. Pin and stitch 1cm (⅜in) from the seamed edge, to complete the French seam.

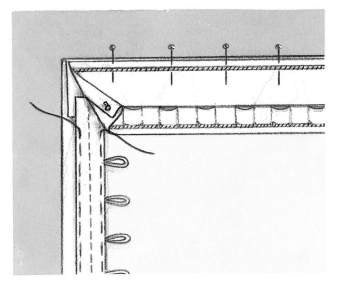

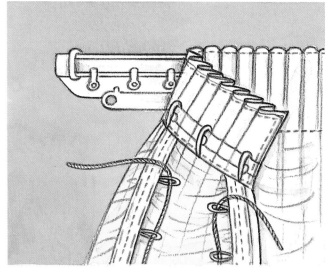

9 **Adding the heading tape** Turn down top edge of blind for width of heading tape. Trim vertical tapes so there is only 1cm (³/₈in) tucked under the edge of tape. Cut a length of heading tape to fabric width plus 2cm (³/₄in). Position tape to top folded edge. Make sure that the drawn cords on the vertical tapes are left hanging free. At one side of heading tape, pull out drawn cords from the tape and knot.

Turn under the tape end for 1cm (³/₈in) so it is in line with outer edge. At opposite side, pull out cords from the right side of the tape and leave to hang free. Turn under tape end in line with edge, as before.

10 **Stitching the heading tape** Pin and stitch heading tape in place, catching down the knotted cords at one side, but leaving hanging cords free at the opposite edge. Draw up the cords across the heading tape to fit the track. Knot surplus cords together but do not cut off. Wind up surplus cord and knot to hold.

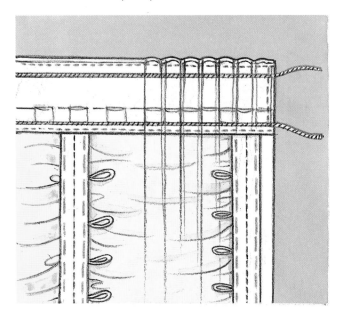

11 **Fitting blind to track** Draw up each vertical tape in turn, until blind measures the window drop. Space the gathers evenly down the whole blind. Knot cords together, but do not cut off. Wind surplus cords up and knot together to hold.

12 **Hanging the blind** Fit curtain hooks through the heading tape, evenly spaced about 8cm (3in) apart. Attach a cleat to the side of the window, near the bottom, on the same side as the cord lock on the track.

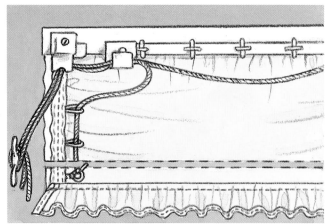

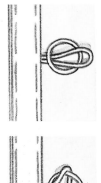

Attaching ring to loop.

13 **Cording the blind** Fasten a plastic ring into the loop at the base of each vertical tape. Insert the loop through the ring, then pull the loop round the outer rim of the ring to hold securely. Cut a length of cord for each length of vertical tape, twice the length of the blind plus one width.

Beginning at the side opposite to the cleat, knot the cord to the base ring. Thread the cord up through the loops on the tape to the top of the blind. Then take the cord through the cord holders on the track and the cord lock at the opposite side, or through the screw eyes on the battening. Repeat, to thread a length of cord through each length of vertical tape in the same way, until all the cords are hanging together at one side.

14 **Adjust the blind** Pull up the blind so it is resting on the sill and knot the cords together just beyond the cord lock, or the last of the screw eyes. Plait the cords together and knot again at sill level. Trim excess cords level. Alternatively, leave cords free and knot together at sill level. A decorative 'acorn' can be added to the ends of the cords.

Window features

A crisp, white curtain with a lacy edging makes the freshest of window dressings. Bright sunlight filtered through the lace creates sun-bright patterns dancing on the wall or floor.

If you are making your own curtains, choose a crisp cotton, fresh linen or, for their easy-care properties, a fabric which includes a man-made fibre such as polyester. Select a boldly patterned and textured lace to go with these fabrics. A chunky cotton lace, crisp crochet edging, or swirling Battenburg lace all look good. Avoid complex curtain headings – a gently gathered fabric will allow the lace trim to show clearly.

Before making up the curtain wash both the fabric and the lace to prevent either shrinking more than the other after they have been sewn together.

The geometric design of many crochet or lace patterns complement coloured fabrics in formal patterns such as stripes, spots and checks, particularly if the background to the pattern is white to match the edging. The contrast between fabric and edging is eye-catching and unusual.

Alternatively, a ready-made table-cloth or dressing table runner with a lace edging or insert could be transformed into a simple flat curtain. Turn a casing at one end and hang it on a curtain wire or rod fixed at the window.

Nothing looks worse than slightly dingy white curtains at a window, so keep them fresh with regular washing – a final rinse in cold water starch before ironing will crisp the curtains and lace up beautifully.

▲ Hardanger embroidery
The edge of this flat curtain has been embroidered using the hardanger technique. Any even-weave fabric is suitable for this type of embroidery in which threads are removed after blocks of stitches have been worked, giving a lacy appearance to the finished cloth.

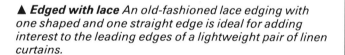

▲ Diamond lace insert
A ready-made table runner has found a new use as a modest curtain by simply turning a cased heading along one edge. The cotton fabric is less see through than a sheer or net, but not as heavy as a lined curtain. There are many types of lacy table runners which could be used.

▲ Edged with lace An old-fashioned lace edging with one shaped and one straight edge is ideal for adding interest to the leading edges of a lightweight pair of linen curtains.

▲ Austrian extravagance
The tape and cords which gather up this blind when raised are started a short way up from the lower edge. This allows a straight lace edging to be stitched to the edge of the blind.

◄ Crochet inserts and edges
Filet crochet can be bought by the yard or, if you are handy with a hook, made to measure. Turn narrow double hems along the panels before machine stitching the lace in position. The edging along the lower edge is added at the end.

Cupboard curtains

Glass-fronted cupboards, cabinets and bookcases are elegant additions to any room, enabling the contents to be seen and admired, while keeping them safe and free from dust. Books, ornaments and collections of small items look particularly attractive displayed behind glass, yet there are some occasions when you will want greater privacy, and here a curtain is ideal, casting a veil over the contents without obscuring the beauty of the glass doors.

Wardrobes, bathroom cupboards and cabinets with glass doors which are used for general storage, can all benefit from a lightweight curtain, which not only covers the contents but provides a decorative finish into the bargain. In bedrooms in particular, a curtain in a glass-fronted wardrobe has a soft and feminine look, with the richness of the grand country house style.

Unlike a standard net or sheer curtain, which is hung from the top, but left to hang freely at the bottom, a cabinet curtain is fixed at top and bottom, creating a more tailored, fitted shape. Since the curtain is held in this way, it is kept in place, even when the door is opened.

The fixed position of a cabinet curtain means that it can be used success-

▲ Fabric finish
A curtain in a fresh, flowery fabric is the perfect touch in this bathroom cabinet. The blue in the fabric echoes the blue lines on the cabinet mouldings, while the yellow enhances the warmth of the creamy paint.

fully not only on cupboard doors but also on larger room and house doors. On a door with a glass panel, it can be fitted on the inside, just covering the glass. On a door which is completely panelled with glass, as on french windows or patio doors, the curtain should be full length.

Fabric choices

Curtains for cupboards and cabinets can be made in any sheer, lacy, light or mediumweight woven fabric. The fabric can be generously gathered, or hung flat, like a blind. For preference, choose a fabric with a woven pattern, so that it is reversible, making it attractive from both sides.

Suitable fabrics include voile, broderie anglaise, net, cheesecloth, madras cotton, sprigged muslin, lining fabric or even fine silk. Sheer fabrics, such as muslin or voile look best when tightly gathered, while fabrics with large pictorial patterns or lace panels are often best displayed hung flat.

Curtain styles

Gathered curtain The fabric falls into soft folds, creating a very pretty, feminine style. Fine to mediumweight fabric is gathered on to a rod or plastic covered curtain wire at top and bottom. A small stand forms a frill. The fabric should be two to two and a half times the width of the rods to give sufficient fullness to the curtains.

Flat panel This is an ideal way of showing off a pretty lace panel, or an attractive piece of crochet or embroidery. It can be used when the fabric has a large pattern, or to display a stencilled design, painted on to an economical fabric like calico, and used to echo features in the room. Like a gathered curtain, a flat panel is fixed on two rods, but without fullness.

Hourglass curtain This attractive version of a gathered curtain adds interest to very plain, inexpensive fabrics such as muslin, voile or polyester cotton sheeting. The curtain is shaped on the top and bottom edges, and then gathered in with a ribbon at the centre to form the hourglass shape.

Materials

Two **curtain rods** or **curtain wires** for each curtain. On a wide curtain, wire may sag a little in the middle, so place it well above the glass so that the wire and casing do not show through the glass from the front.
Furnishing fabric.
Matching sewing thread.

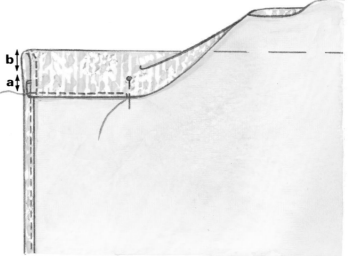

GATHERED CABINET CURTAINS

3 Making the curtain Turn under a double 1.5cm (⅝in) hem along each side edge of the curtain; pin and then stitch. At the top and bottom edges, turn under 1cm (⅜in) and then the depth of the casing **(a)** plus stand **(b)**, pinning and then stitching close to the inner fold.

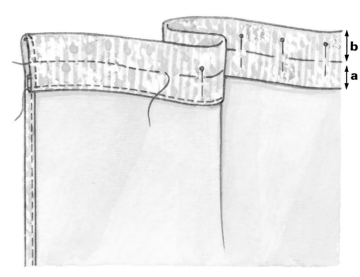

1 The heading allowance Although you can make these curtains with a simple cased heading they look more attractive with a stand. Measure the width of the rod or wire and add 5mm (¼in) for ease – this is the casing depth **(a)**. Decide on the depth of the stand, 3-5cm (1¼-2in) is usual **(b)**.

Add the casing and stand depths, multiply by two and add a 1cm (⅜in) seam allowance **(c)** for the total heading allowance.

2 Cutting out Position the rods or curtain wire inside the cupboard doors just above and below the glass; fix in place. Measure between the rods and add twice the heading allowance (for top and bottom) for the cut length. The cut width should be 2-2½ times the length of the rod. Cut and join pieces of the cut length using selvedges or with french seams in order to make a piece this width. Remember to match the pattern repeats.

4 Making the casings Measure from the stitching line towards the folded edge and mark a point the depth of the casing away from it **(a)**, using tailor's chalk. Draw a chalk line at this position at top and bottom edges, then pin and stitch along the chalk line.

5 Finishing off Lightly press the curtain, then slide a rod or curtain wire through each casing, gathering up the curtain as you do so. Fix in place at the door.

UNGATHERED CABINET CURTAIN

This is a simplified and economical version of the gathered cabinet curtain, and is usually made without a stand.

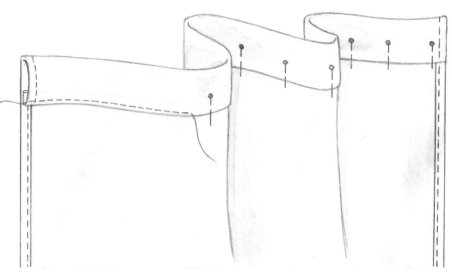

1 Cutting out Fix the two rods or curtain wires in place, and measure between them. If the rods or wires are no more than 1cm (3⁄8in) thick, the total cut length will be this measurement plus 8cm (3in). If the rods are thicker, measure the circumference and add 1.5cm (5⁄8in) for ease and turnings; double this and add to the measurement between the rods. For the cut width, measure the length of one rod and add 6cm (2½in) for side hem allowances, plus 5cm (2in) for ease.

2 Making the curtain Turn under 1.5cm (5⁄8in) double hems along both side edges; pin and then stitch. At the top and bottom edges, turn under 1cm (3⁄8in), then 3cm (1⅛in) or the depth of the casing, if deeper; pin and stitch close to the fold. Lightly press the curtain, then slide the rods into the casings.

◀ **Lace panelling**
The pattern on these lace curtains shows up beautifully when the fabric is hung, ungathered, behind the glass doors of the cabinet.

▼ **Gathered curtain**
Lightweight fabric falls into attractive, gentle folds when gathered on to rods in this hall cupboard, and when the door is closed, it hides the contents.

MAKING HOURGLASS CURTAINS

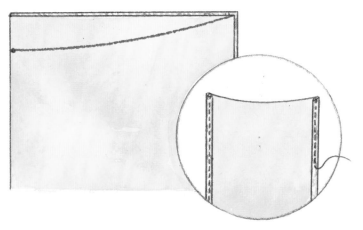

1 Cutting out Fix the curtain rods or wire at the glass door. Calculate the heading allowance as in step 1 for a gathered cabinet curtain. Measure from the top rod to the bottom one, pulling the tape measure inwards at the middle, as shown, then add twice the heading allowance for the cut length. Cut out fabric widths this long to make up a piece 2-2½ times the length of one rod. Join the fabric pieces together using the selvedges to prevent fraying or with french seams. Make sure any pattern repeats match.

2 Making the curtain Fold the curtain in half lengthways with right sides together, to find the centre on the top and bottom edges. Mark a point at the centre, 7.5cm (3in) from the edge, then draw a gentle curve from this point to the corner, as shown, using tailor's chalk. Cut along the line at the top and bottom of the curtain. Stitch double 1.5cm (⅝in) side hems as in step 3 for a gathered cabinet curtain.

3 Finishing the curtain At the top edge, turn under 1cm (⅜in) and then the depth of the casing plus stand, pinning and then stitching in place close to the inner fold. Then complete the curtain, following steps 4 and 5 for a gathered cabinet curtain.

4 The final touch Hang the curtain and tie a length of wide ribbon round the centre of it to gather in the fabric; tie the ribbon in a bow.

▶ *Ivory elegance*
A strip of ivory fabric, used to tie back these elegant hourglass curtains, is topped with a pair of flamboyant rosettes made to match.

PART FOUR

DECORATIVE SOFT FURNISHINGS

Cushion cover~ups

Cushion pads need not always be encased in their traditional zipped covers, but can be wrapped in a number of ways, using various decorative fastening techniques. Generous bows, fabric-covered buttons, Velcro studs topped with silk flowers, and laced ribbon ties are all practical, but stylish ways of securing a cushion cover. Rather than concealing these fastenings as you would

a zip, make them a main feature of the cushion cover design.

Most furnishing cottons are suitable for making the cushion covers, but choose a fabric to complement the cushion design; for example, a soft floral print is ideal for the silk flower cushion, while a striped or checked fabric works well with the geometric lines of the envelope design.

▲ Creative covers
Leave ordinary zipped covers in the shade by making full use of decorative fastenings and your favourite fabrics to create a range of eye-catching cushions. Any one of these imaginative designs will give an instant lift to a plain chair, sofa or even a bedspread.

DOUBLE BOW CUSHION

Materials

Fabric measuring 104 × 43cm (41 × 17in); a print with a small and simple repeated motif works well with this design

Grossgrain ribbon in a contrast colour, 4m (4½yds) long and 4cm (1½in) wide

Sewing threads

Cushion 40 × 40cm (15¾ × 15¾in)

1 Cutting and hemming Cut the rectangle of fabric into two pieces, each one measuring 52 × 43cm (20½ × 17in). Along one of the short edges of one piece of fabric, turn in a 1.5cm (⅝in) hem to the wrong side and stitch in place; repeat on the other piece of fabric.

2 Joining the pieces Place the cushion pieces together, right sides facing and with the hemmed edges matched up. Stitch down the remaining short edge to join the front and back pieces together, allowing a 1.5cm (⅝in) allowance.

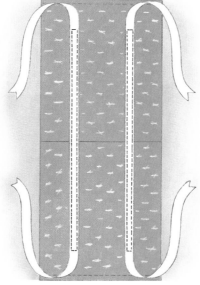

3 Attaching the ribbons Open out the cushion pieces to lie flat with right sides face up. Cut the ribbon into two equal lengths of 2m (2¼yds), and shape the ends by cutting out a small 'V'. Pin one length down each long side of the cushion, 10cm (4in) in from the edge and parallel to it; stitch down both sides of the ribbon, stopping with a line of stitching across it, 12cm (4¾in) from the top and bottom edges of the cushion.

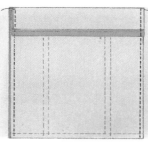

4 Finishing the cushion Refold the cushion with right sides together, tucking in the unstitched ends of the ribbons. Fold over 9cm (3½in) of the top edge of the cushion and stitch down both sides, 1.5cm (⅝in) in from the edges to join the sides and form a flap. Turn through to the right side and insert the cushion pad, tucking it under the flap. Tie the ribbons into two generous bows.

ENVELOPE CUSHION

Materials

Patterned fabric 43 × 42cm (17 × 16½in)

Plain fabric in a contrasting colour, measuring 80 × 42cm (31½ × 16½in)

Binding in a contrasting colour, 2m (2¼yds) long

Ribbon to match the binding, 80cm (31½in) long and 2.5cm (1in) wide

Sewing threads

Cushion 40 × 40cm (15¾ × 15¾in)

1 Preparing the centre piece Lay out the patterned piece of fabric, wrong side up. Turn in a 1.5cm (⅝in) hem along the two short sides.

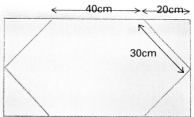

2 Cutting out the outer piece Cut off the corners from the plain fabric rectangle to form a hexagon of the dimensions shown: measure 20cm (8in) in from both short sides along the top and bottom edges, and mark with tailor's chalk; then measure halfway up the short side edges and mark the spot. Join these points to form the hexagon and carefully cut it out.

3 Sewing on the binding Lay out the plain fabric and centre the patterned piece of fabric over it, with wrong sides together. Pin and tack the two pieces together along the top and bottom edges. Beginning at one of the far tips of the hexagon, pin and then sew the binding around the raw edges, joining the patterned and plain fabric together along the top and bottom edges.

Double bow cushion

Lace-up cushion

Envelope cushion

Silk flower cushion

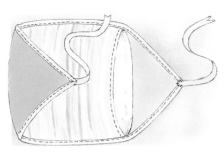

4 Attaching the ribbon Cut the ribbon into two lengths of 40cm (15¾in). Take one length and stitch it to the wrong side of one of the outer flaps; use tiny stitches which do not show on the right side. Repeat for the second ribbon length. Shape the ribbon ends by cutting out a small 'V'. Slip the cushion pad in behind the patterned panel, fold in the two flaps and tie the ribbons in a bow.

SILK FLOWER CUSHION

Materials

Fabric measuring 75 × 71cm (29¼ × 28in); an all-over floral print complements this design perfectly
Six fabric flowers in silk or imitation silk and in a toning shade; if you prefer, use bows or fabric-covered buttons instead of flowers
Six pairs Sew 'n' Sew Velcro coins
Sewing threads
Cushion pad 45 × 36cm (17¾ × 14¼in)

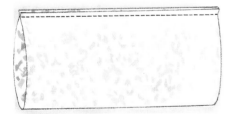

1 Forming a tube Fold the fabric in half, with shortest edges and right sides together. Pin and stitch these edges together to form a tube, taking a 1.5cm (⅝in) seam allowance.

2 Hemming the ends Turn in a 1.5cm (⅝in) hem to the wrong side, along the raw edges of the fabric at both ends of the tube; stitch in place.

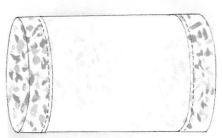

3 Folding in the cushion sides Fold back 7cm (2¾in) of the fabric at each end of the tube towards its centre; do not stitch, but press the folds to hold the fabric in place. This will eliminate the need for a seam running down the sides of the finished cushion cover.

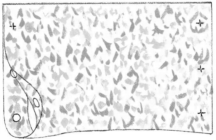

4 Securing the cushion sides Stitch three pairs of Velcro coin fastenings down each side of the cushion, over the folded hems, 4cm (1½in) in from the outer edges; the stitching will secure the folded sides. Turn the cushion through to the right side.

5 Adding the flowers Stitch one flower over each Velcro coin to hide the stitching. Slip the cushion into the tube and press the Velcro coins together to seal the cover.

LACE-UP CUSHION

Materials

Patterned fabric measuring 86 × 43cm (33¾ × 17in)
Plain fabric in a contrasting colour, measuring 55 × 10cm (21¾ × 4in)
Binding in a co-ordinating colour, 320cm (3⅝yds) long
Ribbon in a contrast shade to binding, 190cm (2yds) long and 2cm (¾in) wide
Basic eyelet kit available from most haberdashery departments
Sewing threads
Cushion 40 × 40cm (15¾ × 15¾in)

1 Cutting out Cut the rectangle of patterned fabric into two squares of 43cm (17in). Cut one square in half diagonally; the two triangles will form the front flaps of the cushion.

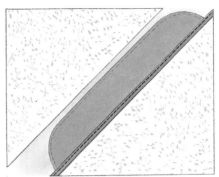

2 Attaching contrast strip Trim both ends of the contrast strip into a curve and turn under a 1.5cm (⅝in) hem along the curved edge. Pin and stitch the binding to the longest edge of one fabric triangle. Place the bound triangle edge over the raw straight edge of the contrast strip, so that they overlap by 2cm (¾in) and both lie face-up; tack together. Stitch the contrast strip to the triangle, but leave four gaps next to where the four eyelets will lie – ribbon will be laced through these gaps. Stitch binding to long edge of the other fabric triangle.

3 Joining front to back Position the triangles over the patterned fabric square, wrong sides together. Pin then stitch binding around cushion edges, joining front and back pieces. Slip-stitch diagonal slit together for 2cm (¾in) only, at both ends.

4 Adding the ties Use the eyelet kit to make four holes down each side of the diagonal slit in the front of the cushion, 8cm (3¼in) apart. Insert the cushion pad via the slit. Cut the ribbon into two equal lengths and shape the ends as usual. Thread the ribbon through the eyelets as shown and secure the cover with two bows.

BRODERIE ANGLAISE BOLSTER

Materials
Broderie anglaise fabric measuring 89 × 63cm (35 × 24¾in)
Fabric for the lining in a pastel shade, the same size as the broderie anglaise; use a reasonably stiff cotton fabric
Narrow broderie anglaise trimming 130cm (1½yds) long
Ribbon to match lining fabric, 150cm (1¾yds) long and 2.5cm (1in) wide
Sewing threads
Bolster 47cm (18½in) long and 18.5cm (7¼in) in diameter

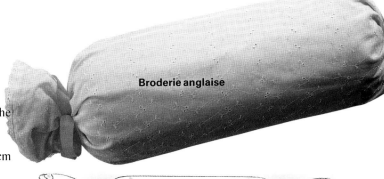

Broderie anglaise

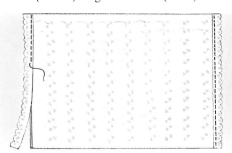

1 **Joining the lining and trimming** Place lining and broderie anglaise together, right sides facing and edges lined up. Pin and stitch along short edges, 1.5cm (⅝in) in from edge; turn through to right side. Cut broderie anglaise trimming into two equal lengths. Turning 1cm (⅜in) of the trimming's raw edge to the wrong side, if necessary, pin then stitch one length of trimming along one short end of the fabric, overlapping the two slightly and stitching through both the lining and the broderie anglaise; repeat on other short end.

2 **Forming the bolster tube** Fold the fabric in half lengthways, with the broderie anglaise sides together, and pin and stitch along the raw edge to form a tube, allowing a 1.5cm (⅝in) seam allowance.

3 **Tying the ends** Slip the bolster into the cover so that it lies in the centre. Cut the ribbon into two equal lengths of 75cm (29½in). Gather up the fabric at each end of the bolster and secure it with a ribbon bow.

MOIRE BOLSTER

Materials
Moiré fabric measuring 117 × 63cm (46 × 24¾in)
Velvet ribbon 150cm (1¾yds) long and 2.5cm (1in) wide
Narrow cord or **fabric tape** 170cm (1⅞yds) long and no wider than 1cm (⅜in)
Sewing threads
Bolster 47cm (18½in) long and 18.5cm (7¼in) in diameter

2 **Making a casing for the pull cord** Stitch round one end of the tube, 1.5cm (⅝in) out from the raw edge of the hem, leaving a small opening through which you can insert the pull cord. Measure 1.5cm (⅝in) out from the first line of stitching and stitch a second line around the end of the tube, to form a casing. Repeat at the other end of the tube. Cut the fabric tape or cord into two pieces of the same length and thread one through the casing at each end of the tube.

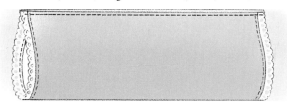

1 **Forming the bolster tube** Fold the fabric in half lengthways, with right sides together. Stitch the long edges together allowing a 1.5cm (⅝in) seam allowance. Fold in a 15cm (6in) hem at each end of the tube and press to hold it in place.

Moiré cushion

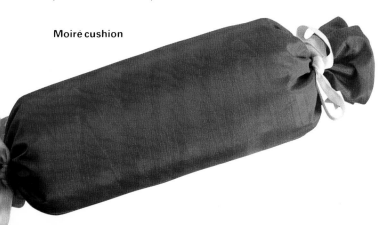

3 **Finishing the bolster** Turn the cover through to the right side and slide it over the bolster so that the bolster lies centrally. Slip your hand into one end of the bolster and draw up the pull cord or tape tightly, securing the ends with a loose knot; repeat at other end. Cut the ribbon into two equal lengths and tie each one in a bow around the gathered fabric at each end, covering the casings.

Piped cushions

Cushion covers are one of the simplest soft furnishings to sew and one of the quickest ways to update an existing scheme – either by introducing a new colour or a new style. Piped or frilled, lace-edged or bordered, each finish will give a different character to a room.

First, decide on the cushions' function – are they just a decorative addition to a sofa or a bed, or will they need to be more practical, for example, to soften hard dining chairs, or to provide additional seating? The size and shape of the cushion depends on the answers to these questions.

Secondly, choose the fabric – match the cushion cover fabric to your other furnishings or go for a complete contrast of colour and pattern. Brighten up a neutral colour scheme with a riot of colourful covers or add just a subtle hint of colour with a paler hue taken from the main colour in the room.

Cushion pads and fillings

Nowadays it is easy to buy cushion pads in a range of shapes and sizes – square, rectangular and round, with or without gussets. You can choose the filling to suit your needs – most purchased cushion pads contain either a natural feather mixture or a synthetic filling such as polyester. A feather-filled pad will give a cushion that soft, inviting look and can be quickly plumped back into shape. Polyester filling is more practical as it is completely washable and is a must for people with allergies.

▼ **Piped perfection** *Piping made from a contrast colour picked from the cushion looks smart; made from the same fabric it gives a classic finish; while striped or checked fabric cut on the bias adds a jaunty touch.*

Adding piping

One of the simplest ways of transforming a plain cushion cover is with a line of piping round the outer edge. Piping will give the cushion a good outline, a professional finish and add strength to the seams. Decorative piping can be bought ready-made or you can make your own by covering a length of cord with a bias-cut fabric strip.

Piping cord comes in a range of thicknesses from 00 to 6; sizes 3 or 4 are the most suitable for decorative sofa cushions, but try to match the thickness to the size of the cushion. Take the covering fabric with you to the haberdashery department and wind it round the cord to gauge the effect. If you prefer a more prominent piping or have large cushions to edge, you can use a thick cord or a roll of wadding, which will give a fat piped edge. Traditionally, piping fabric covers the cord smoothly, but you can also gather the fabric, giving a slightly frilled edge to the cushion.

The covering strip is cut on the fabric bias – across the grain – so it will have enough 'give' to go round the cord and round the cover without puckering.

▼ *A neat finish A piped trim is perfect for these formal cushions.*

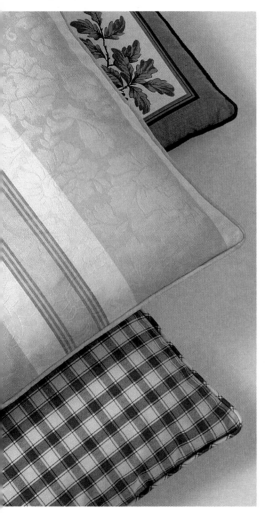

MAKING UP PIPING

1 Fabric quantities For the width of the covering strip, measure round the cord and allow an extra 2.5cm (1in) for seam allowances. For the length, measure round the cushion cover, allowing an extra 2cm ($^3/_4$in) for joining.

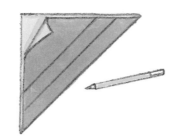

2 Cutting the bias strips Fold the fabric diagonally, so the cut edge lies along the selvedge. With your hand flat against the fabric fold, cut along the fold. Both diagonal edges are now cut along the fabric bias. Mark the required strip widths along the diagonal edges and cut out.

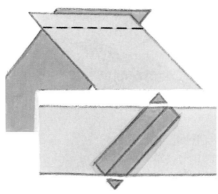

3 Joining strips together Fabric strips must be joined together on the straight grain. Place strips with right sides together; pin and stitch with a 6mm ($^1/_4$in) seam allowance. Press seam open. Trim off points.

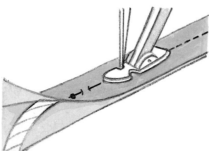

4 Covering the cord Fold the fabric strip in half round the cord with wrong sides together. Pin and stitch close to the cord using a zip foot attachment on the sewing machine to keep stitching close to the cord.

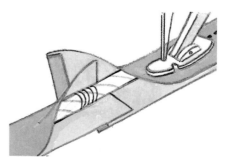

5 Joining piping To join piping together to fit round the cover, trim off both cord ends so they butt together. Bind over the ends to hold them firmly in place with sewing thread. Trim the covering fabric so one side overlaps the other for 2cm ($^3/_4$in). Turn under 1cm ($^3/_8$in) and place over raw edge. Pin and stitch over join.

Square cushions On a square cover, pin the covered piping to the right side of the top cover piece, with cut edges together and the stitching on piping 1.5cm ($^5/_8$in) from the outer edge of the cover. At each corner, snip into piping fabric up to stitching. Using a zip foot, stitch along first side to the corner, work one stitch across corner and then stitch along next side. Repeat for the other two sides. If the fabric is thick, work two or three stitches diagonally across the corner to help cover to turn through the corners.

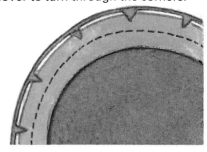

Round cushions On a round cover, place the covered piping to the cover in the same way as for square cover. Snip into the piping fabric up to stitching at about 2.5cm (1in) intervals, to help curve the piping round the edge. Stitch around piping using zip foot.

HOW TO MAKE GATHERED PIPING

1 Cutting fabric strips Measure the width of the piping fabric in the usual way. Measure round cushion and add ¹/₂-1 times extra for the length. Cut out the fabric strips on the bias in the usual way, joining to make the required length.

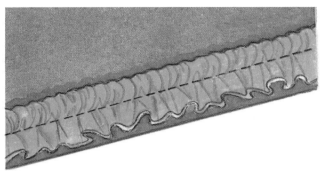

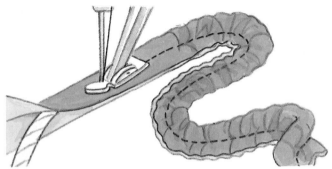

2 Gathering up the piping Fold the covering fabric in half round the cord and pin the cord to hold. Stitch for 15cm (6in) using the zip foot but do not stitch right up against the cord, as the tube needs to be loose enough to be gathered. Leaving the needle in the fabric, raise the pressure foot and gently pull the cord through the tube to gather up the fabric. Check the gathers are even, lower the foot and repeat, working in 15cm (6in) sections, until the end of the cord is reached.

3 Completing the cover Apply the gathered piping to a cover piece, joining the ends together in the same way as before. Stitch the gathered piping to the first cover piece, before adding the second cover section, checking the gathers are even as you work. Complete as for basic piped cover.

▼ *A gathered finish A thick cord has been used in the piping to make a bold gathered edge to this attractive cushion. The fabric is a pretty glazed cotton with a floral pattern; the piping fabric is picked from one of the colours in the pattern.*

MAKING A ZIPPED PIPED COVER

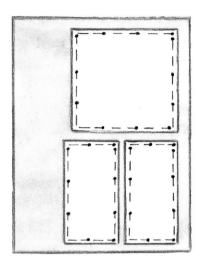

1 Cutting out Measure the cushion pad and cut a paper pattern to this size adding 1.5cm (⅝in) all round for seams. Using the pattern, cut out one piece of fabric for the front. Fold and cut the pattern in half and pin the two halves to the fabric leaving 2.5cm (1in) between them. Cut out the back cover. Fold back cover in half and cut down fold to make two back pieces.

2 Joining the backs Place back pieces with right sides together; pin and tack a 1.5cm (⅝in) seam. Stitch in from each end for 4cm (1½in), fastening off threads by back stitching for a short distance. Neaten edges of seam allowance by zigzag stitching or oversewing, then press seam open.

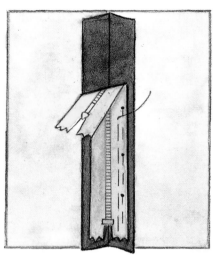

3 Inserting the zip Choose a zip 8cm (3in) smaller than centre back seam. Place zip right side down over wrong side of seam, matching teeth section of zip over tacked section of seam. Pin and tack in place. Using the zip foot, stitch zip in place. Remove tacking stitches.

4 Completing the cover Make up covered piping and set round front cover piece as described above. Place cover pieces with right sides together. Pin, tack and stitch all round cover, using zip foot to position stitches on, or just inside previous stitching line. Trim and neaten edges. Turn cover to right side through zip. Insert cushion pad and close zip.

◀ **Contrast edging** A shiny glazed cotton has been used for this piping. If you are using a patterned fabric, piping breaks up the edges of the cushion so that you don't have to match the design and can use up remnants of fabric economically.

Frilled cushions

Cushions, the most versatile of home furnishings, are synonymous with comfort, colour and style. Wherever they are placed, cushions have an immediate softening impact. Yet by trimming cushions in one of a variety of ways, they can be specially tailored to enhance individual rooms in your home.

Even the most basic frill can be adapted to different decorative styles. For example, a lace-frilled cushion brings frivolity and romance to a bedroom,

while a piped frill in a contrasting fabric adds a bold, cheerful finish to a cushion on a kitchen chair. Later chapters will cover more formal modifications of the cushion frill – pleated frills, for example.

The simplest frills are made from a single layer of fabric with a neatened outer edge. They can be bound with a contrast edging, finished with a double hem, or with decorative machine stitching such as closely worked zigzag stitch, or one of the attractive edge

▲ Piped and frilled
Insert the piping with the frill – the method used is the same for circular or square cushions.

stitches found on the newer machines.

A single frill produces a crisp finish while a double frill gives a fuller, softer edge. It is made from a folded strip of fabric and is stitched to the cover in the same way as a single frill.

MAKING A SINGLE-FRILLED COVER

1 Calculating the frill Measure round the cover and allow twice this for the frill length. The frill width is a matter of personal choice, but you will find that a frill wider than 7.5cm (3in) will be too floppy unless you are working with lace for bed cushions. Add an additional 3cm (1in) for double hem and seam allowance. Any extra needed for joining strips together should be included in the frill length.

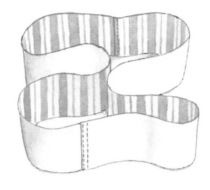

2 Cutting out the strips Cut the fabric strips on the straight of the grain – across the fabric width, from selvedge to selvedge. Working from the wrong side, using a metre stick and tailor's chalk or marking pencil, measure and mark the strips across the fabric. Cut out carefully along the marked lines.

3 Joining the strips together The frill strips must be joined together into a ring to fit round the front cushion cover piece. Pin and stitch the frill strips together with narrow French seams (see page 85). If the pattern is distinctive, try to match the designs over the seam.

4 Hemming the frill Turn under 1cm ($^3/_8$in) all round the outer edge of frill. Turn under another 1cm ($^3/_8$in), forming a double hem. Pin and tack hem in place. Either machine stitch or hem the frill by hand with small invisible stitches.

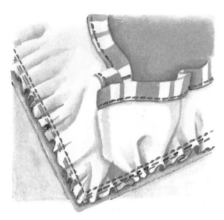
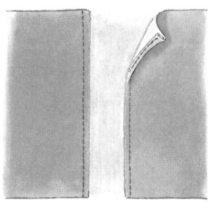
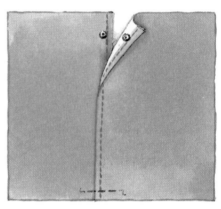

6 Stitching frill to front cover Cut out one cover piece in the same way as for piped cushions (see page 190). With right sides together and raw edges matching, pull up gathering stitches to fit round the cushion cover and pin. Check that the gathers are evenly spaced. On square covers it may be necessary to allow extra gathers to go round each corner. Tack and stitch the frill to the cover.

7 Making a non-fastening back opening Fold paper pattern in half and cut as for piped cushions. Place pattern on fabric and cut out, adding 6cm (2in) to both centre edges. Turn under and stitch a double 1cm ($^3/_8$in) hem along both centre edges.

8 Completing back cover To keep opening taut after pad is inserted add press studs or velcro to the opening. With right sides up, overlap the hemmed edges for 4cm (1$^1/_2$in) and attach fastening; then pin and tack together along outer seamlines.

▶ **Double up with lace**
Purchased lace, slightly narrower than the frill, can be added for a softer finish. Pin the lace to the frill after it has been hemmed but before gathering. There are so many different designs of lace – soft and romantic, bold and chunky – so choose a style to suit the furnishings in the room.

5 Gathering the frill Work two rows of gathering stitches along the length of the frill.

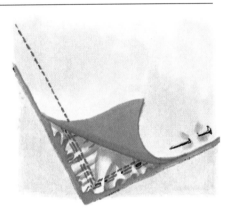

9 Finishing off Place back to front with right sides together, sandwiching the frill. Pin and stitch together all round, making sure that the stitching matches or is worked inside the previous line of stitching. Trim seam to reduce bulk of gathering and turn cover right side out. Insert the cushion pad through back opening.

▲ *Piped detail* *Taking a lead from the upholstery, this pair of cushions shows two variations of piped and frilled finishes. A length of covered piping cord can be inserted between the frill and the cover. Make up the* *piping and tack round the front cover before adding the frill. The fabric is quite stiff so hemmed single frills have been used with the one-sided printed fabric backed with the reversible plain.*

tip

Perfect gathering
Heavy fabric If your chosen fabric is medium to heavy weight, the long gathering threads may break when they are pulled up. Stitch the gathering rows in short sections and position the rows on either side of any seams. It is difficult to pull gathering threads through the seam thickness.

Frill fullness When gauging the amount of fullness in a frill, take account of the fabric's weight. For a thick fabric that gathers more bulkily than the standard-weight furnishing cotton, one-and-a-half times the length will be sufficient, while for very fine fabrics, such as lawn, you may need two to three times the measurement.

A contrasting edge Single frills can be finished with a bound edge using contrasting ribbon, tape or bias binding. Fold binding in half over the raw frill edge and machine stitch in place. For a wider edging, hem the frill then place the binding on the edge and stitch along both sides.

MAKING A DOUBLE FRILL

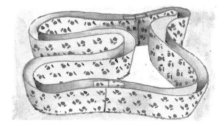

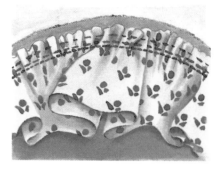

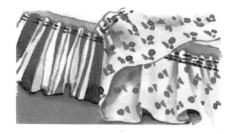

Making the frill A double frill is a folded strip of fabric which does not need a finished edge. If the fabric used is firmly woven, a double frill may need extra give. In this case cut the strips on the bias of the fabric (see page 188). Decide on the frill depth and length and cut out strips to twice this depth plus twice the seam allowance, by the chosen length, as for single frills.

Adding the double frill to a cover
Join strips together into a ring with plain flat seams; trim and press open. Fold strip in half lengthways, wrong sides together; pin raw edges together and press along fold. Gather up through both layers and stitch to cover as for single frills.

Working with more than one frill
Make up two or more frills in the same way as for single frills, making each one slightly smaller in size – about 2cm (³/₄in). Match the raw edges together and gather up as for a single fabric.

▼ *Doubling up*
A double frill is ideal for reversible cushions.

Beautiful bolsters

Long, firm bolster cushions fit easily into any decor. Traditionally used at each end of a sofa or to provide a prop for other pillows on a bed, they can also be used to transform a bed into a sofa or as a support on window seats, easy chairs or sofas.

If you already have a bolster cushion you can re-cover this, or buy a bolster-shaped cushion pad to the size you require. These only come in a limited range of sizes, however, but you can make your own quickly and economically by cutting about 1m (1yd) of wadding as wide as the length of the bolster and rolling it into a pad. Sew the end in place with loose slipstitches to hold, then make a cover to fit.

▲ Plain and simple
On a tailored sofa where the other cushions are plain or with a flange, a simple bolster with piped seams at each end is perfectly in keeping with the style.

Materials

Bolster pad or 1m (1yd) **wadding (batting)** made into a pad.
Matching **zip** 6cm (2¼in) shorter than the bolster.
Matching **sewing thread**.
Optional **piping** and other trimmings.
Lining or remnant for the bolster with gathered ends.

HOW TO MAKE A PLAIN BOLSTER

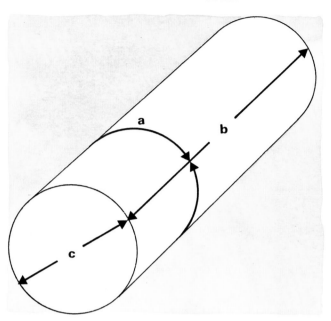

1 Cutting out Measure round the bolster to find its circumference (a) – measure loosely so that the cover will have an easy fit. Cut a piece of fabric this measurement plus 3cm (1¼in) by the length of the bolster (b) plus 3cm (1¼in). Measure across the end of the bolster (c) and cut two circles this measurement plus 3cm (1¼in) across.

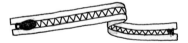

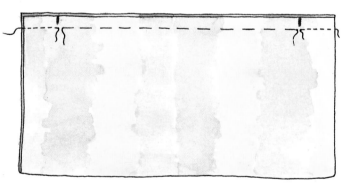

2 Stitching the main piece Place the zip centrally along one lengthways edge of the rectangle and mark each end on the fabric with tailor's chalk. Fold the fabric lengthways, right sides together and with edges matching, then machine stitch the ends of the seam past the marks, taking a 1.5cm (⅝in) seam allowance. Tack the remainder of the seam together.

3 Inserting the zip Insert the zip, centred in the seam as for square cushion (see page 190). Remove the tacking.

▶ *Daydream*
On a pretty day-bed, the bolsters give support to the cushions to make it look more like a sofa. The gathers on the ends of the bolsters fit in beautifully with the other frilled cushions used.

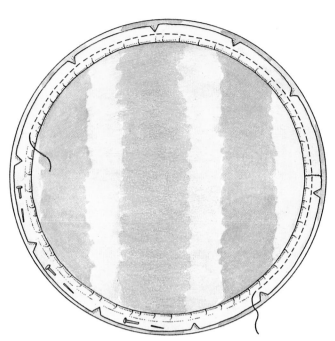

4 Attaching the piping Make up enough covered piping cord to go round the two circular end pieces (see page 12). Snip into the seam allowance of the bias strip used to cover the cord at 2.5cm (1in) intervals for ease and stitch to each end piece with seamlines matching, using a machine zip foot.

5 Attaching the end pieces At each end of the main piece, snip into the 1.5cm (⅝in) seam allowance at 2.5cm (1in) intervals for ease. Then, with right sides together, pin, tack and stitch a circular piece to each end of the main piece. Turn right side out through the zip opening and insert the pad. Close zip.

BOLSTER WITH GATHERED ENDS

1 Cutting out Cut out the main piece and insert the zip as in steps 1-3 for a plain bolster. Cut out a circle for each end from lining fabric as in step 1. Cut two strips of fabric one and a half times the circumference of the bolster, with a width half the measurement across the end plus 1.5cm (⅝in).

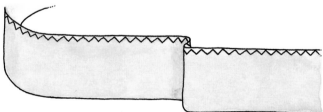

2 Making the gathered ends Neaten one raw edge of each strip of fabric with tight zigzag or overlock. If fabric frays badly, turn a narrow 5mm (¼in) hem. Fold each strip in half widthways, with right sides facing, and stitch the ends together to make a ring, taking a 1.5cm (⅝in) seam allowance. Press the seam allowances open.

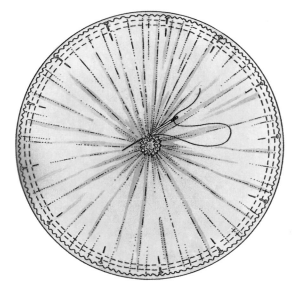

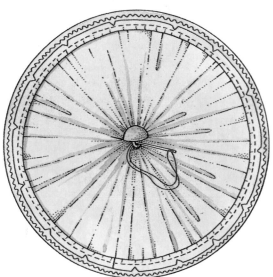

3 Gathering up Run two rows of gathering threads close to each long edge of each strip. Gather up the unfinished edge to fit the outside edge of each circle of lining fabric; pin. Pull up the other gathering threads tightly so that the fabric lies flat on the circle; pin. Tack the gathered fabric, right side up, to the right side of each circle round the edge and at the centre. Remove the gathering threads.

4 Finishing off Stitch the piping to the end pieces, as in step 4 for the plain bolster, stitch the fabric in place at the centre, then remove the tacking. Cover a large button with fabric and stitch to the centre of each end to cover the meeting edges of the gathered fabric. Attach the ends to the main piece as in step 5, for the simple bolster.

BOLSTER PILLOW

The soft, feminine styling of this type of bolster cover makes it particularly appropriate for the bedroom. It is quick and easy to make since it is gathered in at each end with a ribbon or length of coloured cord instead of having a zip fastening.

Buy or make the bolster the width of a pillow or long enough to go across the whole bed. Each cover also requires 1.5m (1½yd) of 6mm (¼in) ribbon or cord.

1 Cutting out Measure across one end of the bolster and along the length; add 5cm (2in) for the length of the fabric required. For the width, loosely measure round the circumference of the bolster and add 3cm (1¼in). Cut out one piece of fabric this size.

2 Making the casings Fold under 1cm (⅜in) then 1.5cm (⅝in) at each end to form casings for the ribbon or cord. Pin and then edgestitch close to the hem fold.

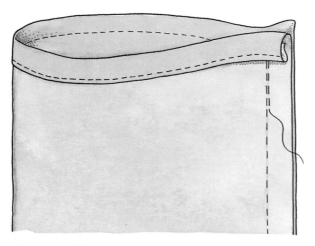

3 Stitching the seam Fold the fabric in half lengthways, with right sides together and edges matching. Pin and then stitch raw edges together taking a 1.5cm (⅝in) seam allowance and leaving casings free at ends. Backstitch at each end for strength.

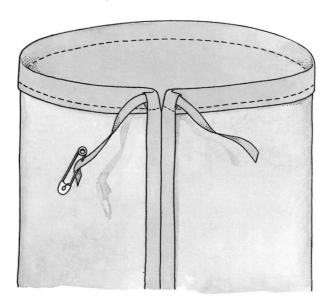

4 Finishing off Cut the ribbon or cord in half and use a safety pin to thread a piece through the casing at each end. Turn the bolster cover through to the right side; draw up one end with the ribbon and tie in a bow, then trim the ribbon ends at an angle. Insert the pad and then draw up the other end and tie.

▲ Fancy that
For the bed, the softer look of gently gathered bolster covers is ideal. Add a lace trimming to the edge for that little bit extra.

tip

Bolster pillow variation

Cut the fabric 3cm (1¼in) wider than the circumference of the pillow by the length of the pillow plus 12cm (4¾in). Fold in half lengthways, right sides together and stitch a 1.5cm (⅝in) seam to form a tube. Hem each end, turning under 5mm (¼in) and then 1.5cm (⅝in). Insert the bolster pillow centrally and tie 80cm (⅞yd) ribbon round the fabric at each end like a Christmas cracker. Tie the ribbon in a bow and trim the ends at an angle for a neat finish.

Buttoned cushions

Buttoning gives gusseted cushions the appearance of over-stuffed luxury, making the cushions look deeper and therefore more comfortable. The buttons, which are usually covered with fabric, can be added to most types of cushions, from simple scatter cushions to deep gusseted chair seats. They are not advisable for very thin squab cushions, however, since the buttons will not sink deep into the pad, making them uncomfortable to sit on.

The idea for buttoning came into popularity in Victorian times, when buttons were widely used on all types of furniture from foot stools to Chesterfield sofas. Perhaps, because of this, buttoned cushions and furniture have an old-fashioned look which is now very much back in style.

Fabric covered buttons
Most buttoning is done with covered buttons, which look and feel softer than ordinary dressmaking buttons. The special buttons used for this can be either plastic or rust-proof metal, but although plastic is fine for dressmaking purposes, the strong metal variety is best for cushions.

Any light or mediumweight fabric can be used to cover the buttons, and you may have some remnants of attractive fabric already, which would be ideal for the purpose. Usually all the buttons are covered with the same fabric, but for added interest you could use a different colour for each one to create a harlequin effect. You can even embroider fabric or use stitched canvas as the button covers.

▼ **Springtime**
Buttoning makes deep cushions look invitingly plump, soft and springy. Here the buttons are covered with bias binding which was used to trim the piping giving a springtime look.

COVERING METAL BUTTONS

1 Cutting the pattern Buy medium to large cover buttons for cushion buttoning – between 19 and 29mm (¾ and 1¼in). Cut out the circle on the back of the pack which is the correct size for the buttons you are covering. This is your pattern.

2 Cutting the fabric Position the pattern on the right side of the fabric and move it around so that the pattern covers a motif. If the motifs are too large for this, decide on the colour you would like to highlight, and position the pattern accordingly. Draw round the pattern and then cut out the fabric; repeat for all the buttons you wish to cover.

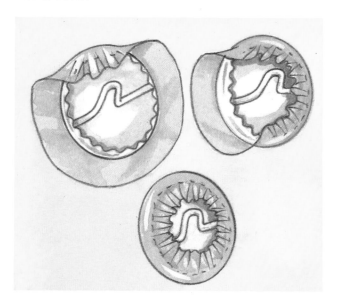

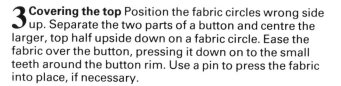

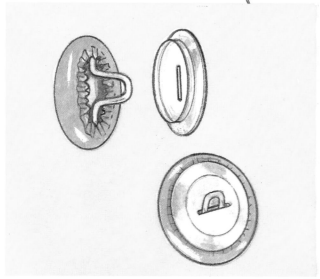

3 Covering the top Position the fabric circles wrong side up. Separate the two parts of a button and centre the larger, top half upside down on a fabric circle. Ease the fabric over the button, pressing it down on to the small teeth around the button rim. Use a pin to press the fabric into place, if necessary.

4 Assembling the button Check that the fabric is smooth on the top part of the button. If so, quickly press the hollow side of the bottom part on to the stem of the button; it should snap together with the top part, neatly covering the raw edges of the fabric. Cover the remaining buttons in the same way.

► *Button focus*
The front of this pretty pillow is made in four triangular sections, trimmed with double-edged lace and then stitched together. The button is the finishing touch, focusing attention on construction of the pillow, and covering the point where the four triangles meet.

COVERING PLASTIC BUTTONS

Unlike metal buttons, plastic ones do not have teeth to secure the fabric, which means that they are covered in a slightly different way.

1 Cutting out Cut out circles of fabric using the appropriate pattern on the back of the pack of cover buttons as in steps 1 and 2 opposite.

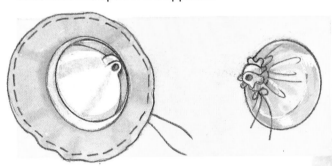

2 Covering the top Run a row of gathering stitches close to the edge of a fabric circle, with the two thread ends pulled out on the right side. Separate the two halves of each button, and position the top part upside down on the wrong side of the fabric. Pull up the thread ends to gather the fabric, and tie in a knot close to the button stem. Trim off the thread ends.

3 Assembling the button Check that the fabric is smooth on the top part of the button and then press the hollow side of the bottom piece on to the button stem; it should snap together with the top piece, neatly covering the fabric edges. Cover the remaining buttons in the same way.

tip

Spare parts
Manufacturers usually supply an extra button on ready-made garments in case a button is lost. For the same reason, its a good idea to cover an extra button when making buttoned cushions, and keep it safely in reserve.

Materials

Covered cushion

Large covered buttons

Furnishing fabric

Button twine, available from the sewing departments of some of the larger chain stores or from specialist upholstery suppliers. It comes in only a few colours, but it will not show on the finished cushion, so an exact match is not necessary.

BUTTONING CUSHIONS

1 Planning For each button on the front of the cushion you will need another one on the back for reinforcement. This can either be a small, inexpensive button, or, if the cushion is reversible, a second covered button. Use tailor's chalk to mark the position of the buttons on each side, making sure that the button marks on the underside are exactly under the ones on the top.

2 Attaching the buttons Thread a needle with button twine and knot the ends together to make a double thread. Pass the needle from the underside of the cushion to the top, making sure the needle goes through the marks on both sides. Thread on a button and stitch back to the underside. Thread on another button and stitch to the top side and through the top button.

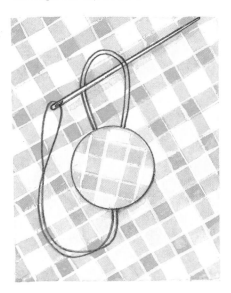

3 Knotting off Pull firmly on the twine to tighten the thread and pull the two buttons into the cushion. Pass the twine round the shank of the button to make a loop and then pass the needle through the loop to secure the buttons.

4 Finishing off Tie another knot in the thread, then trim. Repeat steps 2-4 to attach all the required buttons, pulling them the same depth into the cushion.

▲ *Comfort first*
Buttons add decorative interest to squab cushions, but make sure the cushions are deep enough to allow the buttons to sink in, otherwise they may be uncomfortable to sit on.

Gusseted cushions

Adding a gusset to a cushion cover allows for a deeper, more tailored shape. The gusset strip forms the side between the top and bottom pieces of the cover. The three dimensional shape produced can be emphasized by piping the seams or with a decorative or contrasting gusset. Gusseted cushions can be square, rectangular or round and used on hard chairs, benches or sofas.

The zip is inserted in the back part of the gusset where it will not be seen. The zip usually extends round the sides of the cushion to make it easier to insert the pad or foam. This is especially important if the foam is very firm. The length of the extension will largely depend on the thickness of the foam or pad - the deeper the cushion, the longer the extension each side.

▲ **Terrace seating**
Provençal fabric, in bright colourways, has been used to make a set of cheerful cushions for folding wooden chairs. As the gusset is quite narrow it is made from a single strip of fabric with the zip inserted along the seamed edge, just under the piping.

Choosing the pads

The type of filling you should choose depends on whether you want a firm or soft cushion. For a firm cushion which retains its shape and looks neat, choose block foam. It's easy to use, resilient and washable. The thickness of the foam depends on where the cushion is to be used – seat cushions are usually about 10cm (4in) thick.

If you prefer a softer look, choose a loose filling – feathers, feathers and down, or foam chips. Feathers and down are a luxurious filling, but their extreme softness means that they should only be used for thick gusseted cushions. When using loose fillings, the filling is stuffed into an inner cover. This enables you to remove the outer cover for washing.

Suitable fabrics

This type of cushion will usually get a lot of wear, so choose closely woven, washable fabrics for the cover; furnishing fabrics such as heavy cotton, corduroy, glazed cottons or linen are ideal.

▶ **A perfect fit**
This deep, gusseted cushion fits neatly into the seat of a cane armchair. The washable cotton fabric used matches the wallpaper, and a simple squab cushion with ties adds comfort to the back.

MAKING A GUSSETED CUSHION

1 Making the filling If using block foam, buy or cut it to the correct size. For loose fillings, make an inner cover from downproof cambric in the same way as the outer cover, but omitting the zip, and stuff with the filling.

2 The outer cover Measure the width and length of the top of the foam or soft-filled pad and add 3cm (1¼in) to both measurements for seam allowances. Cut two pieces of fabric this size.

3 Measuring the gusset The gusset is made up of two pieces: the front and sides are cut as one, while the back piece, in which the zip is inserted, is cut separately. Measure the front gusset - the depth of the pad by three quarters of each of the two sides, plus the length of the front. Add standard 1.5cm (⅝in) seam allowances all round.

Measure the back gusset - the depth of the pad by a quarter of each of the two sides plus the length of the back. For seam allowances add 3cm (1¼in) to the length and 6cm (2½in) to the width. Cut two lengths of fabric to these dimensions.

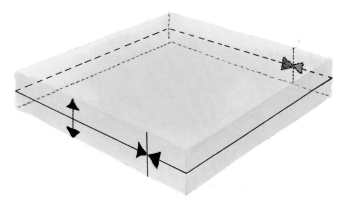

◀ *An inviting corner*
This window seat, made from a single cushion, is just the place to curl up with your favourite magazine. The feather pad has been shaped with the sides angled outwards to fit the area snugly.

Tailored look

For a tailored effect, make the gusset in four pieces instead of two, with seams at each front corner. This requires accurate measuring, cutting and stitching to ensure that the seams are straight and positioned exactly at corners.

When joining gusset pieces together, leave 1.5cm (^{5}/8in) free at each end. The fabric will spread at the corners to aid stitching the gusset to the top and base pieces.

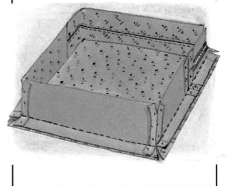

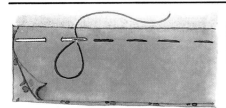

4 Inserting the zip The zip should be 3cm (1^1/4in) shorter than the back gusset section. Cut the back gusset in half lengthways. Place right sides together; pin and tack down the complete length. Press seam open.

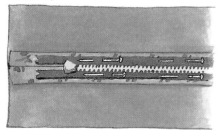

5 Position zip centrally Place zip face down over wrong side of seam. Pin and tack in place. Turn to right side; stitch zip in place.

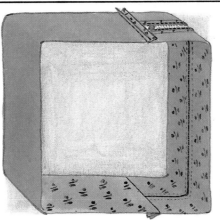

6 Making up the gusset With right sides facing and taking 1.5cm (^{5}/8in) seam allowances, pin the ends of gusset pieces together. Check for fit round cushion pad, then stitch seams.

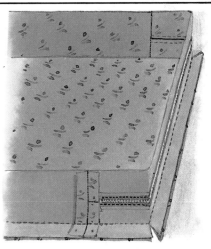

7 Stitching gusset to main pieces With right sides facing, pin and tack one edge of the gusset to one cushion piece. Snip into gusset at corners to help the fabric lie flat. Open the zip, then stitch second cover piece to opposite edge of gusset in the same way. For a crisp look, add contrast piping to these seams (see pages 187–190). Turn right side out and insert pad; close zip.

ROUND GUSSETED COVERS

1 Make a pattern Pin a piece of paper on the chair, and draw round the seat area to make a circular pattern. If you are using a circular foam pad, draw round this instead. Fold into four to check it is symmetrical and trim if necessary. Add seam allowances all round.

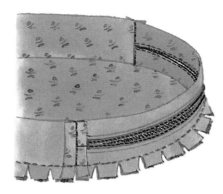

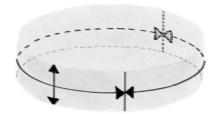

2 Measuring the gusset The gusset is cut in two pieces, like a square or rectangular cushion. Measure up in the same way so that the back gusset extends about a third of the way round the cushion. Add seam allowances as in step 3 of making a gusseted cushion.

3 Inserting the zip Cut the back gusset in half lengthways. Insert the zip in the same way as for square or rectangular cover. With right sides facing and taking 1.5cm (^{5}/8in) seam allowance, pin and stitch gusset pieces together along short edges.

4 Stitching gusset to main cover With zip open and right sides facing, pin and stitch the gusset to one cover piece and then the other. Snip into seam allowances at 2.5cm (1in) intervals all round, to ease the fabric and achieve a neat appearance. Turn cover right side out. Insert pad; close zip.

tip

Concealing the zip
If the gusset can be seen all the way round when the cushion is in position, reposition the zip where it will be less conspicuous. The easiest method is to put the zip on the underside, as in a squab cushion, although this means you cannot turn the cushion over. On a thin, square cushion it can also be positioned on the back gusset in the seam, but the zip should not extend round the corners.

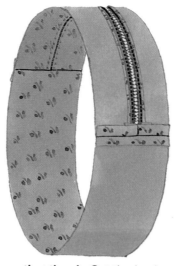

◄ Formal comfort
Deep, gusseted cushions provide comfort on this wicker sofa. The large print has been cleverly matched on the top and front gusset for a professional finish. The seams are subtly piped in green.

Tucked cushions

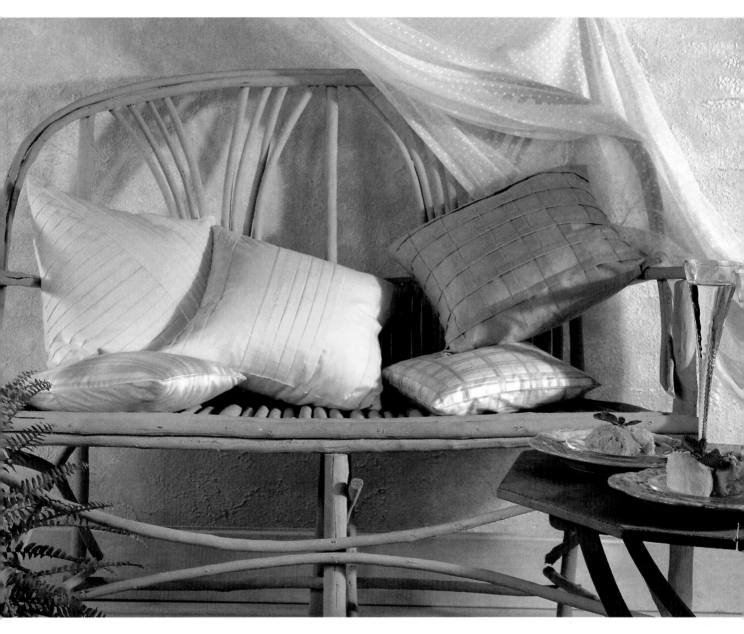

By stitching lines of folds into a plain fabric, you can add surface detail and create a whole range of innovative designs. The tucks are machine stitched either horizontally or vertically along the grain of the fabric, and can vary in width and spacing according to the chosen pattern or personal preference.

Elaborate tucked designs can be shown off to the full on cushion covers, like those shown here, but the technique can also be used to add a simple decorative trimming to the edges of pillowcases, tablecloths and napkins.

Suitable fabrics

Plain fabrics in light shades are best for displaying tucks, as they will allow the eye to focus on the tucked design, rather than on the fabric pattern. Elaborate patterns also become distorted by tucks and can look odd, though with careful planning, simple checks and stripes can produce wonderful results. Check the effect by pleating your chosen fabric into a series of small folds before you buy.

Your chosen fabric should be evenly and closely woven, making it easier for you to ensure that the tucks are accurately folded and stitched along the grain; always cut the fabric along the grain. For the best results, choose a fabric that presses into a sharp crease line, and avoid slippery fabrics which are difficult to work with, like satin and many synthetics. When selecting a fabric, also bear in mind that each tuck takes up three times as much fabric as its

▲ A tuck in time
The beauty of these tucked cushions lies in the simplicity of their designs, which are created from the addition of textured surface detail. Use plain, lightweight fabrics for the best results, and make the cushions in a range of colours.

finished width, so try and choose a reasonably priced fabric, particularly if your design incorporates several tucks.

Lawn or lightweight cotton and linen are ideal. Furthermore, if you use fine fabrics like these, the triple layer of fabric made by each tuck will create strong bands of colour against untucked areas of the cushion, and greatly enhance the overall design.

Materials

Note: The metric to imperial measurements are not exact conversions, but have been calculated so the cushions are easy to make. Follow only one set of figures.

Lemon yellow fabric for the yellow cushion; you will need a piece 91 × 43cm (34¾ × 17in) for the front of the cushion, and 46 × 43cm (18 × 17in) for the back

Pale blue fabric for the blue cushion; you will need a 67cm (25¼in) square for the front of the cushion, and a piece 46 × 43cm (18 × 17in) for the back

Ivory fabric for the ivory cushion; you will need two rectangles of fabric for the front. Piece A – 171 × 31cm (66½ × 11¾in), and Piece B – 87 × 59cm (35 × 23in), plus one piece for the back, 46 × 43cm (18 × 17in)

Pale pink fabric for the ruffle tuck cushion; you will need a piece 119 × 43cm (47 × 17in) for the front of the cushion, and 46 × 43cm (18 × 17in) for the back

Dark pink fabric for the irregularly tucked cushion; calculate the fabric requirements from your design; our cushion was made from a piece 83 × 43 cm (33 × 17in) for the front, and 46 × 43cm (18 × 17in) for the back

Zip 35cm (13¾in) long for each cushion, to match the fabric

Matching sewing threads

Tailor's chalk

Ruler

Square cushion pad 40cm (15¾in) for each cushion

Iron and **pressing cloth**

YELLOW CUSHION

This cushion has a design of regular tucks, each of which is 2cm (¾in) wide from the fold to the stitching line. The tucks are arranged in three bands – two outer bands of three tucks, and one central band of six tucks, with spaces of untucked fabric in-between.

1 Marking a seam allowance Lay out the fabric for the front cover, right side face up. Use tailor's chalk to mark a 1.5cm (⅝) seam allowance along one short edge.

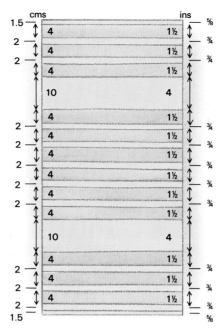

2 Marking the tucks Using either centimetres or inches, work from the diagram, to mark up the stitching lines. Measure and mark the tuck widths down both sides of the fabric, using tailors chalk, then join them with chalked lines ruled across the fabric, finishing with a 1.5cm (⅝in) seam allowance; the shaded areas indicate the pleats.

3 Stitching the tucks Starting with the first tuck, fold the fabric wrong sides together, matching the two stitching lines. Tack and then machine along the stitching line. Repeat for the rest of the tucks.

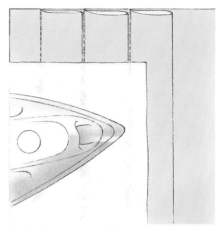

4 Pressing the tucks Use a slightly damp pressing cloth to press the tucks along their folds; this will give a sharp edge, without adding shine or scorching the fabric. Then press the tucks flat, so that they all lie in the same direction.

5 Making the zip opening Cut a 43 × 6cm (17 × 2¼in) strip of fabric from the back cover fabric. With right sides together and long edges matching, pin and tack the strip back on to the main back piece, taking a 1.5cm (⅝in) seam allowance; machine stitch the seam for 4cm (1½in) only at each end, leaving the centre tacked together. Press the seam flat along its whole length.

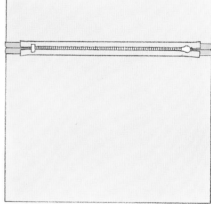

6 Inserting the zip Lay the zip right side down over the wrong side of the cushion back, with the teeth directly over the seam. Tack then machine stitch the zip in place. Remove tacking.

7 Joining front to back With right sides together, pin and stitch the back cover to the front around all four sides, taking a 1.5cm (⅝in) seam allowance. Trim diagonally across each corner, then turn cover through to right side via the zip opening. Press the seams.

IVORY CUSHION

This cushion is made from two triangles of tucked fabric, stitched together on the diagonal to form a square cover. On one fabric triangle (Piece A), the tucks are shorter and stop at the diagonal seam; on the other (Piece B), the tucks extend right across the cushion's diagonal, from one edge to the other. All the finished tucks are 2cm (¾in) wide.

1 **Making the tucks on Piece A** Lay out the 171 × 31cm (66½ × 11¾in) rectangle of fabric with right side up, and mark a 1.5cm (⅝in) seam allowance across one of the short edges. Mark a series of tucks 4cm (1½in) wide, interspersed with gaps of 2cm (¾in) along the length – ie 4cm (1½in), 2cm (¾in), 4cm (1½in), 2cm (¾in), etc. This will give you 28 tucks (or 29 if using inches), ending with a 2cm (¾in) space, plus a 1.5cm (⅝in) seam allowance. Stitch the tucks as before, then press them flat.

2 **Making the tucks on Piece B** Lay out the 87 × 59cm (35 × 23in) rectangle of fabric, right side up, and mark a 1.5cm (⅝in) seam allowance along the short edge. Mark the stitching lines as for piece A to make 14 tucks (or 15 if using inches) across the fabric. Stitch the tucks, and press to lie flat.

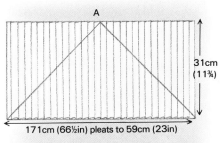

A

31cm (11¾)

171cm (66½in) pleats to 59cm (23in)

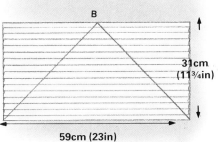

B

31cm (11¾in)

59cm (23in)

3 **Trimming to form triangles** The fabric rectangles are trimmed to make two triangles. Measure halfway across the long side of Piece A, which should now measure 59cm (23in). Mark two lines from this point down to the two bottom corners of the rectangle, and trim the excess away to make a triangle. Repeat on Piece B, whose long side also measures 59cm (23in); note that the tucks lie horizontally, not vertically.

4 **Joining the triangles** With right sides together and longest edges matching, pin then stitch the two triangles together along the longest edge to form a square, taking a 1.5cm (⅝in) seam allowance. Make up as for the yellow cushion.

tip

Ivory cushion short cut
Once confident with tucking, save on time and fabric when making the ivory cushion by working from two triangles of fabric at the start, rather than two rectangles which then need to be trimmed.

BLUE CUSHION

Stunning chequered designs can also be created by stitching lines of vertical, as well as horizontal tucks. This design has six vertical and six horizontal 2cm (¾in) tucks, with 4cm (1½in) squares of untucked fabric in-between.

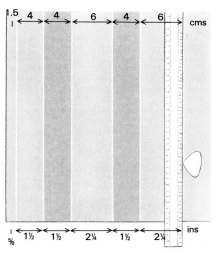

1.5 | 4 | 4 | 6 | 4 | 6 | cms

⅝ | 1½ | 1½ | 2¼ | 1½ | 2¼ | ins

1 **Making the horizontal tucks** With right side up, mark a 1.5cm (⅝in) seam allowance along one edge of the front cover fabric. Then mark up the design. Begin with the first 4cm (1½in) space, then measure 4cm (1½in) for the first tuck; leave a 6cm (2¼in) space before marking 4cm (1¼in) for the next tuck. Continue marking up 6cm (2¼in) spaces and 4cm (1½in) tucks (shaded in the diagram), ending with a 6cm (2¼in) space and a 1.5cm (⅝in) seam allowance. Stitch the tucks, and press.

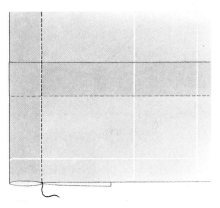

2 **Making the vertical tucks** Turn the fabric so that the tucks lie horizontally. Mark up the vertical tucks exactly as for the horizontal ones. When stitching the vertical tucks, carefully fold and stitch across the horizontal tucks as you go. Press flat with a slightly damp pressing cloth. Make up as for the yellow cushion.

◄ *Matching set*
Make co-ordinated cushions in various shades of the same colour.

2 Making the tucks Mark up the stitching lines for the 4cm (1½in) tucks, with 2cm (¾in) gaps in-between, as for the ivory cushion. This will give you 19 tucks (or 20 if using inches), finishing with a 2cm (¾in) space, plus a 1.5cm (⅝in) allowance. Stitch and press tucks.

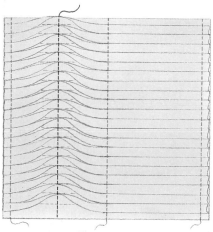

PALE PINK CUSHION

Ruffle tucks look stunning, and are suprisingly easy to stitch. Experiment with this technique on fine, silk-like fabrics which catch the light for a striking two-tone effect. On the cushion all the finished tucks are 2cm (¾in) wide.

1 Getting started With right side face up, use tailor's chalk to mark a 1.5cm (⅝in) seam allowance along one short edge of the front cover fabric, followed by a 2cm (¾in) gap, before marking the first tuck.

3 Creating a ruffled effect Lay out the fabric so that the tucks lie horizontally and face away from you. Tack and stitch down both sides of the cushion front, 1.5cm (⅝in) in from the side edges, and also down the cushion centre, so that the tucks are stitched to lie flat. Turn the fabric around so that the tucks face you. Measure halfway between two rows of stitching and tack and stitch the tucks to lie flat in the opposite direction (a); repeat between the other two rows of stitching. Make up as for the yellow cushion.

DARK PINK CUSHION

Many attractive designs can be made using different sized tucks and spaces. For a symmetrical look carefully plan your design before you begin, or make a more random pattern by inventing it as you go.

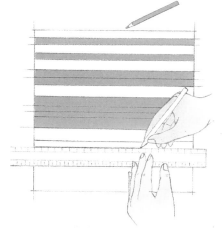

1 Planning a design If planning a design, draw up a scaled-down diagram to work from, shading in the tucks for easy reference. In the design shown here, the tuck width varies from 1.5-2.5cm (⅝-1in).

2 Marking the tucks Lay out the front cover fabric with right side face up and mark a 1.5cm (⅝in) seam allowance along one short edge as usual. Carefully mark up the design from your drawing. You should always finish with a space for the last pressed tuck, plus a 1.5cm (⅝in) seam allowance.

3 Stitching and pressing Stitch the tucks and press them flat as before, so that they all lie in the same direction. Make up as for the yellow cushion.

Re-covering drop-in seats

A dining chair with a drop-in seat, can be smartened up or made to match new furnishings with a change of cover. Choose an elegant damask or needle-point fabric for a formal effect, or a pretty floral for something fresh. As long as the fabric is hard-wearing, any medium to heavyweight furnishing fabric can be used for the purpose.

Re-covering this type of chair need not be a major operation since the seat lifts out for easy handling, and it may be that only the top layer of fabric needs to

be replaced. Just 1m (1yd) of fabric or less will be enough to cover most chairs, and if the fabric has only a small or random pattern, this amount may be enough to cover two chairs.

Start by checking the state of the wood, and if necessary clean and re-finish it before you start on the fabric. Remove the outer layer of fabric, and if the layers underneath are in bad condition, remove them one by one until you get down to a sound layer.

▲ *Quick recovery*
A chair with a drop-in seat can be transformed with a new cover in a few hours. No sewing is necessary, and since all the work is done on the underside of the seat, it doesn't even have to be neat.

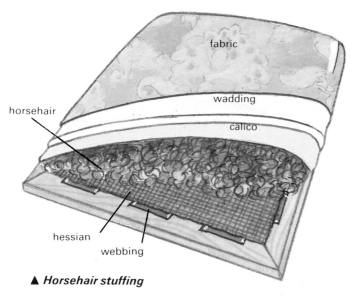

▲ *Horsehair stuffing*

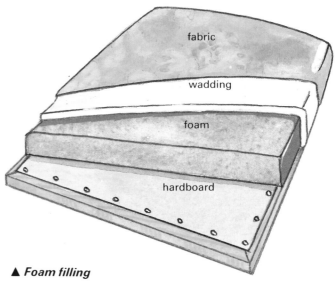

▲ *Foam filling*

Types of upholstery

The traditional drop-in seat comprises various layers of fabric and stuffing which give the seat its firm, but comfortable shape. Strips of strong webbing are stretched across the wooden seat frame in each direction to give the chair its base. A layer of hessian goes on top of this and then the horsehair or fibre mixture which makes up the main part of the seat. A layer of calico secures the horsehair and helps to prevent it working its way out. Cotton or polyester wadding on top of this add extra insulation for the horsehair and soften the overall effect, providing a smooth surface for the furnishing fabric which goes on top.

◄ *Pretty in chintz*
A floral chintz gives this chair a fresh but informal look, ideal for a cosy sitting room or kitchen.

Some modern chair seats are padded with foam which is placed on a hardboard or chipboard base and then covered with polyester or cotton wadding and then fabric. This is a quicker way of upholstering a seat, but not as durable or as comfortable as a traditionally upholstered seat.

Materials

Furnishing fabric of upholstery weight, 10cm (4in) larger all round than the fabric section of the chair seat.

An old **screwdriver** and a pair of **pincers** to remove old tacks or staples. A **tack** or **staple remover** will make this easier, but it is probably not worth buying one unless you plan to do several items.

Hammer and **16mm (⅝in) upholstery tacks** or a **staple gun** and **staples**. Staples are easy to use, but hard to take out. Professionals swear by tacks which can be partially nailed in for a temporary positioning and then knocked home when the arrangement has been finalized.

Fabric protector (optional).

If the layers underneath the main fabric are not in good condition, peel them apart to see what you need to replace. If the seat is upholstered with traditional materials, it may be necessary to replace the **wadding (batting)** and possibly also the **calico**, but it is unlikely that you will need to replace the remaining layers unless the chair is in very bad condition. If the chair is upholstered with **foam**, this can be replaced quite easily, especially since many suppliers will cut it to shape as part of their service.

RE-COVERING A DROP-IN SEAT

1 Removing the old fabric Push the seat up and out from underneath. Turn it upside down and remove the tacks or staples holding the fabric to the wooden frame. A staple or tack remover makes this easy, but tacks or staples can also be removed by carefully levering them up with a screwdriver and then pulling them out with pliers. If they are difficult to remove, try ripping off the fabric round them to make space underneath for the screwdriver. If a tack has lost its head, hammer the remains into the wood so that it does not catch on the new layers.

2 Arranging the fabric If the foam or wadding under the fabric is in good condition, all you need to do is replace the main fabric. Wrap the fabric loosely round the seat and stand back to survey the effect. If it has a large pattern or stripe, rearrange it to find the most pleasing effect. Always centre a large motif.

3 **Temporary tacking** With the lengthways grain running from front to back, and with the pattern arranged as required, place the fabric right side out on the chair seat and then turn the whole thing upside down. Knock a nail halfway into the wood at the centre of each edge as a temporary tack, with the fabric pulled taut. Alternatively fix a staple in these positions.

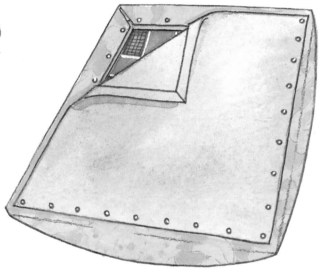

temporary tack

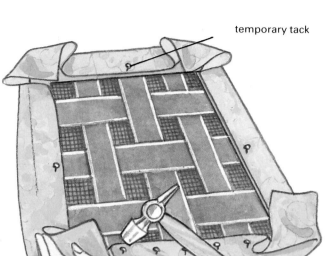

4 **Tacking the edges** Starting at the front of the seat, temporary tack or staple the fabric along the edge with the tacks spaced 4cm (1½in) apart. Tack the opposite edge and then the two side edges, pulling the fabric taut as you work, and leaving the corners free. When satisfied with the effect which should be smooth, hammer all the tacks home.

6 **Finishing shaped corners** Some chair seats have two corners with small square indents which accommodate the chair legs. Make a temporary tack in the centre as for a standard corner, pulling the fabric taut in the gap. Fold the excess fabric under to make pleats at each of the outer points and tack or staple in position; remove the temporary tack.

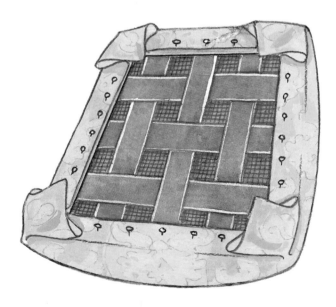

5 **Finishing the corners** Open out the fabric at the corners and hammer a temporary tack in the centre to hold (omit this stage if using staples). Fold the excess fabric on each side to the centre to make a pleat and tack or staple in place; remove the temporary tack.

7 **Neatening the underside** If required, take a piece of spare fabric – hessian, calico, or lining fabric will do – and cut it 2.5cm (1in) larger all round than the frame. Turn under 3cm (1¼in) all round so that it is slightly smaller than the seat, and tack to the base of the frame to cover all the raw edges and to protect the stuffing layers from dust.

8 **Preserving the fabric** Once the seat has been re-covered, spray it with fabric protector to extend its life. Any marks which do get on the fabric should be removed with fabric dry-cleaning fluid.

Planning ahead
Tacks which are hammered deep into the chair frame are difficult to remove when it comes to re-covering the chair again. To make it easier to remove the fabric later, do not hammer the tacks completely flush with the fabric.

Replacing the layers of padding

On a seat padded with foam, it may be worthwhile replacing the foam at the same time as the cover in order to extend the life of the seat and give it a fresh appearance.

On a seat traditionally upholstered with horsehair, it probably won't be necessary to replace all the layers unless the chair is in particularly bad condition. However, sometimes the wadding can wear thin and the horsehair starts to come through the calico, so these should both be replaced.

If the horsehair underneath the calico is in bad condition, it may be possible to top it up with new horsehair without completely renewing it; to renew the whole layer requires a bit more skill – this will be covered in a later chapter. Calico and wadding are widely available, but horsehair or its equivalent is available only from upholstery suppliers.

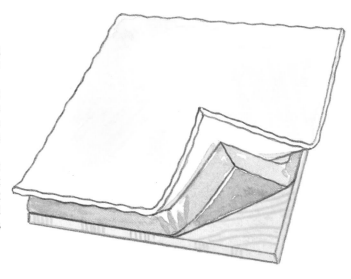

REPLACING FOAM

1 Measuring up Remove the old fabric and foam from the chair seat but leave the hardboard or chipboard in position. Draw round the seat on a piece of card to make a template for the new foam. Send the template to the foam supplier and get them to cut the foam to size.

▼ *Calico cover A fresh calico cover keeps the horsehair stuffing underneath in place and provides a secure base for the wadding and main fabric cover.*

2 Completing the seat Place the cut foam on the seat and cover with a piece of cotton or polyester wadding to soften the edges, 1cm (⅜in) larger all round (optional). Attach the fabric cover in the usual way (see previous pages).

REPLACING THE CALICO

Remove all the layers on the chair until you get down to the horsehair stuffing. Cut a new piece of calico to size and then fix to the chair in the same way as the main fabric, following the instructions on the previous pages but keeping the tacks well back from the inside edge where the tacks for the main fabric will go. If the frame is full of holes from previous tacks, the calico can be fixed to the sides of the frame instead, but make sure that the seat will still fit in the chair.

REPLACING THE WADDING

Traditionally cotton wadding is used on top of the calico to give the seat a soft, smooth finish, although 70g (2½oz) polyester wadding is an excellent alternative. Simply cut to the shape of the pad, adding 1cm (⅜in) all round to cover the sides of the seat. Position between the main fabric and the calico or foam and fix the main fabric on top, following the instructions on the previous pages.

Easy bedlinen

A duvet cover and pillowcases in fresh colours make the bed look bright and cheerful, and can invigorate the whole room. Made in fabrics with a white background, they look clean and cool for summer, while in rich, dark colours they look warm and luxurious.

By making the duvet cover and pillowcases yourself, you can choose exactly the fabrics you want to get just the right effect, and if you make the cover reversible, you will have two pattern options in one. Combine fabrics that tone in with the other fabrics used in the room, or fabrics in the same colours, but with different patterns. Try a plain or striped fabric on one side, and florals or other country motifs on the other side.

To co-ordinate the pillowcases, make two sets – one to go with each side of the duvet cover. Alternatively, make the pillowcases from one fabric and trim with the other.

No complicated stitching is required to make either the duvet cover or the pillowcases, since all the seams are straight and hemming can be done on the machine. They shouldn't take you long

▲ Reverse to stripes
Stripes and florals are mixed together in this reversible duvet cover to provide two decorative options instead of one. The fabrics share the same colour and floral theme, making them co-ordinate well.

to make, either, and moreover the end results should be a lot more satisfying and will have cost you a lot less than ready-made versions.

Fabrics

Although still loosely called bed-linen, most sheets, pillowcases and duvet covers are now made from pure cotton or polyester-cotton. Pure linen and linen and cotton mixes are expensive and crease too easily to be popular for general use.

Polyester-cotton This is the most widely-used bedding fabric, being easy to wash and requiring little or no ironing. It can be bought in sheeting widths of 230cm (90in), which is wide enough for one side of a king-size duvet cover. Often manufacturers produce co-ordinated ranges of plain and patterned polyester-cotton sheeting, making it easy to mix and match.

Pure cotton This is a more luxurious fabric than polyester-cotton, and feels crisp and cool in summer. However it is more expensive than polyester-cotton, and you may find you need to join fabric widths across each side of a double or king-size duvet cover.

Duvet covers

Basically duvet covers are just large bags, sewn all round with a fastening in one short edge. Use whichever fastening you prefer – press fasteners or velcro are easiest, but you could use buttons or zip bought off the roll if preferred.

Sheeting fabrics can be used across the full width of each side, but narrow fabrics should be joined in the centre, with cut edges at the side. If your preferred fabric is expensive, make the duvet reversible, with a cheaper fabric on the underside. However, when mixing fabrics, always make sure they have the same fibre content, or they may shrink at different rates in the wash.

Estimating fabric requirements

Make the cover the same size as the duvet, so that the duvet fills it out completely to look plump and warm. Measure up and add 10cm (4in) to the length and 3cm (1¼in) to the width for seam and hem allowances. You will need

▲ **Floral flair**
Two co-ordinating floral fabrics in pinks and greens on a cream, background turn the bedroom into a riot of colour. One of the fabrics has a border pattern which has been cleverly used at the top end of the cover to give the effect of a sheet turned down. The fabric is used again to make a deep, flat bed valance.

two pieces this size – one in each fabric if making it reversible. Buy extra to match patterns.

To help estimate the fabric requirements and the length of fastening required, here are the standard duvet sizes, and the sizes that the openings should be in covers:

Single 140 × 200cm (55 × 78in). Make the opening 98cm (38½in) long.
Double 200 × 200cm (79 × 79in). Make the opening 148cm (58in) long.
King-size 220 × 230cm (86 × 90in). Make the opening 158cm (62in).

MAKING A REVERSIBLE DUVET COVER

1 Cut out and hem Using the measurements given opposite, cut out two pieces of fabric the size of the duvet, adding 10cm (4in) to the length and 3cm (1¼in) to the width. This includes ease. On the bottom, short end of each piece, turn a double 2.5cm (1in) hem; pin and machine stitch.

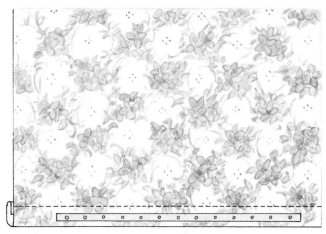

2 Prepare chosen fastening Cut press fastener tape or velcro for the opening – 100cm (39in) long for a single duvet cover, 150cm (59in) for a double and 160cm (63in) for a king-size. Separate the two parts of the fastening, and pin one part to the right side of each piece of fabric, over the hem.

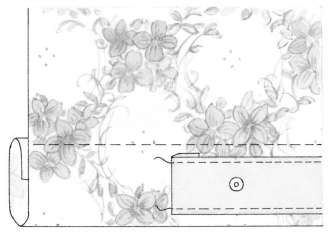

3 Stitch the fastening Place the two pieces together and check that the press fasteners correspond. Adjust if necessary. Turn under raw ends of press fastener tape and machine stitch down the long edges of each tape, using a zip foot. If using velcro, stitch along both long edges, without turning the ends under.

4 Finish the opening edge Place the pieces right sides together and join press fasteners or velcro. Tack from each side to 1cm (⅜in) past the tape, close to the hem edge. Stitch along the tacking, then at right angles across the hem and tape, as shown. Stitch twice for extra strength.

5 Stitch french seams With wrong sides together, stitch a 5mm (¼in) seam down both sides. Snip off corners. Turn wrong sides out, and stitch the seams again with a 1cm (⅜in) allowance to complete the french seams. Stitch remaining edge with a french seam in the same way. Turn cover right side out and press.

tip

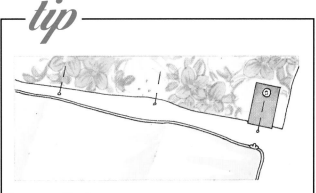

Prevent slipping
Prevent the duvet from slipping or from bunching at one end of the cover by using press fasteners. Cut a 6cm (2¼in) strip of ribbon, fold in half and stitch a press stud through both thicknesses near the folded end. Stitch the cover end of the ribbon to the corner of the cover. Sew the other half of the press stud to the corner of the duvet.

Pillowcases

New pillowcases give good results in the minimum of sewing time, and can be made to match either the sheet or the duvet cover. If you like to have two pillows, you can make the cover for the lower one to match the sheet, and the upper one to match the duvet.

Housewife pillowcases are the most straightforward to make and do not require a lot of fabric. Unlike duvet covers, there is no need for a complicated fastening – a flap inside the case is all you need to hold the pillow in place.

The pillowcase is cut in one piece, with one end folded over to form the flap which keeps the pillow in place, and the raw edges neatly enclosed in french seams.

As with all styles of pillowcase, a housewife pillowcase should fit the pillow loosely for a smooth effect. For this reason, when measuring up, add about 3cm (1¼in) to the length and width of the pillow for ease. Then add seam and hem allowances. A standard pillow is 75 x 50cm (29½ x 19¾in), so you will need a piece of fabric 174 x 56cm (68¾ x 22¼in) for each pillowcase.

▶ *Inspired details*
The question of how fancy to make an item is often determined by the fabric. Here, the pretty gathered frill on the top pillowcase perfectly complements the floral trellis design, while the more geometric combination of flowers and stripes, is better suited to the simple housewife style of pillowcase underneath.

SIMPLE HOUSEWIFE PILLOWCASE

1 Cut out and hem Cut a piece of fabric the same width as the pillow plus 6cm (2½in) by twice the length plus 24cm (9¾cm). This includes ease. Stitch a double 1cm (⅜in) hem at one short end. At the other end turn under 5mm (¼in) and then 3.5cm (1½in) and stitch.

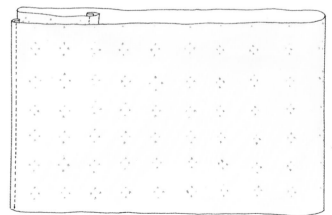

2 Form pocket flap At the end with the narrow hem, press 15cm (6in) to the wrong side to make the flap. Then fold the other end over so that it meets the fold of the flap and pin.

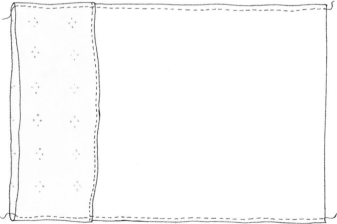

3 Stitch french seams Sew along long edges taking a 5mm (¼in) seam. Turn wrong sides out, press and stitch seams again taking 1cm (½in) seam allowance to complete the french seams. Turn right side out.

Frilled bedlinen

A frilled duvet cover and matching pillowcases are lovely additions to the bedroom, where their generous use of fabric adds a touch of luxury. The frills can be left plain and simple, or further embellished with ribbon, lace, binding or piping to add that extra personal detail.

On a pillow, the frill usually goes all the way round, although it can be placed only on the two short edges if preferred. On the duvet cover, however, it usually runs along the side and lower edges,

leaving the top edge free, where a frill might be irritating at night.

The frills can be either single or double, but if you want the duvet cover and pillowcases to be fully reversible, either bind the edges of the single frills or make double frills. Make the duvet cover from the same fabric on both sides, or with the frill in the same fabric as the front and another co-ordinating fabric on the back. For a really striking effect, make the frills from a pretty contrasting colour.

▲ Crowning glory
This pretty frilled duvet cover and pillowcases, which match the curtains and wallpaper, are the crowning glory of this lovely bedroom. The green and ivory colours in the fabric are picked out in the carpet, net curtains and bed valance to complete the effect.

Choosing the fabric

Sheeting fabric is 230cm (90in) wide and is usually made from cotton polyester which makes it easy to care for. Its extra width means that both the front and back pieces of a duvet cover can be cut in one piece, so you don't have to worry about pattern matching.

Furnishing fabric is usually 120-130cm (48-50in) wide and is available in a huge range of patterns and colours, with a variety of fibre contents. Choose a washable fabric made of cotton or mixed fibres and pre-wash it to prevent shrinking later.

The furnishing fabric will need to be pieced together on the front and back of double or king-size duvet covers to make up the required width. For professional results, use a full width of fabric in the centre of each piece, with a narrower, matched strip along each side.

Fabric requirements

The amounts given below are for frilled duvet covers made from **sheeting fabric** where the frills have a fullness of one and a half times the length of the seam. For fuller frills, add the depth of one extra frill piece.

(If using **furnishing fabric**, allow two lengths of fabric for both the front and back plus the depth of an extra pattern repeat for each piece to allow for matching. Add the depth of the required number of frill pieces. Since a double duvet with double frill requires 10.3m (11¼yd) furnishing fabric, consider making the back piece or frills from a much cheaper fabric.)

For a **single duvet cover with single frill** you will need 5m (5½yd) of 230cm (90in) sheeting fabric. For a single with **double frill** you will need 5.5cm (6yd) of sheeting fabric. However if the pattern on the fabric does not have a specific direction, you can place the main pieces sidweways enabling you to make the cover from less fabric – 4m (3½yd) with a **double frill** and 3.5m (3⅞yd) with a **single frill**.

for a **double duvet cover with single frill** you will need 5m (5½yd) of 230cm (90in) sheeting fabric. For a **double duvet cover with a double frill** you will need 5.5m (6yd).

For each **frilled pillowcase** with single or double frill you will need 1m (1yd) of 230cm (90in) sheeting fabric or 1.7m (1¾yd) of furnishing fabric.

Other materials

Matching sewing thread
Fastening tape – velcro, zip or press fastener type – for the duvet cover
Bias binding and other trimmings are optional

MAKING A DUVET COVER WITH DOUBLE FRILL

1 Cutting out Cut out two pieces of fabric the size of the duvet, adding 10cm (4in) to the length and 3cm (1¼in) to the width. Standard duvet measurements are given on page 216. For a finished frill 12cm (4¾in) wide, cut out fabric strips 27cm (10¾in) wide to make up a piece 1½-2 times the length of the edges to be frilled.

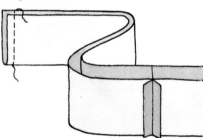

2 Making the frill Join the strips of fabric together with 1.5cm (⅝in) seams. Press seams flat, then fold the frill in half lengthways, right sides together, and stitch seams at the ends. Trim, turn right sides out and press again.

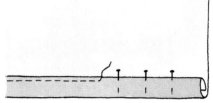

3 Preparing the duvet pieces Turn a double 2.5cm (1in) hem along the bottom short end of each main piece. Pin and machine stitch.

4 Equal parts Divide the frill into six equal lengths, and mark along the long raw edges. Measure the duvet edges to be frilled and divide and mark into 6 equal parts.

5 Gathering the frill Run two rows of gathering threads through both layers of fabric close to the long raw edges of the frill, stopping and starting at the marks.

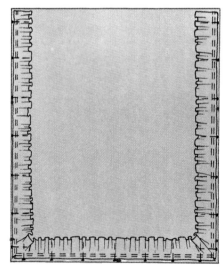

6 Attaching the frill With right sides together and raw edges level, pin the frill to the front, matching the marks. At the top of the front, the finished ends of the frill should be placed level with the seamline. At the bottom of the front, the frill should be placed with the seamline just above the edge of the hem. Pull up the gathers to fit, allowing extra fullness at corners for ease. Snip into corners and tack.

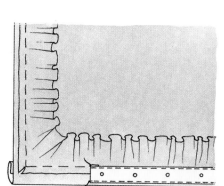

7 **Attaching the fastening** Along the hemmed edge of each main piece attach the fastening as in steps 2 and 3 for a reversible duvet cover (see page 217). On the piece with the frill, the tape covers the raw edge of the frill.

8 **Stitching side seams** Pin the two main pieces right sides together and edges matching. Stitch from the bottom edge, over the tape until you are just past the hem. Then stitch near the hem to the side seam, and along the side seam to the top, as shown. Repeat for the other side.

9 **Finishing off** Tuck the frill away from the top seam and pin to ensure it is not caught in the stitching. Pin and stitch the top seam. Overlock the raw edges together, or trim and zigzag to prevent fraying. Turn the cover out through the opening, spread out the frill and press.

▲ *Country charm*
The charming appeal of the rustic interior lies in its freshness and simplicity. Here, a subtly patterned, creamy fabric is used for the pillowcases which are frilled for feminine attraction.

MAKING FRILLED PILLOWCASES

1 **Cutting out** For the front and back of each pillowcase, cut two pieces of fabric 6cm (2½in) longer and wider than the size of the pillow. For the flap cut a piece 20cm (8in) by the width of the pillow plus 6cm (2½in). For a finished double frill 4cm (1½in) wide, cut strips 11cm (4½in) wide to make a total length 1½ times the measurement round the pillow.

2 **Preparing the frill** Join the frill pieces into one large loop, taking standard, 1.5cm (⅝in) seam allowances. Press seams open, then fold in half lengthways, wrong sides together and press again. Measure the length of the frill, divide and mark into four and run two rows of gathering threads close to the raw edges, stopping and starting at marks.

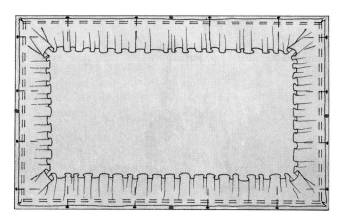

3 **Attaching the frill** Measure round the front piece and mark in four equal sections. Pull up the gathering threads on the frill and pin to the front, raw edges matching. Snip frill at corners and tack in place.

4 Hemming Stitch a double 1.5cm (⅝in) hem along one short edge of the back piece. Stitch a double 1cm (⅜in) hem along the lower edge of the flap.

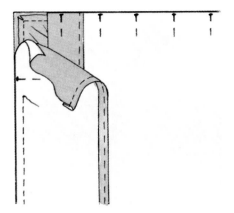

5 Stitching seams Put the back and front pieces together, right sides facing, with all edges matching except the hemmed edge of the back which will fall short. Place the flap right side down on top so that the long raw edge lines up with the protruding front edge. Pin, tack and stitch all round taking a 1.5cm (⅝in) seam allowance.

6 Finishing off Neaten the raw edges with overlock stitch or by trimming the seams and then stitching together with zigzag stitch. Turn the pillowcase right side out, folding the flap inside, and press.

SINGLE FRILLS

Duvet covers and pillowcases can be made with single frills, with the raw edge finished with a narrow hem or bound with bias binding. A contrast binding can be used to highlight one of the colours in the fabric, or to add zest to a plain fabric.

To make the frill, cut strips of fabric the finished width of the frill plus 1.5cm (⅝in) for seam allowances, and cut the main pieces as above. Join the srips with french seams, attach the binding to one long raw edge or turn a narrow double hem. Continue from step 3 onwards (for duvet cover or pillowcase).

BINDING THE EDGES

1 Making the binding Cut strips of fabric on the bias twice as wide as the finished width of the binding plus 1cm (½in). Join strips to make up the required length plus 1.5cm (⅝in). Press the strip in half lengthways. Press the raw edges 5mm (¼in) to the centre. Pressing can be done in one go with a tape maker, or you can use ready-made bias binding which is already folded.

▲ **Attractive ending**
Pillowcases trimmed with frills on the outside ends only, create an attractive and unusual effect.

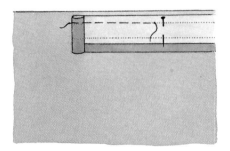

2 Pin and stitch Turn in 1.5cm (⅝in) at one end of the binding. Starting at this end, place one long raw edge of the bias binding to the raw edge of the fabric, right sides together. Pin and stitch, following the first fold in the binding.

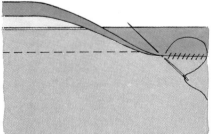

3 Finishing off Fold the binding over to the wrong side so that the centre fold in the binding is level with the edge of the fabric. Tuck the other edge of the binding under along the last fold and hand stitch to the fabric to complete.

Edged pillowcases

The Oxford style, or flanged pillow-case is perhaps the most versatile of all the pillowcase styles, and offers a wealth of opportunity for trimming ideas. Since the flange is ungathered, it shows off ribbon, braid and embroidery to good effect, and since it isn't the part you sleep on, it can be embellished with embossed, or raised trimmings without any discomfort.

An Oxford pillowcase is quite straightforward to make, but it does require careful cutting and a certain amount of hand stitching. If you don't have the time or inclination to make one, you could simply buy a ready-made pillowcase and use the trimming ideas given here to transform it into something to be treasured.

▲ Oxford blue
Oxford pillowcases have a simple charm and elegance which is very appealing. Made from crisp blue and white fabrics such as these, they need very little extra adornment to grace the bed with style.

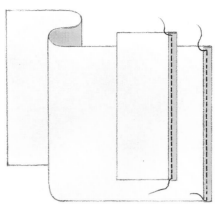

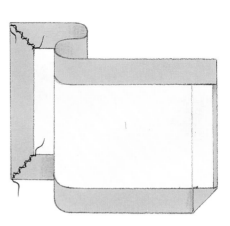

OXFORD PILLOWCASE

1 Cutting out Each 75 × 50cm (29½ × 19¾in) pillowcase requires 80cm (⅞yd) of 230cm (90in) wide sheeting fabric, or 130cm (1½yd) of 120cm (48in) cotton or linen. For the front, cut out a piece of fabric 98cm (38½in) wide and 72cm (28½in) long. For the back, cut a piece 81cm (32in) wide and 52cm (21in) long; and for the flap, cut a piece 20cm (8in) wide and 52cm (21in) long.

2 Stitching the hems On one long edge of the flap, turn 1cm (½in) and then another 1cm (½in) to the wrong side to make a double hem; pin and stitch. Repeat to stitch a double hem along one short edge of the back.

3 Making the flange On the front piece, turn 5mm (¼in) and then 5cm (2in) to the wrong side all the way round. At each corner, fold the fabric under at an angle to make a mitre and trim the excess fabric to reduce bulk; press. Pin the flange, and then carefully slipstitch the mitred corners in place, making sure stitches don't go through to the right side where they will show.

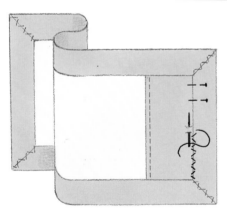

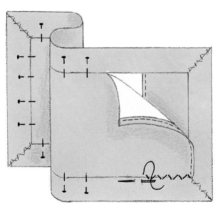

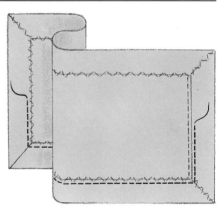

4 Attaching the flap With wrong sides facing, slip the three raw edges of the flap 1cm (½in) under the flange at one end. Pin and then slipstitch together where the flange meets the long edge of the flap.

5 Attaching the back With wrong sides facing, place the back piece on the front so that the hem just overlaps the flange at the flap end. Slip the three raw edges of the back piece under the flange; pin and slipstitch together.

6 Finishing off Working from the back of the pillowcase, machine stitch all round, 3mm (⅛in) from the inside edge of the flange; make sure you don't catch the back opening as you stitch. For added decoration, do this in a close zigzag stitch, using a thread in a toning colour; press to finish.

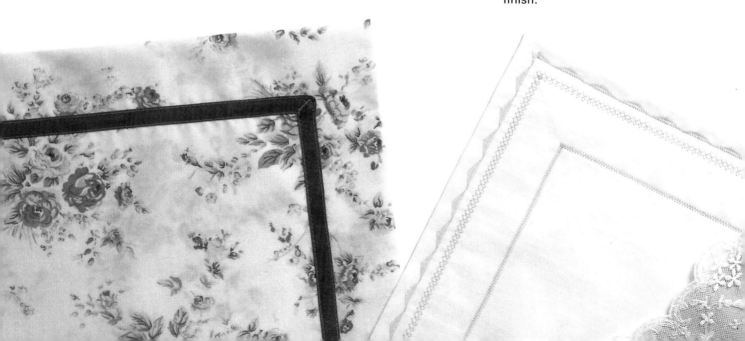

Simple decorative ideas

Whether you have made an Oxford pillowcase yourself or bought one ready-made, a simple trimming will add that personal touch. A row of braid or machine embroidery, or a shaped edge neatened with zigzag stitch, is all you need to transform the pillowcase. For a really pretty finish, nothing is nicer than a lace and ribbon trim, and for more experienced home sewers, a quilted or scalloped flange will be the crowning glory of the pillowcase.

Braids and piping Dressmaking trimmings are usually soft enough to trim pillowcases. Ric-rac braid and double piping work particularly well, and will add a flamboyant touch to bed-linen.

Stitch coloured ric-rac near the outer edge of the flange or in the middle. Double piping, or flexible Russian braid can be pinned in a wavy line or in loops and swirls and then stitched in place.

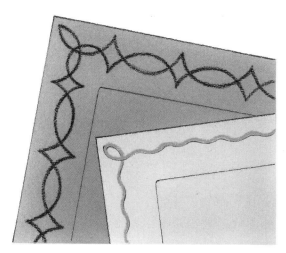

Lace edge Select lace with one scalloped or shaped edge and stitch to the flange on the front of the pillowcase with the shaped edge at the outer edge of the flange. At the corners, fold the lace under in line with the mitre on the flange; stitch and then trim off the excess fabric. Pin satin ribbon over the straight edge of the lace, mitring it at the corners and stitch along both long edges.

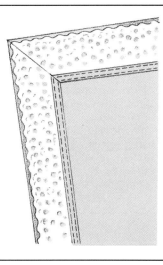

Machine embroidery If your sewing machine does embroidery stitches, pick out a favourite pattern and stitch on the front, close to the outer edge of the flange. If you like, stitch further rows towards the middle.

If your machine only does straight or zigzag stitch, sew rows of close zigzag in different colours for a ribboned effect, or stitch wavy lines in running stitch all round.

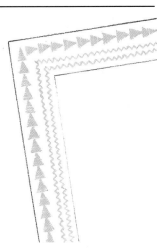

Zigzag edge Shape the edge of the flange by drawing zigzags or scallops with tailor's chalk, and then stitch along the line with a close zigzag stitch. Use a cardboard tube, eggcup or compass to get neat curved lines for the scallops, and for zigzags, use a ruler to measure and mark off even points. Carefully trim the excess fabric close to the stitching. On a plain pillowcase, use the same colour for the stitching round the inner edge of the flange for a really smart finish.

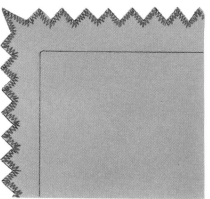

tip

Protective backing
When giving a pillowcase a zigzag edge or doing machine embroidery, tear-away backing will make things easier by providing reinforcement, and preventing stitch distortion. Simply pin the tear-away backing behind the fabric and stitch; then tear off the excess backing when stitching is complete.

QUILTED FLANGE

For a luxurious and unusual effect, add lightweight wadding to the flange, as you make it, slipping it in place after you have stitched the mitred corners.

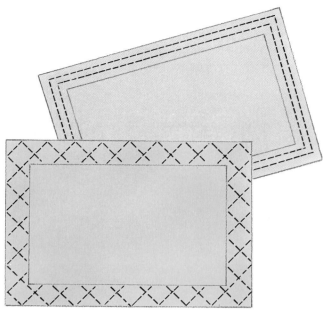

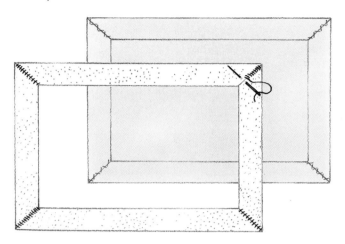

1 Adding wadding Follow steps 1-3 for a flanged pillowcase. Cut strips of wadding 5cm (2in) wide (the width of the finished flange), then place on top of the flange and cut the ends on the diagonal to match the mitres. Butt the two edges together at each corner and stitch together by hand, then slip the frame of wadding into the flange and tuck the 5mm (¼in) turning round it.

2 Quilting the flange Finish making the pillowcase following steps 4-6 for a flanged pillowcase, pinning the flange securely as you sew to hold the wadding in position. Quilt the finished flange in a matching thread, using a quilting bar on the machine for even rows. Stitch in diamond patterns or channels; or if you are more experienced, opt for one of the more complex quilting patterns.

SCALLOPED FLANGE

1 Cutting and stitching Cut out and make up the pillowcase, following steps 1-3 for a flanged pillowcase, but stitching the mitres with very small stitches, and taking particular care not to go through to the front of the pillowcase.

2 Stitching the scallops Carefully turn the flange wrong side out and press. Mark small scallops all the way round the edge, taking care to get a full scallop at each corner, and rounding off the corners if necessary for a good fit. Use a cardboard tube or compass to make even scallops. Pin the flange together, then stitch along the scalloped line taking small stitches.

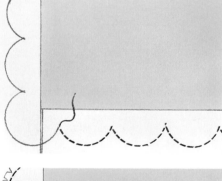

3 Finishing off Trim 1cm (⅜in) beyond the stitching and make snips to, but not through the stitching every 2cm (¾in) for ease. Turn through to the right side and finish making the pillowcase following steps 4-6 for the flanged pillowcase.

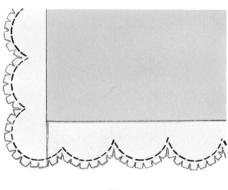

Quilted bedspreads

Quilting gives a bedspread body and shape, as well as providing extra warmth on chilly nights. Even the most basic quilted design, like the simple diamond pattern shown here, will show off your chosen fabric to the full.

When planning a quilt, take the colour and pattern of the fabric into account and choose a quilting pattern and sewing thread accordingly. If the fabric is covered with evenly spaced motifs, emphasize them by centring each one in its own quilted square or diamond. Stripes and checks can be quilted along or in-between their lines, or even at an angle to the main pattern. Plain glazed cottons look stunning quilted with thread in a darker shade, particularly if an intricate design is used, but for all-over patterns keep to a simple quilting design in a toning thread to avoid making the quilt too busy.

▲ Quilted comfort
The simplicity of the diamond quilting design on this bedspread is perfectly suited to the main fabric, giving it fullness and a luxuriously padded look, without detracting from the delicate floral pattern as a more elaborate design would.

Fabrics

Although ready-quilted fabric is available, the choice of fabric and the style of the quilting is limited. Quilting the fabric yourself gives you a far broader choice, allowing you not only to match the bedspread perfectly to other fabrics and colours in the bedroom, but also to experiment with the size and style of the quilted design to achieve different effects.

Firm, closely woven furnishing cottons are best for quilting large items such as bedspreads, as they provide the firm base needed for the stitching. Avoid sheer and loosely woven fabrics, which tend to become distorted when stitched, and through which the wadding underneath is often visible. The choice of fabric colour and pattern is virtually limitless, but do make sure that your chosen fabric is easy to launder, fairly crease-resistant and also reasonably hardwearing.

Joining fabric widths

If making a double, a king-size or even a floor-length single throw-over bedspread, it is unlikely that you will be able to buy fabric wide enough to make these from a single piece; to gain the required width you will need to seam together two or more widths of fabric. Rather than joining these with an unsightly central seam, use a full width of fabric for the centre of the bedspread, with two narrower widths (generally one full width of fabric cut in half lengthways) stitched to each side. Full details on joining fabric widths, and matching the pattern across the seam, are given in *Making a throwover quilted bedspread*.

Materials

Firm furnishing fabric the chosen size of the bedspread, plus a 1.5cm (⅝in) seam allowance all round (see the section on joining fabric widths)
Lining fabric the same size as the main fabric
Lightweight wadding (batting) the chosen size of the bedspread (see step 7 of *Making a throwover quilted bedspread*)
Covered piping cord (optional) to fit around the edges of the bedspread, plus 10-15cm (4-6in) for ease (see step 1 of *Trimming with piping*)
Sewing thread for quilting
Calculator, squared paper and **pencil** to draw up a small-scale plan of the quilt
Tailor's chalk, long ruler and **set square** to mark the quilting pattern on to the fabric
Tape measure

MAKING A THROWOVER QUILTED BEDSPREAD

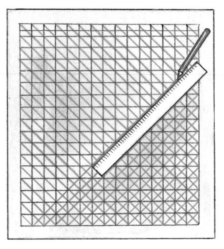

1 Measuring up Always measure up on a made-up bed as the cover will lie over all the bedlinen. First decide how far over the bed edges you want the cover to fall – midway down the side of the bed to reveal a pretty valance, or right to the floor to obscure stored objects or an ugly bed base and legs.

For the width, measure from the chosen depth on one side of the bed over to the same point on the opposite side of the bed. For the length, measure from just behind the pillow at the top of the bed down to the bottom end, taking the tape measure over the edge of the bed to the chosen depth.

Since quilting tends to reduce the overall size of the fabric add 10cm (4in) to both length and width measurements to compensate for this. Also, if you like to tuck the bed cover under the pillows to give a neat appearance, add a further 30cm (12in) to the length measurement.

2 Planning the pattern Decide roughly what size you would like the squares on your quilt to be – as a rough guide, they should be 12-20cm (4¾-8in). To calculate the exact square size needed to fit evenly into your bedspread, divide the width measurement by your desired square size to give the number of squares that will fit the measurement; round up the answer; then divide the measurement by the rounded-up number to give the exact square size.

For example: a bedspread width of 190cm (75in), divided by a square size of 15cm (6in), gives you 12.6 squares, or 13 whole squares when rounded up; divide 190cm (75in) by 13 to give you the exact square size of 14.6cm (5¾in).

As the bedspread is rectangular, you will almost always be left with incomplete squares on the length of the bedspread (if quilting on the diagonal, half-diamonds at the edges are inevitable); plan your bedspread so that incomplete squares lie along

the top edge, where they can be hidden behind the pillows. Draw up a plan of the quilt on squared paper.

3 Cutting out If your fabric is wide enough to make the bedspread from a single piece, simply cut out a rectangle to the required size, adding a 1.5cm (⅝in) seam allowance all round. If you need to join two widths of fabric, cut one piece from the main fabric to the required length, plus a 3cm (1¼in) seam allowance at both ends, and a slightly longer piece to allow for pattern matching.

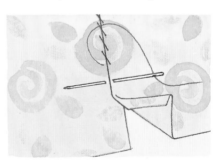

4 Joining widths Cut the longer length of fabric in half lengthways. Take one half-width and fold under 1.5cm (⅝in) to the wrong side along the selvedge; with right sides face up, position the folded edge of the half-width over one selvedge of the main fabric piece, overlapping the two by at least 1.5cm (⅝in) and matching the pattern if necessary. Slip-tack together: bring the needle up through the three layers of fabric on one side of the join, and out at the fold; make tiny stitches across the join through the single layer of fabric and the fold. Trim side pieces to same length as the main piece.

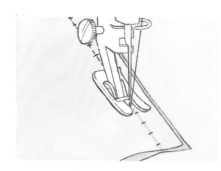

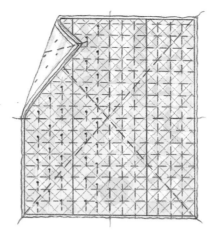

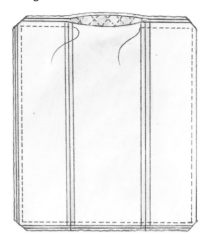

5 Stitching widths together Turn the side piece over to lie wrong side up, unfold the seam allowance and stitch through the centre of stitches formed along the folded edge. Remove tacking stitches. Attach second half-width to other side of panel. Snip into selvedges and press open. Trim equal amounts from sides to make quilt required width, plus a 1.5cm (⅝in) seam allowance on each side.

6 Marking the pattern Lay the top fabric out flat, with right side up. Use tailor's chalk and a long ruler to mark out the quilting design on the fabric, using your mini-plan as a guide. Begin by marking out the longest diagonals, then mark up all the shorter diagonals, making sure they are perfectly parallel and at an equal distance apart. Use a set square to ensure that all the angles of the diamonds are perfect right angles. If you can use a quilting bar confidently, do not chalk in every line, but only the main diagonals and a few others as reference points.

7 Joining widths of wadding To make up a piece of wadding the same size as the bedspread, you will probably need to join widths together. Line up the wadding pieces, with side edges butting, and stitch together with a wide herringbone stitch.

8 Seaming the wadding Lay the wadding out flat and centre the main fabric over it, right side up. Starting at the centre of the bedspread, pin and tack out to the corners and to the middle of each side edge. Then pin and tack a series of parallel lines 20cm (8in) apart, running across the quilt from one side to the other, and down it from top to bottom; you will find that the wadding spreads out a little as you tack. Finally, pin and tack around the outer edges of the quilt.

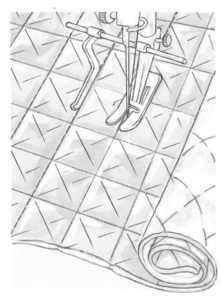

9 Quilting the fabric Experiment on spare pieces of fabric and wadding to find a suitable stitch size – you will need to use a size slightly larger than average. With the fabric face up, begin the quilting by straight-stitching along one of the two longest diagonals, following the chalked line (see machine-quilting tips). Then swing the quilt round and straight-stitch along the other longest diagonal.

Following the chalked pattern and, if you have one, using a quilting bar set to the desired distance, stitch along all the diagonals going in one direction, before swinging the quilt round and stitching along those running in the opposite direction.

If you are quilting a particularly large bedspread, work the longer diagonals from the centre of the quilt out to the edges. Remove all the tacking stitches.

10 Attaching the lining Make up the lining to the same size as the bedspread, including a 1.5cm (⅝in) seam allowance all round, joining widths if necessary.

Lay out the quilted fabric, fabric side face up, and place the lining over it, matching the edges and with right sides together. Pin, tack and stitch round the edges, taking a 1.5cm (⅝in) seam allowance and leaving a 45cm (18in) opening in the middle of one edge.

Trim the corners and seams, cutting off the wadding close to the stitching, and turn the bedspread through to the right side. Turn in the opening edges and slip-stitch them together.

tip

Machine-quilting tips
Supporting the fabric When machine-quilting a large item like a bedspread, make sure the bulk of the quilt is supported as you stitch. If it is allowed to hang free over the edge of the table, it will pull during stitching and result in uneven stitch lengths; either work on a very large table or drape the bedspread over a second table or chair.
Working the centre To work the centre of the bedspread, keep the sides rolled up, with the largest section of quilt to the left of the machine foot, and the smaller section tightly rolled to fit under the arm of the sewing machine. If the bedspread is very large, work it from the centre out to the edges, rather than from one side to the other.

TRIMMING WITH PIPING

Trimming the bedspread with fabric-covered piping gives you the opportunity to link it to other fabrics and colours in the bedroom, as well as giving the outline of the quilt added definition and a professional finish.

1 Making the piping Make up the quilt as usual, following steps 1-9. Measure right the way round the outer edge of the quilt to assess how much piping is needed. Follow the instructions for making fabric-covered piping (see page 188) to make-up the required length, plus 10-15cm (4-6in) for ease; use fairly thick piping cord, with a toning or contrast fabric for the bias strips.

▼ *Topping idea*
Added length allows this quilted cover to tuck beneath the pillows.

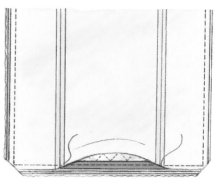

2 Attaching the piping Lay out the quilt, with fabric side face up. Pin and tack the covered piping around the edges of the bedspread, with the cord lying innermost and with the stitching line along the piping 1.5cm (⅝in) from the outer edge of the bedspread; to help the piping fabric lie flat, snip into it at the corners, up to the stitching line.

3 Finishing the quilt Make up the lining as usual and place it over the bedspread, matching the edges and with right sides together. Pin, tack and stitch round the bedspread edges through all layers, taking a 1.5cm (⅝in) seam allowance, and leaving a 45cm (18in) opening in the middle of one edge. At the opening, stitch through all layers except the lining. Remove tacking stitches, trim corners and seams, and turn the bedspread through to the right side. Turn in the open edges and slip-stitch the lining to the main fabric.

Pattern quilting

Quilting has always been valued as much for its decorative appeal as for its more practical qualities of warmth and durability. It gives a fabric body and volume, and can also enhance the design if used to outline single motifs or the overall pattern. Emphasize the images on a floral fabric by quilting around flowers and leaves, or stitch around the shapes and splashes of colour in an abstract design to add impact.

Although quilting around motifs is less straightforward than quilting a basic trellis design, it can still easily be done by machine, provided the motifs are not too small and intricate. If your fabric is patterned with large and small motifs, only quilt the former to make up the dominant part of the design. If you wish, the more delicate motifs can be quilted afterwards, either by hand or machine.

With a strong or elaborate pattern, use a thread that blends in with the background; on more subtle designs, accent the motif outlines with a contrasting colour. For items like a bedspread, use a firm, closely woven furnishing cotton, which gives a firm base for the quilting. Make sure that your chosen fabric is easy to clean and reasonably hardwearing.

▼ *Freestyle quilting*
Stitching around the motifs on a fabric brings its design to life, giving it body and movement. Follow the outlines of each motif, or deviate from them slightly to create complementary patterns.

▲ *Textured flowers* *The leaf and floral motifs on these bedspreads have been carefully quilted, giving the fabric design a textured, three-dimensional effect.*

Materials

Firm furnishing cotton – see steps 1 and 2 for quantity
Lining fabric the same size as the main fabric
Backing fabric for quilting, the same size as the main fabric
Lightweight 2oz wadding the same size as the main fabric
Sewing thread for quilting
Tape measure
Scissors

QUILTED MOTIF BEDSPREAD

1 Measuring up Make sure the bed is fully made up before you begin to measure it. Decide how far over the edge of the bed you would like the cover to fall – midway down the base or right to the floor. For the length, measure from just behind the pillows down to the bottom of the bed, taking the tape measure over to the required depth. For the width, measure from the required depth on one side of the bed over to the same point on the opposite side.

2 Cutting out When you have established the finished size of bedspread, cut out the fabric to the correct size, adding a further 6cm (2½in) all round for seams and shrinkage during quilting; join fabric widths where necessary, making sure you match the pattern across the seams. If you wish to tuck the bedspread under the front of the pillows for a neater appearance, add a further 30cm (12in) to the length. Cut out and make up the lining fabric and the wadding to the same size. (For full details on joining fabric and wadding widths, see pages 228–229.)

5 Stitching around the motif Carefully stitch around the outline of your chosen motif, trying to maintain a steady rhythm and speed – this will be easier if you plan your stitching sequence in advance. When stitching around sharp curves and points, such as leaf tips, make sure you stitch right to the edge of the motif, and pivot the needle to avoid distorting the fabric.

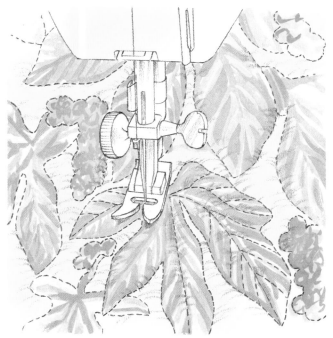

6 Emphasizing the design To add further interest and emphasis to the motifs, quilt in any details that immediately catch your eye, such as the edges of the petals within a rose motif, or the veins on a leaf. As well as adding a touch of realism, this will give the bedspread a wonderfully textured appearance. For natural motifs, like flowers, use a matching thread to fill in detail, so that the eye is drawn to the enhanced design rather than the colour of the thread.

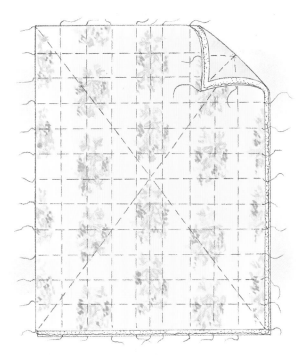

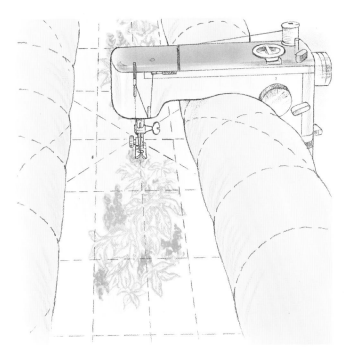

3 Tacking the wadding to the fabric Sandwich the wadding between the backing fabric and the main fabric, with the main fabric right side up. Starting at the centre of the bedspread, pin and tack through all layers, working out to each corner, and then to the middle of each side edge. Then pin and tack a series of lines across and down the quilt, spaced about 20cm (8in) apart, to form a grid.

4 Getting started Before you begin, practise quilting around motifs on a spare piece of fabric and wadding, until you find the correct stitch length and tension. When you are satisfied, it's best to start with a fairly large motif at the centre of the bedspread. Tightly roll up the sides of the quilt and slip one roll under the arm of the sewing machine – this will make it easier for you to manipulate the quilt while working the centre. If possible work on a large table.

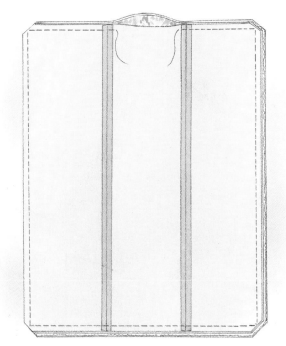

7 Attaching the lining Quilt the whole bedspread, working from the centre out to the edges. Then lay out the quilted bedspread with the right side up, and centre the lining over it, with right sides together. Pin and stitch round the edges, taking a 1.5cm (⅝in) seam allowance and leaving a 45cm (18in) opening in the middle of one edge. Trim the corners and seam allowances, then turn through to the right side. Turn in the opening edges and slipstitch together. (For details on piping the bedspread, see page 230.)

▼ *Motif detail The dominant motifs are quilted in a thread whose colour matches the background exactly. The smaller motifs are left unquilted to avoid the design becoming too fussy.*

Quilted appliqué

By combining your quilting skills with basic appliqué, you can create stylish fabric borders for a set of pillowcases. For fully co-ordinated bedlinen, use motifs from leftover bedspread fabric, or from a similar design. Quilting the motifs before you appliqué them to the pillowcases gives them a soft, contoured look, perfectly suited to plump pillows.

Make up a design from a series of motifs scattered down the side of the pillow or, for a more subtle effect, use a single motif in a corner. On a small project like a pillowcase, hand-quilting is always an option, so feel free to choose dainty, intricate motifs. For comfort's sake, always stitch motifs down the side of the pillowcase.

MOTIF PILLOWCASES

1 Cutting out the motifs Plan a rough design and decide which motifs you want to use. Roughly cut out each motif from the main fabric, leaving a 5cm (2in) border all round. For each motif, cut out a piece of wadding and one of backing fabric to the same size.

2 Stitching the motifs Sandwich the wadding between the backing fabric and the wrong side of the motif, and pin and tack together around edges. Straight stitch round the motif, carefully following its outline and stitching through all layers. Stitch in any detail within the motif as well, to add interest and texture. Trim the fabric and wadding to just outside the stitching line.

3 Attaching the motifs Pin each motif separately in position on the pillowcase, arranging the design to achieve the best effect. If the pillowcases are intended to match the bedspread, place the motifs in a similar layout as the original pattern. Use a machine or handworked satin stitch to stitch the motifs in place, working round the outside of each one and covering the raw fabric edges.

tip

Relief effect
To create different areas of relief on a motif, add layers of wadding or cut sections away; for example, give the petals of flowers a fuller effect by cutting wadding away at their base.

▼▶ *Sweet dreams*
Plain pillowcases are greatly enhanced by the addition of quilted motifs. If short of time, simply stitch a strip of decorative fabric, down the side of the pillowcase to create an equally stylish effect.

Gathered bed valance

A gently gathered valance is an attractive addition to the bed, softening its hard lines and giving it a touch of luxury. It will conceal a bed base which no longer co-ordinates with the room's colour scheme and will cover the gap between the bed base and the floor – ideal if you use the space under the bed for storage.

The valance is made from two main pieces – the base and frill – with the frill attached to the base piece so that it will run along both sides and the foot of the bed. Since only the frill is seen when the valance is in place, the base piece can be made from a cheaper piece of fabric, or even an old sheet. For even more economical results, the frill can be attached to a strip of fabric which tucks under the mattress.

By carefully choosing the fabric for the valance, you can make it into a real feature of the bed. Make it in a plain or patterned fabric, matching the main

▲ Mix and match
Two fabrics used on the bed drapes and pillowcases have been cleverly joined in the valance so that the stripe alternates with the main motif.

colour to the colour of the pillowcases or to one of the colours in the duvet cover. If the duvet cover is piped, then match the main colour in the valance to the piping.

▶ *Old world charm* A lovely double bed with iron bedsteads has been given a long, very full valance for an old-fashioned effect which is in keeping with the style of the bed.

Measuring up

For the base piece measure the length and width of the bed base, and add 4.5cm (1¾in) to the length and 3cm (1¼in) to the width for hem and seam allowances. For the frill measure from the top of the bed base to the floor, and add 6.5cm (2⅝in). Cut and join strips this wide to make up a piece one and a half to twice the length of two sides and the foot of the bed.

Here are the average bed base sizes:
Single 90 x 190cm (3 x 6ft 3in)
Double 140 x 190cm (4ft 6in x 6ft 3in)
Queen-size 150 x 200cm (5ft x 6ft 6in)
King-size 180 x 200cm (6ft x 6ft 6in)
Valance drop 30-35cm (12-14in)

MAKING A GATHERED VALANCE

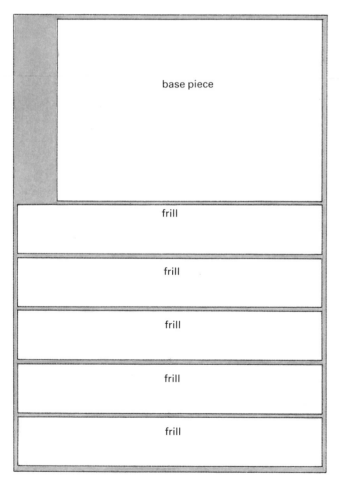

1 Cutting out For a single bed you will need a base piece plus 4 frill pieces cut across the width of the sheeting fabric. For a double, queen or king-size bed you will need a base piece plus 4-5 frill pieces cut across the width of the fabric, depending on the fullness of the frill required.

2 Preparing the base piece At one short end (the end which will go at the head of the bed) turn a double 1.5cm (⅝in) hem. Pin and stitch.

3 Preparing the frill Join the frill pieces together with french seams to make one long strip. (See *Window Treatments*, page 173.) Pin and stitch a double 1.5cm (⅝in) hem at each end.

4 Sectioning the fabric Measure the length of the frill piece and divide into six to eight equal sections. Measure the sides and lower end of the base piece, and divide the total length into the same number of equal sections. Mark off the sections on the wrong side of the base piece and at the top edge of the frill.

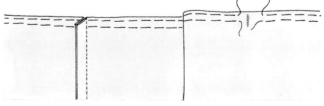

5 Preparing the frill Turn a double 2.5cm (1in) hem along the unmarked edge of the frill. Run two rows of gathering stitches close to the other edge, either side of the 1.5cm (⅝in) seamline. Stop and start the stitching at the chalk marks.

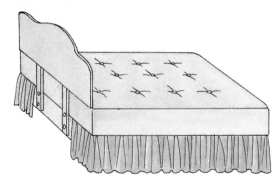

▲ *Patterned valance* Plain white bedding is crisp, clean and fresh looking, but it may sometimes look rather cold. Brighten up the effect by using a patterned fabric for the valance.

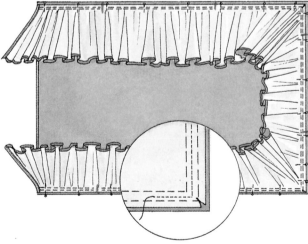

6 **Pin and stitch** Pin the frill to the base piece at marks so marks match, with right sides facing and raw edges together. Draw up the gathering stitches to fit and arrange gathers evenly, allowing extra fabric at the corners. Snip into seam allowance of frill at corners, then tack and stitch between the rows of gathering stitches. Trim seam allowances and zigzag together.

tip

Neat finish

To hide the edge of the frill at the head of the bed, and to give the valance a neater, more tailored appearance, position the frill so that it wraps round to the head end of the base piece by 5cm (2in) on each side. If the bed has a headboard, the frill should stop just at the outside edge of each of the headboard supports.

▶ *Pretty cover-up*
A bed valance gives an attractive finish to even the most basic bed base. It covers the sides and legs of the base and neatly hides away any items stored underneath.

AN ECONOMICAL VALANCE

A clever and inexpensive way of making a bed valance is to attach the frill to a flap of fabric which is then slipped between the bed base and mattress. The flap is made in three pieces, one for each side and one for the base. The pieces are mitred at the corners to form a three sided frame which sits on the base.

1 Cutting out the frill Cut out strips of fabric for the frill the depth of the frill plus 6.5cm (2⅝in). You will need enough strips to make up a piece one and a half to twice the length of both sides and the foot of the bed.

2 Cutting out the flap Cut out two pieces of fabric for the sides 30cm (12in) wide by the length of the bed plus 4.5cm (1¾in). Cut a third piece for the end 30cm (12in) wide by the width of the bed plus 3cm (1¼in) for seam allowances.

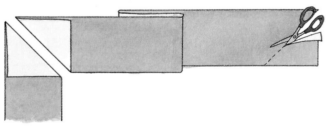

3 Cutting the mitres Take the end piece and fold each short edge over so that it is level with one long edge. Cut along the fold. Fold and cut one short edge of each of the other two pieces so that they will fit at right angles to the end piece.

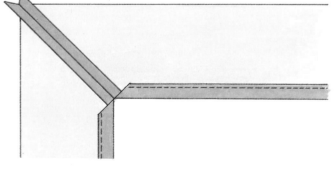

5 Hemming the flap On the inside edge of the flap, turn under 5mm (¼in), then 1cm (⅜in), allowing the fabric to part naturally at the mitres, and stitch. At the two short ends turn under a double 1.5cm (⅝in) hem; pin and stitch.

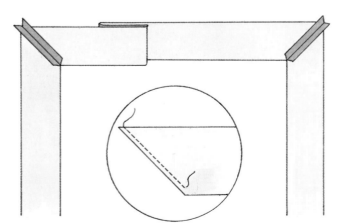

4 Stitching the mitres Place the mitred end of one side piece to a mitre on the end piece, right sides together. Pin and stitch, stopping the stitching 1.5cm (⅝in) from the inner edge.

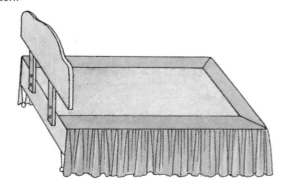

6 Making up the valance Prepare the frill and stitch to the flap as in steps 4-6 above. Press and then fit on the bed between the base and the mattress.

A simple valanced bedspread

The tailored lines of a fully fitted bedspread can be slightly too formal for some bedrooms, so if you prefer a cosier, softer look, opt for the soft frills of a valanced bedspread.

Different effects can be achieved by varying the fullness of the valance skirt, and also its length. To show off a pretty bed valance and create a double layer of frills, let the skirt hang just below the mattress, or make it floor length to hide an ugly bedstead.

Choose a fabric to complement your bedroom's colour scheme and soft furnishings. To add interest and style, use two different though toning fabrics for the skirt and top panel. This is particularly effective if you use two similar fabrics from the same range, keeping to the same colours but with slightly different patterns. For a summery bedspread, use broderie anglaise for the skirt, and place a pastel pink or blue bed valance behind it.

▲ **A perfect choice**
Fabrics with a subtle all-over pattern are ideal for valanced bedspreads, and complement their gently fitted lines far more than strong, symmetrical designs. For extra volume and added warmth, quilt the top panel of the bedspread in a simple square or diamond pattern.

Estimating fabric requirements

Details on measuring up the bedspread, together with seam and hem allowances, are given in steps 1 and 2. If making a double or king-size bedspread, you will probably need to join two or more widths of fabric together to make the top panel, as most furnishing fabrics are only available in widths of 120-130cm (48-50in); buy a little extra for pattern matching across the seams.

The valance strips are cut across the width of the fabric and then joined together, so calculate how many strips you need by dividing the width of your valance by the fabric width; allow extra for seam allowances where two strips are joined, and for pattern matching.

Materials

Fabric for bedspread; use a different fabric for the skirt, if preferred
Covered piping the width of the bed and twice its length, plus a little extra for ease, to make up the piping (see page 188).
Saucer or other round object for shaping corners
Matching sewing thread and **tape measure**

SIMPLE BEDSPREAD

1 Measuring up Make up the bed with all the bedlinen, including the pillows. For the finished size of the top panel, measure the length of the bed from just behind the pillows, and its width; add a further 30cm

(12in) to the length if you wish to tuck the bedspread under the front of the pillows for a neater appearance. For the height of the valance skirt, measure from the top of the bed to either just below the mattress or right to the floor, depending on preference. The width of the skirt is twice the bed length, plus its width, multiplied by 1½, 2 or 2½, depending on how full you would like the valance to be.

2 Cutting out For the top panel, cut out a rectangle of fabric to the correct size, adding 4.5cm (1¾in) to the length and 3cm (1¼in) to the width, for seam and top hem allowances; if joining two fabric widths, cut one to the required length, plus 4.5cm (1¾in), and one slightly longer for pattern matching if required. For the skirt, cut out as many strips as are needed to make up the required width; add 4.5cm (1¾in) to the skirt height for a top seam and hem allowance, and 1.5cm (⅝in) to both ends of each strip for seam and side hem allowances. Add extra for pattern matching as necessary.

6 Sectioning the fabric Measure the length of the valance strip and divide it into eight equal sections – this will make gathering the strip easier. Then measure the sides and lower end of the top panel, and again divide the total length into eight equal sections. Use tailor's chalk to mark off the sections around the edges of the panel and along the top edge of the valance skirt, on the wrong side.

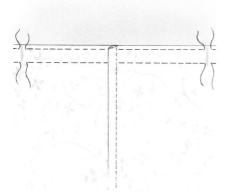

7 Preparing the frill Run two parallel lines of gathering stitches, 2cm (¾in) apart, along the top edge of the skirt, stopping and starting the stitches at each chalk mark. The top thread should lie 6mm (¼in) in from the edge.

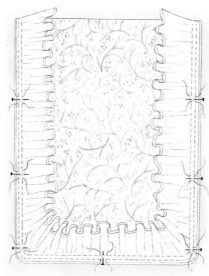

8 Pinning and gathering With right sides facing and raw edges together, match up the chalk marks on the top panel and skirt, and pin together over each mark. Working on one section at a time, pull the gathering threads to draw up the skirt fabric to fit the top panel. Check that the folds are evenly spread over each section, and pin in place. Secure the threads by winding them around pins.

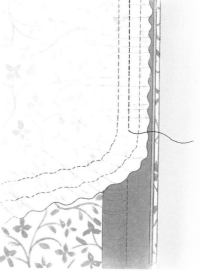

9 Stitching together Tack and stitch the valance skirt to the main panel, stitching between the two rows of gathering stitches, 1.5cm (⅝in) in from the edges of the fabric, and close to the piping cord. Snip into the valance seam allowance at the corners for ease. Trim the seam allowances and bind or zigzag together to neaten all the raw edges.

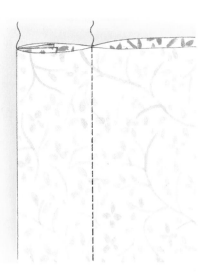

3 **Preparing the top panel** If necessary, join the fabric widths together to make the top panel, making sure you match any pattern across the seams. Using a round object, such as a saucer, as your guide, mark and then trim the two lower corners of the top panel to form a gentle curve – this will give the bedspread a softer finish. (For details on joining widths together, see pages 228–229.)

4 **Adding piping** With the panel right side up and with edges matching, lay the covered piping over the side and bottom edges of the panel, with the stitching on the piping 1.5cm (⅝in) in from the edge. Pin and tack in place, snipping into the piping at the rounded corners for ease. Stitch a double 1.5cm (⅝in) hem along the top edge of the panel, turning under the ends of the piping as you go, for a neat finish.

5 **Joining the valance sections** Join the ends of the skirt sections, enclosing the raw edges with French seams; take 5mm (¼in), then 1cm (⅜in) for the seams, matching any pattern. Pin then stitch a double 1.5cm (⅝in) hem at each end of the strip, and along its bottom edge.

▼ *Keep in trim*
Add a splash of colour to a plain bedspread with a piping trim.

Attaching side gussets

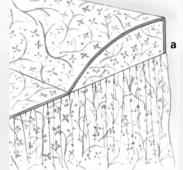

For a perfectly tailored fit over pillows, insert two triangular gussets, one at each side of the bedhead. Make a paper pattern by measuring the height and width of the pillows and drawing these on paper, then joining the two with a soft curve; cut out the pattern and the fabric, adding seam and hem allowances.

Starting at **a**, stitch the straight back edge of the gusset and then the curved edge to the top panel, snipping into the seam allowance to accomodate the curve. Attach skirt to panel as usual.

DAYTIME IDEAS

Pillows can be put in attractive daytime covers and placed on top of the bedspread for a comfy, welcoming look. This will also allow the bedspread to lie perfectly flat for a neat finish at the head of the bed and is a wonderful way to add style to an ordinary bedhead. Make the covers in the same fabric as the bedspread, or in one or more matching fabrics. They can be as simple or extravagant as you wish, so make the most of colourful fabrics and decorative trimmings to enhance a plain or dull bedspread. For extra comfort and variety, cover a few different sized cushions, and scatter these over the bed.

◄ Comfy cushions
A selection of small cushions, covered to match the bedspread, can be scattered over the pillows at the top of the bed, and simply discarded at night. These cushions have been trimmed and decorated with a combination of dainty lace, broderie anglaise and satin ribbon.

▲ Mix and match
A selection of fabrics, shapes and styles has been used to make this charming set of daytime pillow covers, each of which is made from a different patterned fabric, but in the same colours as the bedspread. Large cushions with a matching frill add to the soft, comfy effect.

▼ Plain as can be
Simple, untrimmed daytime covers add softness without being too obtrusive.

Bed coronets

A coronet-style canopy sitting high above the pillows can transform the plainest of beds and give it real designer style. Depending on the choice of fabric and trimmings, and on the fullness of the bed curtains, you can make the coronet as simple or extravagant as you wish, adapting the style to suit the bedroom.

Most coronets consist of a back curtain which sits against the wall behind the bed, and two side curtains which fall in graceful drapes from the front of the coronet. The side curtains are held back at each side of the bedhead by tiebacks or holdback poles, positioned level with the top of the headboard. A semi-circular fabric roof panel is also made to neaten the coronet ceiling, and a valance

pelmet is usually fitted to give the coronet a soft finish.

While it is possible to make your own coronet frame, it is simpler to buy one of the readily available coronet kits currently on the market. These supply you with a pre-shaped semi-circular curtain track, wall brackets and curtain wire to hold the back curtain.

Fabric options

Any fabric that is used in curtain-making is suitable for the coronet. Floral prints will bring a breath of the country into the bedroom, while heavier, darker fabrics in rich colours will give it an opulent, luxurious feel. Experiment with lace, voile and net to achieve a dreamy,

romantic look, ideal in a small bedroom where heavy or busy fabrics can be a touch oppressive.

To add colour and interest to the coronet, use a contrast fabric for the back curtain and to line the side curtains, as suggested in the instructions given. Choose a fabric to suit the colour scheme and other furnishings in the bedroom, or use a decorative trimming or tiebacks to make the link.

▼ Shades of blue
By carefully choosing fabric which blends with other colours and furnishings in the bedroom, you can create a coronet that looks stunning, but does not dominate the setting.

Fabric requirements

The amount of fabric used depends on the height of the coronet and the bed size. These instructions use two 120cm (47¼in) fabric widths for the back curtain and one 120cm (47¼in) width of main and contrast fabric for each curtain. For a fuller effect, use 2½ widths for the back curtain and 1½-2 widths for the sides, ensuring the coronet track is long enough to hold them.

Materials

Coronet track set which should include wall brackets, a curved track for the side curtains, a curtain wire for the back curtain, curtain and valance hooks, holding hooks for tiebacks and fixing screws, a pattern for cutting the roof panel and Velcro Hook and Loop to fix it in place

Fabric for the side curtains and valance (see steps for quantities)

Contrast lining fabric for the back curtain and ceiling panel, and to line the side curtains and valance (see steps for quantities)

Heading tape 2.5cm (1in) wide for the side curtains, and 7.5cm (3in) wide for the valance; you will need 2.5m (3yds) of each

Matching threads

▲ *Crowning glory*
A fabric-covered bedhead to match the coronet is a wonderful way to link the bed to your canopy.

MAKING THE CORONET

The cutting out instructions given here are based on the standard furnishing fabric width of 120cm (47¼in). If your chosen fabric is narrower, cut out and join extra widths where necessary.

1 Fixing the track and tieback hooks Decide on the position of the coronet above the bed – the standard height is 213cm (7ft), but take into account the proportions of your bedroom which may dictate a different height. Assemble and fix the track to the wall above the centre of the bedhead, following the manufacturer's instructions. Position and fix the two tieback hooks level with the top of the headboard, one on each side of the bed.

2 Cutting out the back curtain Measure from the curtain wire to the floor, and add 13.5cm (5¼in) for hems and the top casing; cut out two widths of your contrast lining fabric to this length, allowing extra for pattern matching if necessary.

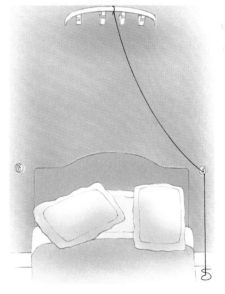

3 Cutting out the side curtains Use a length of string to measure the drop of the side curtains: measure from the curtain track down the side of the bed to the floor, allowing the string to form a gentle drape over the holding hook. Add 3.5cm (1⅜in) to this length for hems and headings. For each side curtain, cut out one width of your main fabric to this length, and one of your contrast lining fabric; allow extra for pattern matching.

4 **Making up the back curtain** Join the two fabric widths together, with two side seams rather than a central one, and make sure you match the pattern across the seams where necessary (see pages 228–229). Neaten the raw edges and press open. Pin and stitch a double 1.5cm (⅝in) hem down each side edge of the curtains.

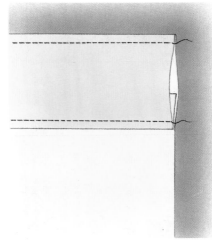

5 **Adding a top casing** To form the top casing, turn down 1cm (⅜in) and then a further 2.5cm (1in) to the wrong side, along the top edge of the back curtain. Pin and stitch along the hemline, and also along the top folded edge. Pin and stitch a double 5cm (2in) hem along the bottom edge of the curtain. Thread the curtain wire through the casing and hang the curtain right up against the wall.

6 **Stitching the roof panel** Using the pattern supplied with the kit, cut out two pieces of the contrast fabric. Place the pieces right sides together and pin then stitch all round, leaving a small opening for turning through. Trim the seams and snip into them around the curve. Then turn right side out, fold in the fabric edges of the opening and slip stitch to close.

7 **Fixing the panel in place** Cut the supplied Velcro strips to the correct length. Stick one side of the Velcro to the track brackets. Pin the other side in position on the fabric roof, then stitch in place. Fix the roof panel in place by pressing the Velcro strips together.

8 **Making up the side curtains** With right sides together and taking a 1.5cm (⅝in) seam allowance, pin and stitch one length of contrast lining fabric to one length of main fabric down both sides and along lower edge. Snip into seam allowances at the corners and turn right side out. Press the seam to the edge, so no contrast fabric will show on right side. Repeat for second curtain.

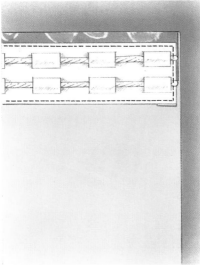

9 **Adding the heading tape** Treat the two fabrics as one at the top edge. Turn down 2cm (¾in) of top edge to the lining side. Pin the 2.5cm (1in) heading tape over the raw edges, 3mm down from the folded top edge. Knot the tape cords at the front edge and turn under, so that the tape edge is in line with the front edge of the curtain. At the back edge of the curtain, unpick the tape cords and turn under the raw end of the tape in line with the curtain edge. Stitch in place. Repeat on second curtain. Pull up each curtain to required length and hang on track.

10 **Cutting out the valance** Once the curtains are in place, decide how long you would like the valance to be – generally 30-50cm (11¾-19¾in). Cut two widths of both your main and contrast fabric to this length, plus 3.5cm (1⅜in) for hems and headings, allowing extra for pattern matching if necessary.

11 **Stitching the valance** Pin and stitch the two main fabric widths together, and the contrast fabric widths, matching the pattern across the seam where necessary. With right sides facing and taking a 1.5cm (⅝in) seam allowance, pin and stitch the main fabric to the contrast fabric down the sides and along the bottom edge. Turn through to the right side and attach the 7.5cm (3in) heading tape exactly as for the two side curtains. Pull up the valance heading tape and hang on to the hooks at the front of the track.

ANOTHER HEADING

Rather than making a valance for your coronet, stitch an attractive stand-up frill along the top edges of the side curtains, as shown in the opening picture. This looks particularly effective if the same heading technique is used on other curtains in the room.

Simply allow an extra 20cm (8in) on the curtain length for turning back above the heading tape, then stitch and gather up the tape as usual. To conceal the join of the curtains at the front of the coronet, attach a fabric rosette where they meet, and complete with matching tiebacks.

tip

Frilled finish
To add style and fullness to a plain coronet, trim the two side curtains and the bottom of the valance with a decorative frill in the same or a co-ordinating fabric.

DECORATIVE TIEBACKS

Imaginative tiebacks or holdback poles provide the finishing touch for a coronet, and greatly enhance the overall impression given by the drape. Position them carefully on a level with the top of the bedhead, and arrange the curtains to fall in a gentle drape at each side of the bed.

▶ Pretty bows
If you choose to use metal holdback poles, but want to keep the effect soft and feminine, disguise their metal ends with a full fabric bow. The bows are easily made up in the same fabric as the side curtains, and can then be simply glued to the ends of the holdback poles. To add the final touch, cover the poles with the contrast curtain fabric so they blend into the background.

▲ Tailored tiebacks *For a classic finish to your coronet, make a pair of elegant tailored tiebacks in the same fabric as your curtains or contrast lining. Alternatively, opt for one of the more unusual tieback designs, such as a plaited, ruched or bow tieback, or use heavy tassel-trimmed cords for a more luxurious effect. Details on making tiebacks can be found in Window Treatments, pages 131–138.*

▲ Ornate rosettes *Fashionable rosettes will add grandeur to a stately coronet, and can be used as a clever cover-up for metal holdback poles (as here), or to add style to plain tiebacks. Make two-colour rosettes in a combination of your main fabric and contrast lining for a perfectly co-ordinated look, or introduce a new colour to add interest where the coronet fabrics are plain. A third rosette placed centrally over the valance makes a majestic finishing touch.*

Cushion collections

Cushions are the perfect finishing touch. They can enhance a colour theme, turn a dull room into a lively one, or transform an ordinary bedroom into a boudoir.

Cushions are an easy way to pull together the decorative scheme in a room. For instance, if you have patterned curtains, cushions of the same fabric on the sofa or chairs will add a co-ordinated touch; take the theme one step further by choosing two or three colours from the curtain pattern and buy or make scatter cushions in plain fabrics in these colours. If you have patterned upholstery, cushions in a toning or complementary plain colour will be effective but cushions in a distinctive accent colour will really draw the eye.

If your room has a neutral colour scheme then you can dramatize it with your choice of cushions. Try using lots of different fabrics and textures: silk, hessian, tapestry, velvet, patchwork, cotton, lace – the range is limitless. The remnant counters of fabric shops provide happy hunting grounds for cushion-sized pieces; all you need to take into consideration is the probable wear on your planned cushions – for instance, if you have children and pets you'll need to choose a washable fabric.

▲ Love-knot variations
The pillows on this attractive button-backed bed are decorated with appliqued bows cut from the fabric used for the headboard. Tiny cushions are either covered in old lace to match the lace-edged sheets or stencilled following the same design theme.

The co-ordinated look ▶
The colour scheme of the room is based on creamy apricot walls and blue wood furniture. The plain lines of the sofa are softened with a mass of co-ordinating scatter cushions – a framework of large square cushions supports three smaller circular ones. Floral gingham and patterned chintz pick up the apricot and blue and add a warm accent of coral.

▲ **Cushioned cane**
A low cane chair is attractively decorated and softened with an appliqued cushion. The garland is created by the appliqué perse method where the motif is cut from a patterned fabric and applied to a plain background.

◀ **Under the eaves**
A plain attic room with a simple iron bedstead is magically transformed into a pretty Victorian bedroom with piles of deeply-frilled, lace-edged cushions.

Patchwork cushion

The craft of patchwork has been used for centuries to make use of odd scraps of fabric around the home. Many of the patch shapes and arrangements are complicated but the square patch used for this cushion is a very basic shape and can be sewn together by hand, using a small oversew stitch, or by machine making the patchwork effect very quick and simple to achieve. All fabrics used, in one item should be either of cotton or a cotton mix, with a similar weight and the same care instructions. It is advisable to collect all the fabrics that will be used first, and then wash and iron them before beginning the work.

▼ Square patches
The cushion has been made in a blue and pink colour scheme, but you could choose colours to suit your bedroom. Once you have mastered the craft of patchwork you may decide to make the quilt too.

Materials

Cotton polyester fabric 25 patches in a selection of light colours and 24 patches in a selection of dark colours, each measuring 8cm (3¼in) square

Cotton polyester fabric of the same weight and laundering instructions to match the dominant dark colour of patches 44cm (17¼in) square

Sewing thread in both light and dark shades

Embroidery needle size 7

Cushion pad 40cm (16in) square

Dressmaker's marking pen

Fabric scissors

TO MAKE THE COVER

1 Preparing the patchwork fabric Iron all the fabric to be used and lay it out flat to avoid creasing, ready to use.

2 Arranging the patches With right sides upwards lay the patches out on a flat surface, following the diagram for the arrangement of the light and dark patches. Re-arrange the patches within the light and dark areas until you are pleased with the overall effect.

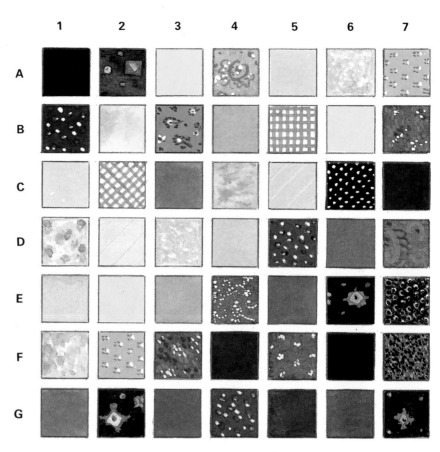

3 Stitching the patches Working along row A, taking a 1cm (⅜in) seam and with right sides facing, stitch patches A1 and A2 together. Join the opposite edge of patch A2 to A3 in the same way, then continue to join all the patches in row A in number sequence. Join rows B, C, D, E, F and G as for row A. Trim the seams. Press all the seams in rows A, C, E and G in one direction and all the seams in rows B, D and F in the opposite direction.

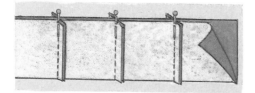

4 Joining the rows With right sides facing and aligning the seams pin rows A and B together. Using a straight stitch and taking a 1cm (⅜in) seam, sew the rows together. Join rows B, C, D, E, F and G together in the same way. Trim the seams and press to one side.

5 Making the cushion cover With right sides together, lay the patchwork on top of the backing fabric and using a straight stitch, sew a 1cm (⅜in) seam around the edge leaving a 30cm (12in) gap along one side.

6 Inserting the pad Snip the corners, then turn cover to right side and press. Insert the cushion pad and using small slip stitches, close the opening.

tip

Patch ideas

If you enjoyed making the patchwork cushion cover and feel that a quilt for your bedroom would complete the look, give it a try, you'll be surprise just how quickly the work will grow. Once finished add a border, then back and quilt the work to finish.

Stylish designer patchwork

Made in brilliant contrasting colours, a patchwork cushion adds a fresh new look to a chair. The fun of patchwork is choosing different fabrics that look good together, then arranging them for a really special design. On a grand scale, bedspreads or throws can be made to match a particular room, but experimenting with a cushion cover is a good way to learn the craft.

Materials
Medium weight patterned and plain cotton fabric 100 x 122cm (39½ x 44¼in) of each
Sewing thread to match plain fabric
Pencil, ruler and **set square**
Thick card template 7cm (2¾in) square
Craft knife
Tape measure
Fabric scissors
Press studs x 4
Chunky piping cord 2m (2¼yds)
Iron and **ironing board**
Cushion pad 40cm (16in) square

▼ Dotty appeal
Bright, freshly coloured fabrics are stitched together in simple squares to create a cushion that will bring a sunny touch to any room.

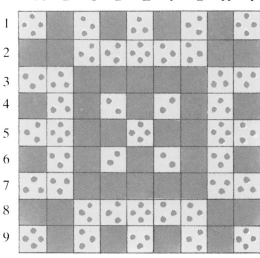

A B C D E F G H I
1
2
3
4
5
6
7
8
9

◀ *Play with patches*
Add a professional touch to your patchwork, by cutting out the dotty fabric paying attention to the arrangement of the dots; like dominoes.

MAKING THE COVER

1 Making the template Draw a line 1cm (⅜in) inside the edges of the square card template to mark a frame. Then cut out with craft knife.

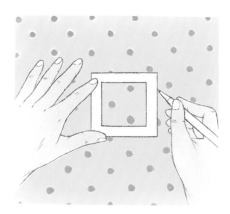

2 Cutting the patches Centre any motifs in the frame and use the template to cut 44 patterned patches and 36 plain (for this design).

3 Arranging the patches Following the layout diagram, arrange the patches on a flat surface.

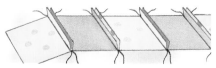

4 Stitching the patches Starting on row 1 join patches A and B along one side – with right sides facing stitch a 1cm (⅝in) wide seam allowance – then add patches C, D, E, F and so on. Stitch remaining rows.

5 Pressing the seams Press the seams on rows 1, 3, 5, 7 and 9 in one direction, and those on rows 2, 4, 6 and 8 in the opposite direction.

6 Joining rows of patches For a good result the seams must match exactly. Stitch rows 1 and 2 with a 1cm (⅝in) seam then join row 3 to row 2. Continue until design is complete. Press seams open.

7 Preparing the cushion back Cut two pieces of plain fabric 29 x 45cm (11½ x 17¾in). Turn and stitch a double hem 1cm (⅜in) wide to wrong side along one long edge of both back halves. Lap one back half over the other for 9cm (3½in) so back measures 45cm (17¾in) square. Pin then tack the halves together.

8 Making the ties Cut eight lengths of printed fabric each 56 x 14cm (22 x 5½in). With wrong sides facing, fold one piece in half lengthways and trim one end at an angle. Stitch a 1cm (⅜in) seam down the edge and along the angled end to make a point. Trim seam allowance on the corners; turn right side out and press. Make other ties the same.

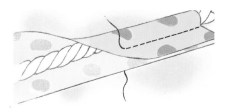

9 Covering the piping Cut four bias strips of patterned fabric 6 x 50cm (2¼ x 19¾in). With right sides facing seam short ends of strips together; press seams open. With right side outside wrap the strip lengthways around the piping cord, and using the zipper foot, stitch the strip as close to the cord as possible.

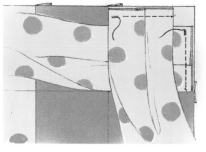

10 Positioning the ties Pleat the raw ends of each tie to a finished width of 4.5cm (1¾in). Match the side of the tie with the corner patch seam and the raw ends of both tie and patch, pin and tack.

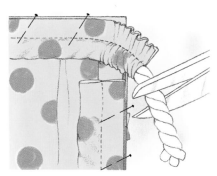

11 Positioning the piping Gently pull the casing so that it is 1.5cm (⅝in) longer than the cord, then beginning at one corner and matching raw edges, pin piping around patchwork cushion cover. Finish piping by pushing back the casing, trimming the cord to fit end to end. Reposition casing and trim to 4cm (1¾in) longer than cord. Hand stitch the casing so that it neatly covers the cord. Tack the piping in place.

12 Completing the cover With right sides facing, pin the back to the front. Stitch a 1cm (⅜in) seam around the edge close to piping cord, snip seam allowance at corners; turn right side out and press. Stitch evenly spaced press studs along back opening. Insert the cushion pad.

Patchwork lace tablecloth

The textures of satin and lace complement each other beautifully and using ready-made lace napkins, this delightful top cloth can be made quickly to transform a plain table.

If you have difficulty finding suitable square napkins, use hemmed fabric pieces of the same measurements. Whichever option you choose it is most important that the corners are truly square, or the finished top cloth will be uneven. Bows stitched to the end of each ribbon strip add the final flourish. If you want you could add extra bows to the corners of the cloth.

▲ **Adding colour**
The satin ribbon enhances the top cloth, highlighting the delicate lace. Try placing the top cloth over a pale tablecloth in a colour that complements the ribbon's colour. Plain and patterned cloths work well.

Materials

Square lace napkins four × 48cm (19in) square

Double sided satin ribbon 5cm (2in) wide × 6.5m (7¼ft)

Fusible webbing (Wundaweb) 2.5cm (1in) wide x 2.25m (3ft 6in) long

Sewing thread to match ribbon

Embroidery needle size 7

Iron and **ironing board**

Pressing cloth

Ruler and **pins**

MAKING THE TABLECLOTH

1 Preparing the napkins Press the napkins to remove any creases. Check the napkin corners are square and if they are not, use other suitable napkins to ensure a flat tablecloth.

2 Preparing the ribbon Cut two lengths of ribbon each measuring 110cm (43½in). Fold one length in half lengthways and widthways, then tack a line of stitches along the folds. Work second ribbon length as for first.

3 Positioning the Wundaweb Cut the Wundaweb in half lengthways, then cut one strip 48cm (19in) long. Lay the ribbon flat on the ironing board and position the short strip of Wundaweb on the ribbon, 6mm (⅜in) from the tacking stitches.

4 Attaching one napkin With the wrong side downwards, lay napkin over Wundaweb positioning edges 6mm (⅜in) from the tacked lines. Make sure that the Wundaweb is along the edge of the hem, then use a damp pressing cloth and warm iron to press in place. Turn work over and use a warm dry iron to press the ribbon securely in place.

5 Attaching the remaining napkins Cut three more narrow Wundaweb strips each 48cm (19in) long and using the tacking stitches as a guide, fix the remaining three napkins in place along the ribbon as before.

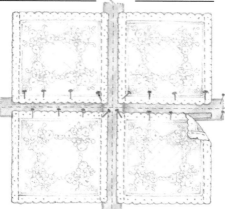

6 Joining the last piece of ribbon Lay the second ribbon on the ironing board and place the cloth over it so the ribbon fills the gap. Line up the napkin 6mm (⅜in) from the tacking stitches and pin to the board to prevent slipping. Tuck the Wundaweb between the ribbon and napkins, then iron.

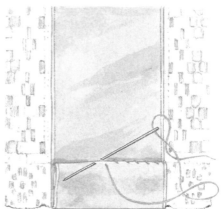

7 Neatening the ribbon ends Trim ribbon ends to within 5cm (2in) of napkin hems, then fold the ribbon to the wrong side with a double hem so that it is level with the napkin hems. Press ribbon hem and taking care that stitches do not show on the right side of the work, use tiny slip stitches to sew hem into place.

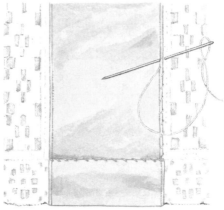

8 Stitching the napkins If the cloth is to be used and washed frequently it is a good idea to stitch the ribbon and napkins together using tiny slip stitches on wrong side of the work.

9 Fixing the bows in place Cut the last ribbon into four equal lengths and tie each to form a bow. Trim the ends and stitch each bow to a ribbon end, between two napkins.

tip

Sew easy
If you have access to a sewing machine, stitch the cloth with small machine stitches. Check for pucker by machine stitching a double thickness of ribbon before sewing the cloth.

Cut~through appliqué

Cut-through, or reverse appliqué is worked by cutting away areas from a top layer of fabric to reveal a contrast colour beneath. The fabric layers can be padded, lined and quilted, so the technique is ideal for working home accessories like the comfortable throw and matching cushion design.

Simple geometric patterns are the easiest to sew and these, worked in contrast colours create striking effects. Choose natural fibre fabrics such as light to midweight cotton for reverse appliqué, as this handles well. The cut edges of the design are turned in and handstitched, so you need a non-slippery fabric which does not fray easily. Dark colours can be worked over lighter shades, and vice versa; but if using a light top colour like we have, make sure the fabric is dense enough to prevent the darker under-layer from showing through.

▼ Casual comfort
Bold contrasting colours effectively display the simple geometric shapes of this wonderful throw, which has been worked using the technique of cut-through appliqué.

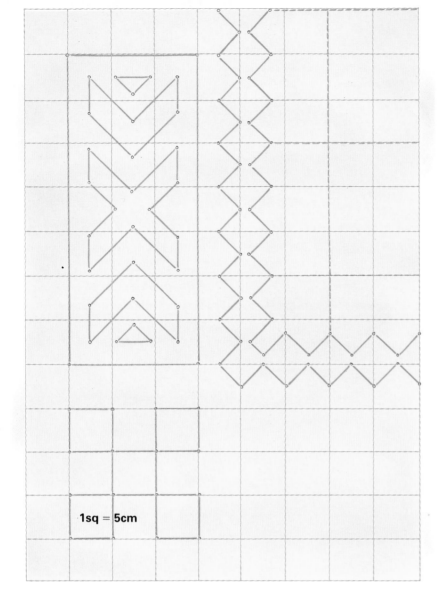

1sq = 5cm

◄ *Geometric border*
The border pattern is used for both the throw and the cushion. Scale it up on dressmaker's graph paper, and use the pattern, repeating it as necessary, to fit around the edge of the throw. For the cushion use the corner piece as the centre, and edge with the inner motif.

The throw

Finished size 146cm (57½in) square.

Materials

Unbleached cotton fabric For the top and base layer you will need 3m (3⅜yd) of 150cm (60in) wide cotton fabric in cream, or another light-coloured but dense cotton fabric

Contrast cotton fabric 1.90m (2⅛yd) of 150cm (60in) wide lightweight cotton in terracotta, or your chosen appliqué colour

Domette 1.50m (1⅝yd) of 140cm (55in) wide domette for interlining

Embroidery cotton Stranded thread for central quilting, to match the contrasting fabric

Sewing threads to match throw colours

Embroidery scissors

Dressmaker's metric graph paper

Wad punch or **bradawl**

Pencil

Ruler

Water or **air erasable dressmaker's marker pen**

MAKING THE THROW

1 **Transferring the pattern** Scale up the design from the diagram on to dressmaker's graph paper. Punch a hole in the paper pattern at each corner point of the design using a wad punch or bradawl.

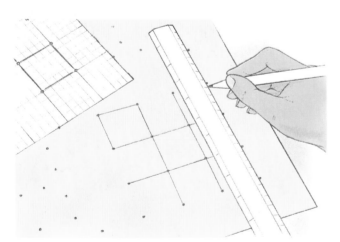

2 **Marking design** Cut a 145cm (57in) square from the cream, top layer fabric (A). Lay paper pattern over, lining up all edges. Transfer the design on to the fabric by marking dots through the punched holes with a pencil. Remove pattern, and join up the dots with ruler and pencil. Mark the corner sections first, then repeat the design once more to join the corner sections.

3 **Adding layers** Cut a 145cm (57in) square of terracotta cotton (B), and cut away an 80cm (31½in) square from the centre. Cut another 145cm (57in) square from cream fabric (D), and a 145cm (57in) length of domette (C). Lay (D) fabric flat with wrong side facing upwards, and centre the domette (C) on top. Place contrast fabric (B) over this with right side upwards. Tack the layers together round the inner edge of the contrast fabric.

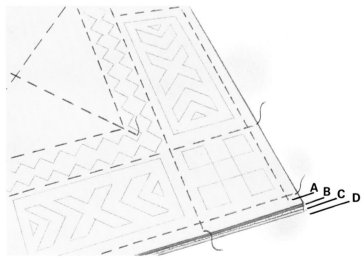

A B C D

4 **Adding the top layer** With right side facing upwards, lay the pattern-marked fabric (A) over the others, and tack through all layers.

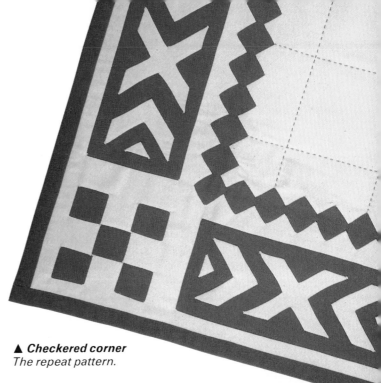

5 **Working the diamond border** Starting on the inner edge of the border, and within the outline of the diamond, carefully cut a small hole through the top layer of fabric (A). Cut a turning allowance of 6mm (¼in), parallel to the drawn line. Snip into this allowance at corner points to ease the fabric around the corners. Turn the fabric under along the drawn line, pin the turnings in place and secure them with very small stitches and matching thread. Repeat with the opposite edge of the diamond border.

▲ *Checkered corner*
The repeat pattern.

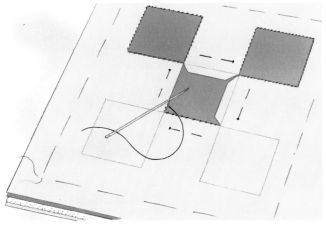

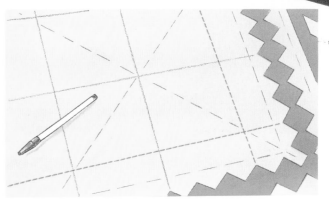

6 **Checkered motifs** Cut and stitch the eight checkered motifs in the same way, allowing 6mm (¼in) for turnings. Work one square at a time to prevent fraying.

8 **Quilting lines** Using the erasable marker pen, mark the quilting lines on the top fabric (A). With stranded cotton work 6mm (¼in) evenly spaced quilting stitches across these lines.

9 **Binding the edges** Cut two 145 x 10cm (57 x 4in) and two 148 x 10cm (58½ x 4in) strips of terracotta fabric. With throw right side up, pin and machine stitch a shorter strip to one side (right sides facing) with a 2.5cm (1in) turning. Turn under 2.5cm (1in) and handsew binding strip to wrong side to cover machine stitching.

7 **Rectangular panel motifs** First pin the inner sections of the design in place before you begin cutting and stitching the main outer sides. Cut round the pinned pieces allowing 6mm (¼in) for turnings. Turn edges in and stitch in place.

10 **Completing the throw** Repeat on the opposite side of the throw, then bind the two remaining sides in the same way, using the longer terracotta strips. Fold under and handsew the excess 1.5cm (⅝in) at each end. Remove all the tacking stitches.

▲ *Checkered cushion* The rustic brown and cream of the matching cushion merges easily into a country interior.

The cushion

Made using the same fabric and design as the throw, this cushion cover is just as decorative on its own. The finished cover size is 40cm (16in) square.

Materials

Fabrics; 50cm (⅝yd) or 150cm (60in) **wide unbleached cotton** or another light, but dense colour, 50cm (⅝yd) of 150cm (60in) **wide contrast cotton** (if you have made the throw, you could use the 80cm (31½in) square that was cut from the centre of the terracotta contrast fabric), and 50cm (⅝yd) of 140cm (55in) **wide domette**

Nylon zip 30cm (12in) midweight zip for insertion in the back of the cushion cover in a similar shade to the main cushion fabric

Matching sewing threads as listed for the throw

Stranded embroidery thread to match the contrasting fabric as listed for the throw

Cushion pad, 35cm (14in) square

Design and **sewing aids** as listed for the throw

MAKING THE CUSHION

1 Transferring the design Cut a 40cm (16in) square of cream top fabric (A) and transfer the checkered motif to the centre. Surround with the diamond border, leaving a 1.5cm (⅝in) gap between the motif and the border.

2 Working the design Cut one more 40cm (16in) square of cream fabric (D), one 40cm (16in) square of contrast fabric (B) and one of domette (C). Layer these in the same formation as for the throw, with (A) on top, and work appliqué as before.

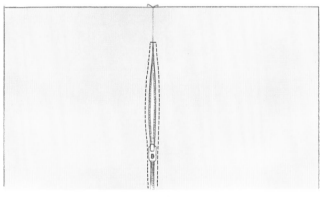

3 Cushion back Cut two 40 x 21.5cm (16 x 8½in) pieces of cream fabric. Taking a 1.5cm (⅝in) seam allowance, stitch together 5cm (2in) in from each end on one long side. Press seam open, and insert zip.

4 Finishing cushion Pin the zipped back piece to the appliquéd front piece, with wrong sides facing. Cut two 40 x 10cm (16 x 4in) and two 43 x 10cm (17 x 4in) strips from contrast colour (B), and bind the cushion edges as for the throw, starting with the shorter strips.

Joining domette

If the domette is not the required width, join a strip to one side to make up the difference. Overlap the two edges very slightly, and join them by working an evenly spaced herringbone stitch through both layers taking care not to pull the stitches tightly.

PART FIVE

FINISHING TOUCHES

Braids and tassels

▲ **Needlework pastimes**
*Tapestry designs are ideal for
making up into decorative cushions.
To give them a real 'heirloom' finish
use cords and tassels in colours
picked out from the design.*

Silky ropes and tassels catch the light and add lustre to rich, high gloss fabrics. For a less formal look, choose braids and trimmings made of heavy cotton, in more muted colours so their effect is more homely and cottage-like. If you decide to trim one item in a room – curtains, for example – why not extend the theme elsewhere, on to the sofa cushions. By repeating an interesting detail, you will give the room unity.

If possible, take a sample of the base fabric along with you when you are choosing trimmings. For the best visual results it's usually safer to aim for an interesting contrast rather than a perfect match. Many of the heavier home furnishing trimmings require dry cleaning, while trimmings designed for clothes are more likely to be hand washable. Before applying cotton trimmings, pre-shrink them by soaking in hot water for ten minutes. Dry on a towel and press with the right side down on the towel to avoid flattening the texture of the braid.

Frayed ends
Silky braids tend to unwind or fray easily. To prevent this happening while working with them, bind the cut ends with adhesive tape which is trimmed off when you are ready to finish the trimming.

◀ *Grand tassels*
The rich red in the floral pattern on these textured curtains is highlighted by the opulent rope and tasselled trimming and tiebacks. The thick cord is knotted at every pleat on the curtain heading and then tied in a bow where the curtains meet. The ends are finished off with big, bold tassels.

▼ *Rustic charm*
This softly fluttering macramé fringe makes an instant valance for a cottage window. To re-create the idea in your own home use deep purchased braid or look for old trimmings in junk shops.

▼ *Unusual handles*
Large chunky tassels, with crocheted bases, make an interesting alternative to knobs on this wooden cabinet.

Adding bows

The supple, flowing shape of fabric bows gives a lift to soft furnishings and other decorative items around the home, drawing attention to a particular feature or providing the focal point themselves. Use them on pelmets and valances, cushions, tablecloths, chair covers and for a host of other decorative applications.

To give neutral furnishings vitality, attach bows in warm or vibrant colours, and add touches of the same colour elsewhere in the room. Where the furnishings don't quite co-ordinate, use the bows as a link, adding them for example, to the window dressing to tie in with a contrasting sofa.

The bows can be made in one or more pieces, producing a more tailored look the more pieces used. For a dramatic or formal effect they can be starched, interfaced or padded with wadding to give them more body and to hold their shape. For a softer, more informal look, a length of lightweight fabric such as chiffon or a piece of satin

▲ Double delight
Simple double bows like these are easy to make and can have a major impact on the decorative scheme of the room. Here, they are made in a pretty blue and white fabric to tie in with the china and chair seats.

ribbon can be tied into a soft, floppy bow. The fabric and setting will usually dictate whether a grand, tailored bow is best or something more soft and simple.

DECORATIVE BOW

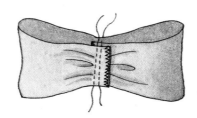

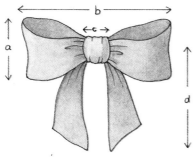

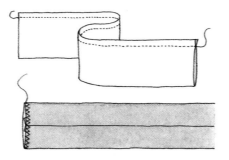

1 Cutting out For the loops, cut out a piece of fabric twice the finished depth **(a)** by twice the finished width **(b)** of the bow, adding 1cm (⅜in) seam allowances all round. For the tails, cut two pieces of fabric the finished width of each tail by twice the finished length from the centre of the knot to the tip **(d)**, adding 1cm (⅜in) seam allowances all round. For the knot, cut a piece of fabric twice the finished width **(c)** by 13cm (5in), adding 1cm (⅜in) seam allowances all round.

2 Making loops and knot Fold the loop fabric in half with right sides facing so that the long edges match. Pin and then stitch the long raw edges together, taking a 1cm (⅜in) seam allowance. Open out the fabric and position the seam at the centre; press with seam allowances open, then turn right side out. Repeat to stitch the knot piece. Neaten the raw edges of both the loop and knot with overlock or zigzag.

3 Finishing the loops With the seam on top, fold the ends over to the middle, overlapping by 2cm (¾in). Run two rows of gathering stitches up the centre of the overlap, taking the stitches through all layers. Gather up and knot the threads to secure.

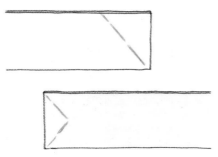

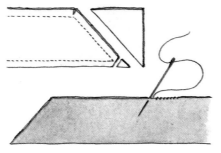

4 Preparing the tail pieces Pin or tack the tail pieces together all round with raw edges matching and right sides facing. To shape the ends, either turn the fabric up at each end so that the end is level with one long edge, or fold in half lengthways and then turn each end up so it is level with the raw side edges. Unfold the fabric and draw along the foldlines with tailor's chalk.

5 Stitching the tails Stitch the tail pieces together all round, taking a 1cm (⅜in) seam allowance and stitching 1cm (⅜in) inside the chalk line at each end; leave a 10cm (4in) gap in the centre of one long edge to turn through. Trim the excess fabric at the ends, and snip to, but not through the stitching at the points. Turn right side out through the gap, then neatly slipstitch the gap closed.

6 Attaching the tails Run two rows of gathering stitches up the centre of the tail piece and gather up to the same width as the centre of the bow. Place the loop piece face down and centre the tail piece on top, then stitch together along the centre to hold, using a double thread. Don't worry about the stitches showing on the front – these will be covered by the knot piece.

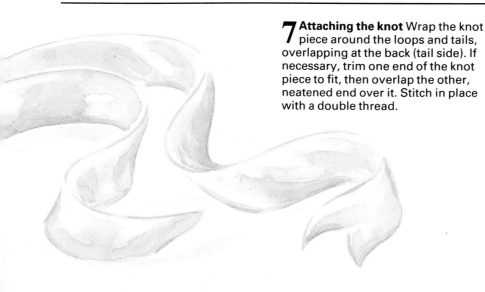

7 Attaching the knot Wrap the knot piece around the loops and tails, overlapping at the back (tail side). If necessary, trim one end of the knot piece to fit, then overlap the other, neatened end over it. Stitch in place with a double thread.

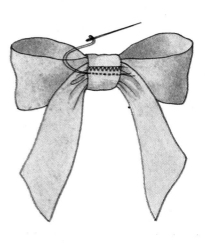

SOFT DOUBLE BOW

This is a soft decorative bow which has two loop pieces instead of one. The loops should be cut slightly longer than the finished size because they are opened out like the petals of a flower in the finished bow, making them appear slightly smaller.

Making the double bow Cut out the fabric (see step 1 for a decorative bow) but cut two loops instead of one. Make up the bow pieces following steps 2-5 for a decorative bow, but omitting the gathering stitches on the loops. Place one finished loop on top of the other, and place both centrally on top of the tails. Wrap the knot round all three pieces and pin at the back. Open out the loops and arrange as required. Carefully trim away the excess knot fabric at the back, then stitch firmly to hold, catching the loops in the stitching to secure.

PADDED BOW

A light padding of polyester wadding will give a decorative bow extra body and shape. Use a padded bow where you want it to create maximum impact. For a crisp look, without the extra bulk of wadding, interfacing can be used instead, ironed on to the wrong side of the fabric pieces.

1 Cutting out Carefully cut out the main fabric as for step 1 of a decorative bow. For the loops, cut a piece of light or mediumweight wadding the finished depth of the loops plus 1cm (⅜in), by twice the finished length plus 2cm (¾in). For the tails, cut a piece of wadding exactly the same size as one of the fabric tails.

▲ Functional bows
Decorative bows in pink and blue add character to the tea table and chairs. Both sets are functional – securing the cushions and covering the gathers on the cloth.

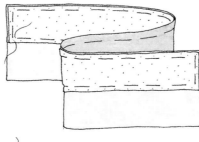

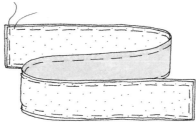

2 Making the bow Tack the wadding to the wrong side of the loop piece, level with one long edge. Tack the remaining piece of wadding to the wrong side of one tail piece. Make up the bow, following the instructions for a decorative bow following the steps 2-7, and trimming the excess wadding at the seam allowances to reduce bulk.

tip

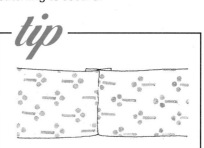

Right direction
If the tails of the decorative bow are long and the fabric has an obvious direction, cut them in four pieces the finished width by the finished length of each tail, adding 1cm (⅜in) seam allowances all round. Join together at the centre with the pattern pointing to the seam. This way the pattern will run vertically in the bow.

TAILORED DOUBLE BOW

A tailored double bow is an elegant variation of a decorative bow, and more formal than the soft double bow. It has two pressed loops, with the top one slightly smaller than the bottom one. The tails can either be positioned behind, as in a standard tailored bow, or folded and stitched to the back to create a T-shaped bow, as pictured above.

1 Cutting out Cut out the fabric as for step 1 of a decorative bow, but cut two loop pieces instead of one. Cut the top loop piece 2-4cm (¾-1½in) shorter than the lower loop so that it will sit neatly on top of the lower loop piece. Now proceed as follows for either style:

▲ T-time
A T-shaped tailored bow adds elegance to an unusual gathered cushion and covers the join where the gathered fabric meets.

2 Standard tailored bow Make up the bow following the instructions for a decorative bow, steps 2-5. Run two rows of gathering stitches up the centre of the tail piece to gather to the same depth as the loops. Centre the smaller loop piece on top of the larger one and then centre the tails behind both. Pin and then stitch together at the centre using a double thread. Wrap the knot piece round the centre of the bow, overlapping at the back and stitch.

3 T-shaped bow Make up the bow pieces as for a decorative bow, steps 2-5. Centre the smaller loop over the larger one and stitch together at the centre. Wrap the knot around the bow and stitch at the back, trimming away excess fabric. Run two rows of gathering stitches up the centre of the tail piece and gather up to the depth of the loops. Fold in half widthways, and pin to the back of the bow. Arrange for a pleasing effect, then stitch.

Picture bows

Pretty picture bows are cleverly designed to give the illusion of holding up the picture, but actually serve a purely decorative function. Use them to add interest to a plain picture frame and to soften its hard lines, or to fill empty wall space around the picture.

The bows are hung on a small hook placed just above the picture, which is then hung in the usual way to cover the tails of the bow. If you choose a style with long tails which extend below the picture – perhaps to provide a decorative link with a second picture directly below the first – simply thread the tails through the picture wire to lie against the back of the picture.

The size of the bow should be chosen in accordance with the picture size, but 18cm (7in) across and 7.5cm (3in) deep is a good average size to work to. Be sure not to make your bows too small and insignificant, or too dominant in size and colour – they should provide decorative detail without detracting from the picture. Relatively stiff fabrics with a slight sheen to them, such as moiré and slubbed silk, work well and make luxurious bows. If using a fine fabric, stiffen it with interlining for a fuller, more shapely bow.

▼ Picture this
A picture bow made from a fabric whose colour and pattern is echoed in other soft furnishings throughout the room, provides a pleasing link between the picture and its surroundings.

Materials
Fabric for making the bow
Tailor's chalk
Matching sewing threads
Two curtain weights for the tails
Small curtain ring for hanging the bow

MAKING A PICTURE BOW

For a perfectly symmetrical shape and neat finish, picture bows are often made up from three separate sections of fabric stitched together, rather than from a single continuous strip. Before you begin, decide on a good size for your bow in relation to the picture, and on a suitable length for the tails.

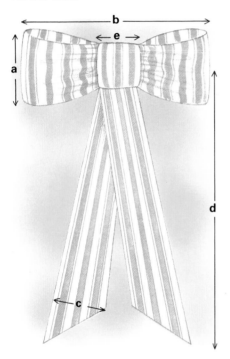

1 Cutting out For the loops of the bow, cut out a strip of fabric twice the depth of the finished bow not including tails (**a**), by twice its width (**b**). For the tails, cut out a strip of fabric twice the width of each finished tail (**c**) by twice the length from the centre of the knot to the tail tip (**d**). For the knot, cut a piece of fabric twice the width of the finished knot (**e**), by 12cm (4¾in). Add a 1cm (⅜in) seam allowance all round each piece. Cut out along the straight grain.

2 Stitching the loops With right sides together, fold the strip of fabric for the loop in half lengthways. Taking a 1cm (⅜in) seam allowance, pin and stitch along the long raw edges and across one short edge. Turn the strip through to the right side and press, keeping the seam on the lower edge. Turn in the raw ends and slipstitch to close, then stitch the two short ends of the strip together to form a loop.

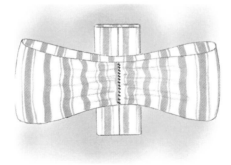

3 Forming the bow Fold and stitch the long edges of the fabric strip for the knot in same way, centre the seam, then stitch across one short edge. Turn through to right side. With the seamed side against the loop, wrap the knot piece around the centre, so that it pulls the loop in to form a bow. Trim raw end of knot piece if it is too long, then turn in the raw edges and slipstitch ends of knot piece together. Then stitch in place on back of bow.

▲ *Pretty as a picture*
Depending on the choice of fabric, picture bows can look as informal or sophisticated as you like. The colourful striped fabric shown here makes a wonderfully fresh bow, ideal for both the natural image of the picture and its simple setting.

4 Shaping the tails With right sides facing, fold the strip of fabric for the tails in half lengthways and pin together around the raw edges. The ends of the strip are decoratively shaped into two points. At one end of the strip, use tailor's chalk to mark a diagonal line from the raw-edged corner to the long folded edge opposite, and repeat at the other end, from the folded corner to the long raw edge opposite.

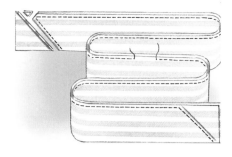

5 **Stitching the tails** Taking a 1cm (⅜in) seam allowance, stitch along the strip and across both shaped ends, leaving a small gap in the long edge for turning through. Trim excess fabric at both ends and snip into corners, then turn through to right side. Insert a curtain weight at each end, and slipstitch the opening to close. Press to lie flat.

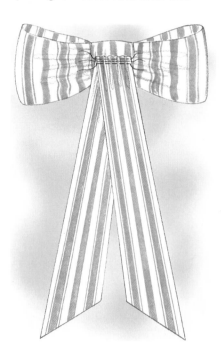

6 **Attaching the tails** Fold the tail strip in half widthways, with the pointed tips at the end of the strip facing outwards; fold at a slight angle so that the two tails spread out along their length. Run two rows of gathering threads across the folded top edge of the tails, and gather up slightly to fit the width of the knot. Secure the threads, then stitch the tails to the knot at the back of the bow.

7 **Hanging the bow** Stitch the small curtain ring to the back of the knot at the centre of the bow; quickly check that the ring is not visible from the front of the bow before you stitch it in place. Hang the bow in position on a picture hook just above your picture. Then hang the picture on its hook below the bow, slipping the tails of the bow through the picture wire to lie against the back of the picture close to the wall.

FULL PICTURE BOW

The style of a picture bow can easily be varied to suit not only the picture, but also the setting. The design featured here is a stunning way to display a picture in a room with a picture rail, by means of a full bow attached to a long, slim fabric strip. Before you begin, hang the picture in place as usual.

1 **Cutting out** Cut out fabric pieces for the loops, knot and tails of the bow as described in step 1 of *Making a picture bow*, but note that the tails are kept quite short in this design. For 'hanging' the picture, also cut a strip of fabric 18cm (7in) wide, by the distance from the picture rail to the top of your picture plus 10cm (4in) in length.

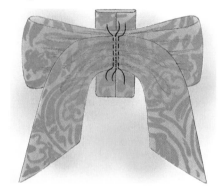

2 **Making up the bow** Make up loops and knot as before, but do not join them together. Stitch tail strip, shaping ends, but mark one diagonal in opposite direction to other; do not insert weights. Run two rows of gathering stitches across centre of tail piece, and gather up slightly. Centre tail piece over join on loops of bow, and stitch in place. Wrap the knot piece around the loops and tails, and stitch in position.

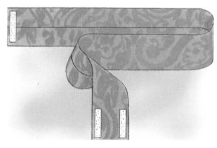

3 **Stitching the hanging strip** Fold and stitch the hanging strip as for the loops, but centring the seam. Sew the stitching half of a length of Sew 'n' Stick Velcro across the top of the strip, on the wrong side, and stick the other half in place on the picture rail ridge. Stitch two lengths of Velcro vertically to lower end of strip, on the right side, and attach a horizontal Velcro strip centrally across top of picture back.

4 **Hanging the picture** Run two rows of gathering stitches across the hanging strip, where the bow will be positioned, and gather the strip up slightly. Stitch the bow in position over the gathered part of the strip, to give the impression that the bow is tied around it. Match the Velcro strips to fix the hanging strip to the picture rail, and to the back of the picture. The strip should lie taut as if holding up the picture – the Velcro will allow you to make adjustments as necessary.

▲ *Hanging high*
This unusual picture bow puts the room's picture rail to decorative use, and draws the eye to the attractive border beneath it. The fullness of the bow counterbalances the wide picture perfectly.

tip

Paper bows
A stylish picture bow can quickly be made from a length of crêpe paper ribbon. Simply tie a loose knot halfway along the crêpe paper strip, and slip first one, then the other end of the strip under and through the front of the knot to form a bow. Tighten by pulling on the back of the bow, and adjust until symmetrical, then glue or staple the tails in place.

Fabric frame-ups

A plain clip-on picture frame can be given a touch of country charm with the addition of a frilled fabric surround. Like picture bows, the frilled trim will serve to soften the hard outline of the frame, give it added interest and highlight the picture. Use a fairly stiff fabric to make the trim, and keep to relatively subdued colours and patterns, which will not draw attention away from the picture.

Materials

Clip-on picture frame, to include **hardboard backing, glass front, white mounting card** and **metal clips;** use a suitable size for your picture
Fabric for the frilled surround – a stiff cotton is ideal; you will need a rectangle of fabric 10.5cm (4in) larger than the frame all round
Iron-on interfacing the same size as the fabric
Spray adhesive
Rubber-solution adhesive
Pinking shears and **matching threads**

▼ Frilled frames

Frilled fabric borders give a soft touch to the hard lines of a plain glass frame, and really draw attention to the picture they surround. Keep to pretty but subtle fabrics for the best results.

MAKING THE FRAME

1 Cutting out Iron the interfacing on to the back of your fabric rectangle, then carefully trim around the edges with pinking shears. Lay the fabric out flat and centre the frame over it. Draw around the frame on to the fabric, then cut away the middle of the fabric rectangle to leave a border.

2 Sticking the border in place Lay out the hardboard backing, inner side up, and pencil a line 1cm (⅜in) in from the edges all round – this will help you achieve a straight border. Place the fabric border, right side up, around the hardboard. Glue the top corners in place on the pencil line, and gather up the inside border edge

to fit the width of the frame; glue the border in place across the top edge of the hardboard backing, taking the pencilled line as your guide. Then stick the two bottom corners in place and gather up rest of border. Only a few gathers are necessary to create the effect and avoid the border becoming too bulky.

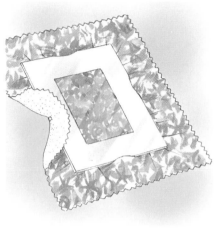

3 Assembling the frame Use the spray adhesive to mount your picture centrally on white card, then place it over the backing board to enclose glued frill edges. Lie glass panel over picture. Clip frame together, carrying the fabric frill forward over the glass with the clips, and then pulling it back outwards to conceal them. Hang picture as usual.

Stylish rosettes

Rosettes are a delightful addition to the country home, adding style and character to pelmets, tiebacks, bed canopies, and many other soft furnishings. In their many handsome forms, they make an attractive alternative to decorative bows, or can be combined with bows in co-ordinated colours or fabrics for a really elegant and sumptuous arrangement.

Like fabric bows, rosettes can be used to highlight a particular feature, to provide added decorative interest, or to cover up gathering stitches or joins in soft furnishings. They are particularly effective on swag and tail arrangements, where they can be used to emphasize the shape of the decoration and to cover the joins or the fixtures.

For the most formal effect, make a pleated rosette in a tartan, striped fabric or elegant mini-print with a co-ordinated covered button at the centre. For a softer effect, choose the simple, but attractive Maltese cross style and combine it with soft fabric bows in the same fabrics. For the softest effect of all, opt for the puff-ball rosette, in a plain or subtle fabric design which emphasizes the soft folds of the cloth.

▲ ***Bedroom splendour***
Splendid double rosettes in the pleated style define the shape of these suptuous bed drapes. The cream fabric on the rosettes, which matches the lining of the drapes, creates a border effect and adds extra body to make the rosettes look all the more soft and luxurious.

Materials for all rosettes
Furnishing fabric for the main part of the rosette and to cover the button at the centre
Medium to large **cover button** for each rosette

Pleated rosettes

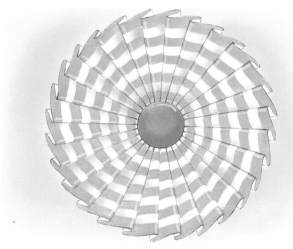

These are the most formal of the rosettes, with a sharply pleated ring of fabric centring on a covered button. The central button can be covered in the same fabric as the pleats or in a contrast: a particularly attractive effect is to use the same fabric as the furnishing for the button, with a contrast for the pleats, or to bind the pleated fabric and use the same binding to cover the button.

MAKING A PLEATED ROSETTE

1 Cutting out Draw a rough sketch of the finished rosette to get an idea of the size. Measure round the outside of the pattern to find the circumference, and cut a piece of fabric three times this measurement by the finished width of the whole rosette.

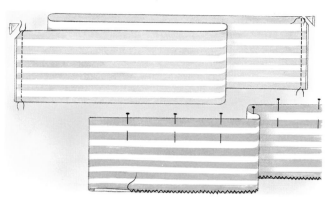

2 Preparing the fabric Fold the fabric in half, with right sides facing. Stitch along the two ends taking a 1cm (⅜in) seam allowance. Trim corners and turn right side out; press. Neaten the raw edges together with pinking shears and a row of straight stitching or with zigzag stitch. Insert pins along the folded edge at 2.5cm (1in) intervals or twice the width of each pleat, if different.

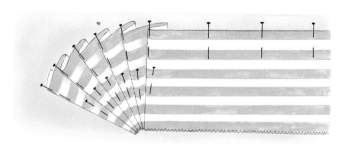

3 Pleating the fabric Pleat the fabric in a curve, with the neatened raw edges at the centre. Use the pins to mark the outer folds of the pleats, and pleat the fabric at the inside edge so tightly that there is only a small amount of fabric showing for each pleat. Finger press the pleats as you work and pin along the length of each one to hold.

Maltese cross rosette

This is a quick and easy alternative to the pleated rosette and is formed with either 2 or 3 bows superimposed and stitched together. It is usually made from one fabric, with a central button covered in the same or a contrasting fabric, however, for added interest the long edges of the loops can be bound with bias binding before the rosette is assembled. Cover the button in the main fabric or in the binding material.

MAKING A MALTESE CROSS ROSETTE

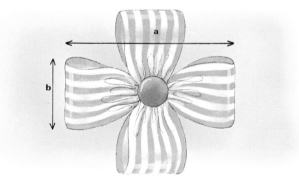

1 Cutting out Cut two or three strips of fabric (depending on the effect you require) twice the finished width of each loop (**a**) by twice the finished width of the rosette (**b**), adding 1cm (⅜in) seam allowances all round. Cut a circle of fabric for the covered button, and cover the button (follow the manufacturer's instructions).

2 Stitching the loops Fold the loops lengthways with right sides facing and pin and then stitch the long raw edges together, taking a 1cm (⅜in) seam allowance. Turn through to the right side, centre seam and press. Bind bias binding to the edges if desired. Neaten edges.

4 Stitching the pleats When you have finished the pleating, tuck the end of the fabric under the first pleat and pin. Hand stitch the pleats at the centre to hold using a double thread.

5 Finishing off Cover a button with fabric following the manufacturer's instructions. Working from the back of the rosette, stitch the fabric to the ring on the back of the button. Finally stitch the rosette in position on the soft furnishing.

tip

Ribbon rosette
Both the pleated and Maltese cross rosettes can be made with ribbon. You only need one layer of fabric instead of two and the edges of the ribbon do not require finishing, making the whole process quicker.

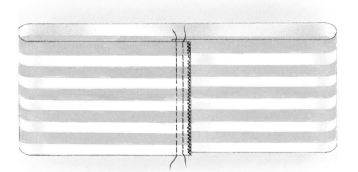

3 Making the rosette With the seam in the fabric uppermost, fold the ends of each loop to the centre so they overlap slightly in the middle, covering the seam. Run two rows of gathering stitches down the centre through all layers and gather up to give the loops their shape. Knot securely and add a further row of stitches to hold, if required. Cross the loops over each other at the centre, with the neatened fabric at the back; stitch securely to hold.

4 Adding the covered button Stitch the covered button to the centre of the rosette where the loops overlap. Finally stitch the rosette to the soft furnishing.

▶ Versatile rosette
A pretty double puff-ball rosette adds character to this petite bedroom chair. This isn't an item that most people would consider putting a rosette on, and it shows how versatile rosettes really are.

Puff-ball rosette

A puff-ball rosette has a voluptuous effect which works equally well in a grand, stately bedroom or a simple, Shaker style decor. Its shape encourages the play of light and shade, which makes it particularly effective with glossy fabrics like moiré, silk or satin, or with plain white linen or cotton.

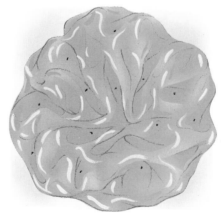

MAKING A PUFF-BALL

1 Cutting out Cut a circle of fabric 2-3 times the required width of the finished rosette: the larger the circle compared with the finished size, the more scrunched will be the finished rosette.

2 Gathering the rosette Thread a needle with a strong thread and knot the ends together to make a double thread. Run a row of running stitches round the circumference of the circle, 1.5cm (⅝in) from the edge, leaving the ends of the thread on the right side of the fabric. Pull up the thread to gather the raw edges into a small circle; knot to secure.

3 Making the rosette shape With a matching thread, take a small stitch in the centre of the rosette. Then, working from the right side, scrunch the fabric with one hand and stitch with the other, taking a small stitch in the hollows, about half way between the edge and the centre. This secures the fabric shape. If required, scrunch again and add further stitches until you are satisfied with the effect.

Fabric picture frames

▲ Perfect pair
These pressed flower pictures have splendid padded frames in damask fabric which picks up the colours from the wallpaper for perfect co-ordination. The tasselled cord completes the elegant effect.

Fabric-covered picture frames are a pretty and economical alternative to wooden frames, and will really draw attention to the pictures. Only the frame has to be covered in the main fabric, so the minimum of fabric is required, and you could probably use light to medium-weight fabric left over from other soft furnishings in the room. Dressmaking fabrics work particularly well, including silks and cottons, so there should be no problem finding an appropriate fabric for your frame.

If the picture is going to be hung, a short length of co-ordinating satin ribbon can be inserted between the frame and the back to hang the picture from. However, if the picture is to be placed on a table, it is necessary to make a back stand to prop up the picture.

Materials

Furnishing fabric(s) to cover the frame and/or mount. For the lining you can either use a separate, cheaper fabric or simply use more of the main fabric.
Squared paper for a pattern.
Stiff card for the frame and back of the picture frame.
Multi-purpose **glue** such as Copydex.
Fusible webbing such as Bondaweb.
Light to mediumweight **wadding (batting)**
Narrow ribbon to hang the picture with.
Plastic sheeting (optional) such as Artcell to protect the picture.

SIMPLE PICTURE FRAME

1 Making a pattern Using the picture as a guide, make a full-size pattern of the finished frame. Cut out the centre, remembering that wide frames are stronger and less fiddly to cover than narrow ones, so start with one at least 3cm (1¼in) deep.

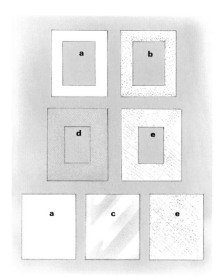

2 Cutting out Cut a piece of card round the outside of the pattern for the back. Cut out a second piece, but this time cut round the inner line as well to make the frame. From lining fabric cut a piece the same size as the back, and from wadding cut a piece the size of the frame. From main fabric cut one piece 2cm (¾in) larger than the frame. From fusible webbing cut one piece the same as the fabric frame, and one the size of the lining. You should have two pieces of card **(a)**, one of wadding **(b)**, one of lining **(c)**, one of main fabric and two of fusible webbing **(e)**.

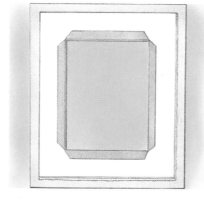

3 Making the frame Take the card frame and glue the polyester wadding to it. Fuse the webbing to the wrong side of the fabric frame. Peel off the backing and place the fabric frame right side down on the ironing board. Centre the wadding side of the card frame on top. Snip into the fabric at the inner corners and then carefully iron the excess fabric on to the back of the card on the inside edges only. Iron the fabric to the wadding on the front of the frame to hold, but do not secure the outer allowances.

4 Inserting the picture Carefully position the picture in the frame. If it is smaller than the outer edge of the frame, stick it to the inside of the frame to hold it in place.

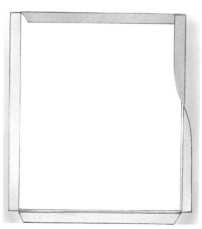

5 Joining the frame Place the remaining card on to the back of the picture and frame. Ease the outer fabric allowance of the frame to the back, encasing all layers, and fuse in place with the iron. Trim the fabric allowances at the corners so the fabric lies flat.

6 Lining the back Glue a piece of ribbon about a quarter of the way from each side on the top edge for hanging. Fuse the webbing on to the wrong side of the lining and then fuse the other side to the back, covering the fused allowances of the main fabric and the ends of the ribbon. The fusible webbing will prevent the lining from fraying.

Protective cover
To protect a favourite photograph in the frame, insert a sheet of clear plastic, such as Artcell in front of the picture. Lighter than glass and certainly not as difficult to use, clear plastic is an excellent alternative to picture glass.

RE-USABLE FRAME

The simple picture frame looks really pretty, particularly when several are arranged together, but once you have inserted the picture, it cannot be changed. This is not usually a problem, but if the frame is designed as a present, it can be made so that the picture can be inserted or changed later.

1 Cutting out Make a pattern as in step 1 for a simple picture frame and cut out the same pieces as in step 2. In addition, cut a piece from main fabric and fusible webbing the size of the card back plus 2cm (¾in) all round and a piece from lining and fusible webbing the same size as the card frame.

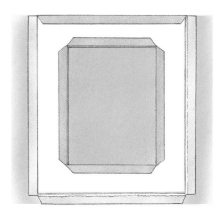

2 Making the frame Glue the wadding frame to the card and leave to dry thoroughly. Fuse the webbing to the wrong side of the main fabric frame and then peel off the protective backing. Place the card frame, wadding side down on top of the fabric and snip into the fabric allowances at the corners. Iron the allowances to the card on the inside of the frame and along the top outside edge only.

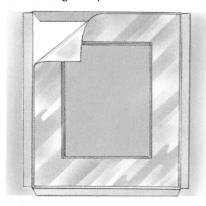

3 Finishing the frame Iron the fusible webbing to the wrong side of the lining frame. Peel off the backing and then iron on to the card frame, covering all fabric allowances except the three outside allowances which should be left free.

4 Making the back Iron the fusible backing on to the wrong side of the main back fabric. Remove the protective backing and then iron on to the remaining card. Turn the allowances to the wrong side of the card and iron these down too.

5 Assembling the frame Place the right side of the back to the wrong side of the frame and fold the free fabric allowances from the frame to the back; fuse to the back. Glue ribbon to the back for hanging as in step 6 for simple picture frames.

6 Adding the lining Fuse the webbing to the wrong side of the lining for the back and then iron this to the back of the card, covering the seam allowances. Slip the picture into place through the gap in the top of the frame.

Fabric mounts

Fabric-covered mounts make a lovely alternative to coloured card and can be used in conjunction with wooden or fabric-covered frames. You could even dispense with the frame and use the mount as a combined mount and frame.

Ready-made card mounts with one or more shapes cut out for the photographs can be bought from picture framing shops and from some haberdashery departments. These simplify making fabric mounts, but you can cut your own from mounting card, available from art shops.

MAKING A FABRIC MOUNT

1 Cutting out Purchase or make a mount from mounting card. Cut the fabric 2cm (¾in) larger all round, including the same allowance on the inside edges of the shapes. Cut fusible webbing the same size as the fabric and fuse to the wrong side of the fabric. If the frame is re-usable, cut lining fabric the same size as the mount.

2 Making the mount Peel the webbing's protective backing off, then place the card centrally on top. Snip into the fabric allowances at curves and trim at corners. Carefully fuse these allowances to the wrong side, ensuring there are no creases on the right side, then turn the card over and fuse to the right side. Fuse the lining over the back, if needed.

MAKING A SHAPED FRAME

Making the frame Cut out the card and fabric as for a fabric mount, but also cut out a piece of wadding the same size as the card. Glue the wadding to the card, and make a back piece as for a simple or re-usable picture frame. Follow the instructions for the type of frame you are making – simple or re-usable – to complete.

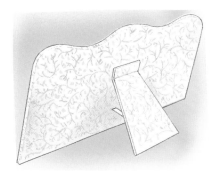

▲ **Back stand**
A back stand is ideal for table-top photographs.

▲ **Two colour damask**
A fabric mount within a padded fabric frame – the cord makes a mock mitre at the corners.

Back stand

If the picture is not going to be hung, it will require a back stand so that it can be placed on a flat surface, such as a bedside table. This is easy to make and requires only a small piece of card, a scrap of the fabric and some fusible webbing and thread.

MAKING A BACK STAND

1 Cutting out Cut a piece of card 4cm (1½in) wide and 1cm (½in) deep. Cut a second piece half the height of the frame and 6cm (2¼in) wide. Trim the larger piece equally on each side so that it tapers to 4cm (1½in) at the top end. Cut a rectangle of fabric and fusible webbing 8cm (3in) wide and the length of the two pieces of card together plus 2cm (¾in).

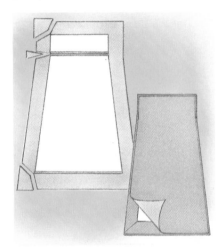

2 Covering the stand Fuse the webbing to the back of the fabric and remove the backing. Place both pieces of card centrally on the wrong side of the fabric with a small gap, no deeper than the thickness of the card, between them. Trim the seam allowances to 1.5cm (⅝in) all round. Fold the seam allowances over, snipping into the allowances for ease, and then fuse to hold. Fuse on the right side too.

3 Lining the stand Cut a piece of lining and fusible webbing the size of the stand. Fuse the webbing to the lining and then fuse the lining to back of the stand.

4 Attaching the stand Glue the top of the stand to the back of the frame so that when the lower end is angled away from the frame, it is level with the bottom. To hold the stand in place, attach a chain of plaited thread, glued to the back of the stand and to the frame.

DECORATIVE IDEAS

Mock mitres Glue strips of Russian braid from the centre corners of the frame to the outside corners before attaching the lining for the back.

Piping trim Cut and cover strips of piping long enough to go round the inside and outside edges of the frame. Glue to the wrong side of the frame on the inside edge before attaching the back, and to the outside edge before attaching the lining. Snip into the fabric covering the piping at corners for ease.

▲ Variety show
Create a variety of effects with padded picture frames.

Lace edge Use lace with one finished edge, and cut enough lace to go round the outside of the frame. Glue it to the back before attaching the back lining. For lace with two finished edges, glue the lace to the back of the frame once it is completed.

Introducing lighting

▲ Night light
Simplicity is the key to this cosy bedside lighting in a country attic.

Lighting is an important, but often overlooked aspect of the appearance, atmosphere and comfort of any home. With clever lighting a dull room reveals interesting nooks and corners, a cold room becomes warm and inviting, and an awkward workspace is suddenly a pleasure to work in. To understand the importance of artificial light in our lives, imagine the world before electricity when the working day was defined by sunset and sunrise. Everyday activities like cooking and sewing were carried out in poor lighting conditions which made

simple tasks difficult and strained the eyes. Candles and later gaslight gave limited illumination and were inflexible compared to the immense range of lighting possibilities today.

Electric light has freed us in a way that is now hard to appreciate. Good task lighting means that we can work comfortably where we want and when we want – you can even work through the night in a windowless basement if it suits you. But where modern lighting really comes into its own is in the creation of atmosphere. As long as you

grasp and apply the basic principles, you can, with a little imagination, create a home that is practical, comfortable and individual. Your hall can be warm and welcoming and your living room a soothing retreat in which to relax. In the kitchen you can combine function with friendliness, while your bedroom can be as cosy and romantic as you could wish.

A lighting checklist

In order to analyze the lighting requirements for a particular room, it is helpful to draw up a checklist.

Does the room have one function or several? Many rooms have to be multi-functional; clever lighting can make one room seem like several, illuminating dining, working, reading and sitting areas in different ways.

What mood do you want to create? In a living room you will want a different mood from that in the kitchen or bathroom. Your requirements must be clearly defined in your mind if you are to achieve them.

How many people use the room? Do any of them have special requirements? Children, for instance, may need somewhere for their homework, in which case you will need a good desk light. If you have an elderly member of the family you'll want an easy chair with a cable-switched reading lamp within easy reach beside it.

Is it a child's room? Always use safety plugs, make sure hot bulbs are out of reach and lamps are stable, and avoid trailing cables. Task lighting shouldn't be too bright – 40 or 60 watt bulbs are quite adequate.

Are there practical limitations? The extent to which you can rearrange the lighting in a room depends on how flexible the existing electrical supply is. Are you prepared for the expense and disruption of putting in new wiring and outlets?

What is your budget? If you decide exactly what you are prepared to spend before you start, you won't find the costs running away with you. Even if the ideal solution is beyond your means, with a little ingenuity you can probably find a cheaper alternative.

Types of lighting

General lighting provides background illumination – it gives you sufficient light to see, to find your way around the room, or to watch television. It can come from recessed ceiling lights, pendants or wall lights.

Atmospheric lighting is used to create mood and to add depth and interest to a room. The country style requires soft, indirect lighting, evoking a period feel of flickering fires and candle-light. Soften lighting effects by concealing lights behind pelmets and objects; consider using uplighters and corner and floor lamps for soft effects.

Task lighting allows you to carry out specific activities, for instance spotlights on kitchen work surfaces, standard lamps for reading, adjustable lamps for close up work on hobbies and sewing.

Display lighting allows you to highlight favourite objects. Undershelf strips will show off the contents of a china cabinet; a spotlight can be beamed on to a large house plant.

Halls and porches

A brightly lit porch is a welcome sight when you return home after dark, and you won't have to fumble in the dark for your key. It also allows you to check who your evening visitors are and helps deter potential burglars.

Lighting in the hall is important because it is the first place that visitors see and it sets the tone for the rest of the house. It should be warm and welcoming – so many thoughtfully arranged homes are let down by bleak and functional entrance halls. When lighting the hall, bear in mind that you need to illuminate the stairs properly. Make sure that you can switch hall and landing lights on from both levels.

▲ **Kitchen lights**
Small strip lights cleverly concealed behind the wooden pelmets in these kitchen units provide excellent lighting for the work surfaces.

◄ **Create a mood**
A pendant over your dining table creates a an intimate pool of light over the eating area – and helps to distract the guest's attention from any possible kitchen muddles behind the scenes.

Lighting the country kitchen

In a kitchen good working light is essential for efficiency and safety. Accidents can happen in poorly-lit kitchens. You need good, comfortable overall lighting – because inevitably the family congregates in the kitchen – and bright task lighting over the work surfaces. These can be lit by downlighters or spots which shed a pool of light on to the working surface and should be placed directly above and slightly to the front of the work surface. If you have wall-mounted cupboards use fluorescent or incandescent tubes which can be hidden behind pelmets under the cupboards.

With fluorescent light, choose a colour-corrected tube – the old-fashioned daylight tubes had a chilly bluish cast. Avoid lights with a pinkish cast in a dining or serving area as these can make meat look undercooked.

If you have a combined kitchen and dining room you can't really get away from the cooking clutter while you're eating. One way to overcome this is to have separate lighting systems for the dining and the kitchen areas. A pendant light hung low over the table, or a rise-and-fall fitting, will shed a pool of light on the eating area, making that the centre of attention. By switching off the lights in the working area you can draw attention away from the pots and pans and concentrate on the meal.

Living rooms

The living room is where you entertain and where you relax to talk, watch TV or listen to music. You should try to achieve an adequate level of background lighting, with additional sidelights and display lights to add interest and create a pleasing, homely atmosphere.

General lighting can be provided by recessed downlighters, wall lights, uplighters or a suitable pendant. Choose fittings appropriate to the country look. For walls look at bracket lights in brass with pretty glass shades, wooden brackets with candle-type fittings, or glass uplighters. There is a wonderful range of these, with designs dating from the 1930s and 1940s, and the lights are often cast from their original moulds.

With enough basic lighting you should now create some interest and variety. Look around your room and note its best features and your favourite objects. If, for example, you are lucky enough to have a fireplace with pretty Victorian tiles, you could put a tiny spot light nearby to highlight them. Or you could fill the grate with dried flowers and hide a light behind it.

If you have treasured objects – a collection of glass in a cabinet, a painting

▼ General and display lighting
Background lighting for the living room is provided by candle wall-lighters with apple white bulbs to enhance the green tints in the room. The china is highlighted by a spotlight concealed in the cabinet.

▲ Atmospheric lighting
A small Tiffany-style table lamp with a tinted apricot white bulb gives a cosy glow to a corner of the living room; consider every available shelf or table as a potential place for soft, indirect lighting.

▲ **Dressing pretty**
A matching pair of table lamps provides most attractive lighting for a dressing table mirror.

Bathrooms

In bathrooms you need a combination of background lighting and task lighting. Look for fittings which will survive a damp atmosphere – choose plastic and glass shades rather than fabric or paper. A glass pendant bowl will give you a soft diffused light, while a concealed strip or an angle light over the mirror will give you enough light to make-up or shave. Wall lights – either brackets or uplighters – are also very attractive in a bathroom setting.

Bedrooms

Aim for soft background lighting which can be provided by central pendants or wall uplighters. You will also need bedside lights to read by. The switches should be easily accessible even when you are lying down, so that you don't have to fumble in the dark. Ideally, it should be possible to switch on the bedside lamps from the door as well as from the bedside – but this complicated wiring arrangement ought to be carried out by a professional.

Table lamps with fabric shades to match your colour scheme look pretty on bedside cabinets or tables. You will also need specific task lighting – if you have a dressing table, for example, or a long mirror. If your dressing table is in a recess, wall lights may be the answer, otherwise choose a pretty table lamp that matches the bedside lamps.

▲ **Light to shave by**
A swan-necked lamp gives a traditional feel to the bathroom and provides good light for the mirror.

▲ **Bedroom glow**
Pairs of glass-shaded wall lights on a dimmer switch give a soft romantic feel to the bedroom.

or a sculpture – arrange your lighting so that they are spotlit in some way. A downlighter, a concealed spotlight or a simple table lamp could all be used to focus attention on the object and allow it to be seen to its best advantage.

Next, turn to practicalities. If children do their homework there you will need a good desk lamp. If one or more people read you should provide adequate lighting of the right type in the right place – a standard lamp behind a chair, or a lamp on a shelf, which sheds light from the side on to the page. If there are hobbyists in the family, they should be catered for – a knitter, for example, should have an adjustable light which shines on to the work.

Fitted lampshades

Fitted lampshades are an elegant addition to graceful lamp bases and light fittings, and look particularly good in dining rooms, living rooms and formal bedrooms. Despite their tailored appearance, they are deceptively easy to make, and you don't need to be a neat seamstress either, since the hand stitching is covered with a trimming such as binding or braid.

A lining on such a shade is optional, but it provides a professional finish by concealing the frame and the raw edges of the seams in the main fabric. It also helps to block out the outline of the bulb and struts when the light is on, and reflects light, giving the finished effect greater brilliance.

Bowed lampshades
Fitted lampshades come in many shapes and sizes – panelled, bowed, tiffany style and with straight or scalloped edges – but of all these, the bowed shape is perhaps the easiest to fit and also one of the most widely used. These shades have circular rings at the top and bottom, with the top ring either the same size or smaller than the bottom one. The sides are panelled off by struts which curve inwards, giving the shade a very elegant appearance.

Fabric selection
Even if the shade is lined, this sort of cover does not require a great deal of fabric, but you do need to make your choice carefully. Soft, easily draped fabric such as fine cotton, silk, satin and crêpe are best for both the main fabric and lining. Stiff fabrics with no stretch should be avoided, as should fabrics which fray easily.

Since the fabric is used on the bias, patterns with an obvious direction should be avoided. For this reason, most fitted lampshades are made from plain fabrics, but some all-over patterns, miniprints and checks can be used if you prefer. Hold the fabric up by the corner to see if the pattern looks good from this angle – if so, you can use it. Remember that even plain fabrics sometimes have a woven pattern, so check these fabrics on the diagonal too.

The fabric colour you choose should go with the colour of the lamp base and décor of the room, but for maximum light reflection, select a paler lining fabric to go with it. If the main fabric is cream or white, with a matching lining, it will radiate a bright light, while a warm colour such as yellow, pale pink or peach will emit a more comfortable glow, making these a good choice for bedrooms or sitting rooms.

▼ **Stretch fit**
Most plain fabrics and some patterned ones can be used to cover bowed lampshades, but they should have a fair amount of stretch on the bias.

Materials
Bowed lampshade frame.
Furnishing fabric.
Stretchy lining fabric.
Matching thread.
Trimmings.
Pins and needle.
Tailor's chalk.
Fabric glue to attach the trimmings.

BOWED LAMPSHADE

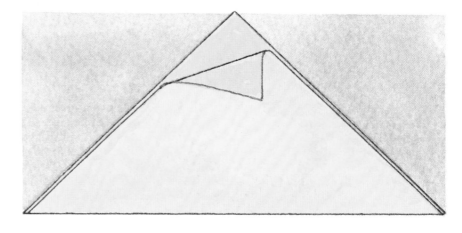

1 Preparation Buy a lampshade frame of the size you want, or remove the old fabric cover from an existing shade. Tape the struts and rings firmly with strong, white cotton tape to make a base on which to stitch the fabric cover.

2 Cutting out Cut a square of fabric on the straight grain, which, when folded into a triangle from corner to corner, will cover half the lampshade with a 4cm (1½in) overlap all round.

A square, one and a half times the length of one strut, should be sufficient, but if the top ring is large, you may require more. Cut lining fabric to the same size.

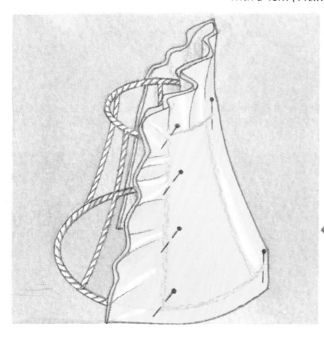

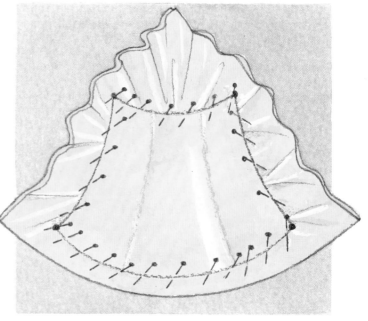

3 Pinning the fabric With the main fabric folded into a triangle, right sides together, and with the fold parallel to the bottom ring, pin the doubled fabric to the frame at the top and bottom of two opposite struts. Pull the fabric taut and add further pins at the centre of the fabric on each of the two struts and each ring. Add more pins in between and adjust the fabric until all wrinkles are smoothed out.

4 Marking the fabric With tailor's chalk, draw along the fabric directly over the two end struts, then mark the position of the top and bottom rings where they meet the struts. Draw lightly along the pinned line of the top and bottom rings. Pin the fabric together at the edges to hold, then carefully remove the pins that fix it to the frame.

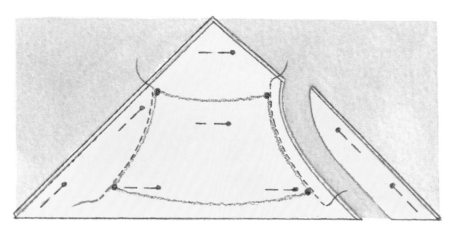

5 Stitching side seams Still with the fabric pinned together, extend the chalk line by 2cm (¾in) on each end, then stitch along the chalk lines. Trim away the excess fabric along the two sides, leaving a 1cm (⅜in) seam allowance. Trim along the top and bottom edges, leaving a 1.5cm (⅝in) gap between the marked line and the edge.

6 Making the lining Fold the lining into a triangle, right sides together, and pull on the two ends to ease out the stretch. Matching the straight grain of lining and main fabric, pin the main fabric to the lining and trim the lining to the same size. Stitch the two side seams, taking a 1.3cm (½in) seam allowance. This makes the lining piece slightly smaller than the main fabric to allow for it being inside the frame. Press the seams open on lining and fabric.

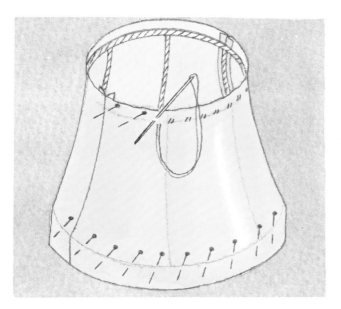

7 Fitting the cover Turn the main piece right side out and slip over the taped frame. Position the two seams exactly over a strut with the marks matching the rings at each end. Pin the fabric to the struts round both rings, pulling smooth to ease out any wrinkles. Using a double thread, oversew the fabric to the tape on the top and bottom rings. The stitches will be covered by the lining or trimmings later. Trim the surplus fabric close to stitching.

8 Positioning lining Slip the lining into the frame, with the right side facing inside. Pin roughly in position with the seams matching the seams on the main fabric and with excess fabric overlapping the frame.

▲ Inside story
A lining gives a fitted lampshade a professional finish, and the strip of lining which neatens the area around the gimbal is the final touch.

10 Attaching the lining Bring the lining over the rings to the outside and oversew to the rings with a double thread in the same way as the main fabric. If trimming with braid or ribbon, ensure the stitches are on the front of the shade, rather than the top so that the trimming will cover them. Trim away surplus fabric close to the stitching and glue on a trimming (see next page).

tip

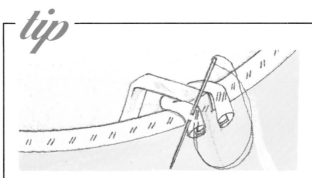

Professional gimbal edge
To finish the lining round the gimbal like an expert, cut two strips of excess lining fabric 2.5cm (1in) wide and 5cm (2in) long. Fold the two long edges of each strip to the centre, then fold in half lengthways. Wrap the strip under the gimbal and stitch to the top of the ring on each side; trim.

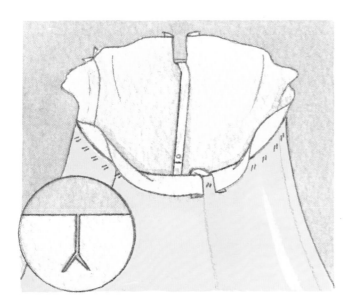

9 At the fitting The upper ring has a light fitting, called a gimbal, round which the lining must be fitted. Mark the position of the underside of the gimbal. Cut the fabric centrally to a point 1cm (⅜in) above it, then cut diagonal slits to each corner. Turn the fabric under at the gimbal to neaten, then finish pinning the lining to the rings, pulling out any remaining wrinkles as you do so.

DECORATIVE TRIMMINGS

Binding It is possible to make your own bias binding. However, it is much easier to use wide, ready-made bias binding. Turn the end of the binding to the wrong side, then with right sides facing, stitch the binding to the shade along the first fold, starting at a seam in the fabric. Turn back the other end of the binding. Flip the binding over to the lining side and glue or slipstitch in place.

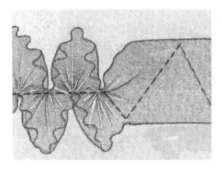

Ruched velvet Cut a length of velvet ribbon twice the length of each ring. Sew across the ribbon in a regular zigzag line taking small running stitches, and drawing up the ribbon at intervals until it fits the shade. Catchstitch the ribbon to the shade so that it slightly overlaps the edge, giving a scalloped effect.

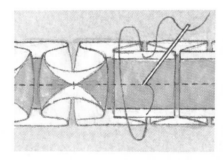

Pleated ribbon Cut two pieces of ribbon, three times the length of each ring, and stitch the narrower piece to the wider one along the middle. Fold the fabric into box pleats of equal size by pleating the fabric first one way and then the other; stitch. Pinch the box pleats together at the centre and catch the edges of the outer ribbon with a matching thread. Glue to the shade.

Braid or fringing Turn one end of the trimming under, then glue in position on the shade, starting at a seam on the fabric. Turn the other end under so that it butts up to the fold of the first end; glue. Bulldog clips can be used to hold the trimming in place while it dries.

A selection of tapes, ribbons and braids suitable for trimming lampshades.

Pleated fabric lampshades

Depending on the type of frame and choice of fabric, a pleated lampshade can take on a number of different looks, and be adapted to suit almost any setting. A plain fabric, pleated into even, crisp folds and mounted on a steeply sloping or drum-shaped frame, will create a shade whose sober charm will be ideal for a smart living or dining room, or a formal bedroom. A patterned fabric mounted on a gently sloping frame, like a coolie, will have a fresher and more modern feel, as the pleats will fan out towards the base of the shade to soften the overall effect.

When making your own lampshade you can afford to be selective, so take some time to choose a suitable fabric which will complement the room's colour scheme, style and existing furn-ishings. An easy option is simply to use the same fabric as the curtains and other existing soft furnishings, but do be wary of creating an overly co-ordinated look – most rooms really benefit from the spark of individuality which small accessories can bring.

Suitable fabrics

As pleated lampshades are often left unlined, try to choose a medium-weight fabric with a fairly dense weave; if the fabric is too fine or has an open weave, both the light bulb and frame will show through. However, thin fabrics can be used successfully if backed with a soft iron-on interfacing before being mounted on to the shade, or if the finished shade is lined. Avoid very thick fabrics, which will be difficult to pleat up

▲ Pleated from top to toe
A fresh floral print loosely pleated over a gently sloping frame makes a charming informal shade. A fabric-covered base completes the effect.

and will allow only a little light to filter through. Pleat up a patterned fabric before you buy it to check the finished effect.

When choosing fabric for making a lampshade, always consider the way in which it transmits light. Beware of some colours, particularly blues and greens, which can make a room feel cold. The safest bets are golden or reddish shades, like peach, apricot and yellow, which create a soft, warm and cosy glow. In the interests of safety, try to choose a non-flammable fabric.

Materials

Lampshade frame with vertical or sloping sides; avoid frames with bowed sides, waisted shapes or shaped edges.

Strong cotton tape for covering the struts and rings of the frame

Fabric to cover the frame (see step 2 for quantity)

Pins

Thimble

Matching thread

Bias binding 2cm (¾in) wide, to fit round the base and top rings of the frame, plus a little extra for ease; either buy ready-made binding, or make up binding from the same fabric as the shade.

Fabric glue to attach the binding

PLEATED LAMPSHADE

These instructions are for an unlined lampshade with gently sloping sides. The fabric is marked off into a series of equal sections, which are pleated up and pinned in place one at a time; by working section by section, you can achieve a perfectly even finish and will find the fabric far easier to work with.

1 Preparing the frame If using the frame from an existing lampshade, first remove the old fabric. If necessary, bind the struts and rings of the frame with strong cotton tape – this will create a fabric base to which the fabric cover can then be stitched.

2 Measuring up and cutting out Measure the circumference of the top ring, multiply this measurement by three, and add a further 6cm (2½in); make sure that this measurement is at least 1½ times the circumference of the base ring. Then measure the depth of the frame, from the top ring to the base ring, and add 6cm (2½in). Cut a rectangle of your fabric to these dimensions. Where you need to cut more than one width to create the required length, do not sew the widths together – they will be overlapped during pleating (see step 7). Allow an extra 5cm (2in) for each overlap.

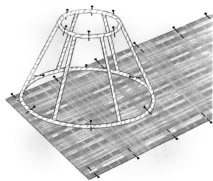

3 Sectioning the fabric Count the number of panels on the frame. Mark off a 3cm (1¼in) allowance at both short ends of the length of fabric, then divide it into the same number of sections as the frame, marking off each one with pins at the top and lower edges. Use a pin to mark the centre of each panel on the frame, and also the centre of each fabric section, on the top and lower edges.

4 Pinning the fabric to the frame Pin the first fabric section over one of the panels on the frame. Make sure that an equal fabric allowance extends beyond the top and base of the frame, and that the 3cm (1¼in) end allowance overlaps the side strut; line up the two section marks and the halfway marks on the fabric with two side struts and the centre point on the frame; pin the fabric in place on the frame.

◄ Colourful checks
With a little experimentation, tartans and checks can be used to great effect on pleated lampshades to create interesting patterns and strong bands of colour. Self-fabric binding cut on the bias to create diagonal checks provides a stylish finishing touch.

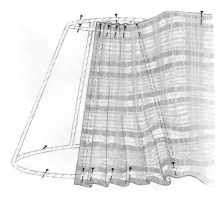

5 **Pleating up the fabric** Gauge how many pleats look best between each strut, and roughly pin in place along the top and bottom rings; adjust the fabric until you find an attractive arrangement, and make sure all the pleats are the same size.

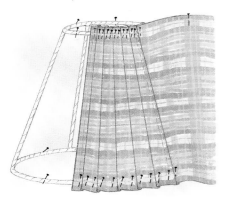

6 **Pinning the pleats in place** When satisfied with the number and size of the pleats, pin them neatly and securely in place along the top ring; the fold of the last pleat should just reach the second strut. To pin the pleats to the base ring, follow the foldline of each pleat down from the top ring, gently pressing it into a soft crease, but pleat up an increasingly small amount of fabric as you near the base ring; with the fabric stretched across the shade, pin each pleat in place. The pleats will then fan out evenly and attractively as the frame widens.

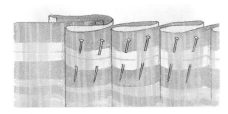

7 **Overlapping fabric widths** Repeat to pleat up the fabric between each strut in the same way. If you need to join on extra fabric widths, slip the edge of the new fabric piece into the last pleat, so that the join will not be visible on the right side of the shade. Then continue to pleat up as usual, making sure the join remains invisible as you fan out the pleats towards the base ring.

8 **A final check** When you reach the final pleat, trim any excess fabric, then pin the pleat in place over the fabric allowance left at the start, turning in the raw edges. Check that all the pleats around the shade are the same size, and make adjustments where necessary.

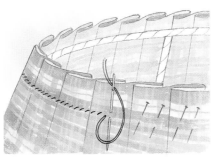

9 **Stitching the fabric to the frame** Using a double thread, oversew round the top of the frame from the outside, making sure each pleat is firmly stitched to the taped ring. Repeat round the bottom ring and remove all pins. Trim the excess fabric from just above the stitching on both the top and the base ring.

▲ A warm glow
Pleated shades in plain fabrics are an ideal choice for elegant settings.

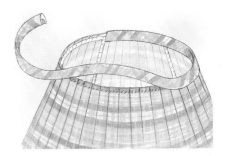

10 **Trimming the shade** Trim the shade with matching or contrast binding to conceal the raw edges. If you are binding in matching fabric, press the raw long edges of your bias strips to the wrong side. Then fold the binding in half lengthways, and glue in place over the raw edges of the fabric, to conceal the top and base rings. Position the binding end at the back of the shade over a strut and in line with the edge of a pleat; turn under 5mm (¼in) at the raw ends and butt together.

Pleated patterns
Using the same technique on a plain fabric, you can create striking pleated patterns, which will stand out when light is shone through the lampshade. Rather than pleating up the whole length of fabric, use a shorter strip and only pleat up groups of two or three pleats, leaving smooth gaps between each group; or create an attractive stripy effect by alternating between single pleats and spaces of the same width.

BOX-PLEATED LAMPSHADE

Box-pleated lampshades are a smart variation on ordinary pleated shades, and are made similarly.

1 Preparing the fabric Prepare a steep-sided or drum-shaped frame. Measure circumference of top ring, multiply by three, and add 6cm (2½in). Measure the depth of the shade and cut out fabric to this size. Divide fabric into sections, marking off allowances at both ends.

2 Marking up the pleats As box-pleats are more difficult to measure and fold evenly, you will find it easier to mark up their positions with tailor's chalk before the fabric is mounted on the shade. Divide the first section into a suitable number of pleats, remembering that each pleat takes three times as much fabric as its finished width. Check the finished effect by mounting the first section on the shade and pinning in place. Adjust the fabric until satisfied with the result.

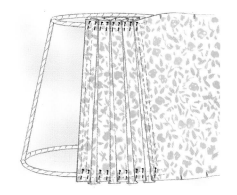

3 Pinning the fabric in place Once satisfied, remove the first section from the shade and mark up the other sections in the same way. Working on one section at a time and pleating the fabric according to the chalk marks, pin the fabric to the frame along the top and then the bottom ring; try to avoid opening up the pleats as you work towards the lower ring – to accommodate the shape of the frame, reduce the amount of fabric behind the pleat.

4 Finishing the shade Make a final check, then stitch the fabric to the shade as before. Cut away the excess fabric, and bind to finish.

◄ **Classically elegant**
Floral prints soften the tailored lines of a box-pleated shade.

▼ **Decorative detail**
Emphasize a smocked shade with ribbon bows in a contrasting shade.

SMOCKED LAMPSHADE

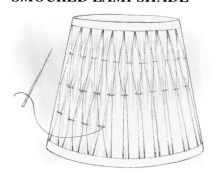

By smocking the pleats of a box-pleated shade, you can transform its tailored lines into ripples of soft folds, and create a wonderfully textured surface.

Starting near the top of the shade and working in a straight line around it, pinch each box pleat to the centre and secure with a few small stitches. Then measure a third to halfway down the shade (depending on its height) pull each pleat apart, and use small stitches to attach it to the neighbouring pleat. Measure an equal distance down the shade and stitch the pleats as for the top line of smocking. Continue with rows of smocking to just above lower ring.

Simple shelving

In any house where space is tight, increasing the amount of storage on offer will help to ease the squeeze. Shelving is the cheapest way to make use of odd corners and unused spaces and requires neither special skills or equipment. Using widely available materials, any competent home decorator can put up a simple shelf with bracket supports.

▼ An extra shelf
This combination shelf and curtain pole is very versatile: the shelf can provide a home for plants and favourite crockery, while the pole, here, is used for drying herbs.

Choosing shelf materials

Select the material for the shelf not just because it looks good but bearing in mind what it is going be used for. Strong materials are needed to take the weight of books, while thin, lightweight shelves are fine for, say, china and ornaments. Any shelf will sag if the distance between the supports is too large, so remember, the thinner the shelf, the shorter the span between the brackets. See the chart overleaf for bracket spacing on solid walls.

Timber There are two types available, either **hardwood**, which is extremely durable, though quite expensive, and softwood, such as pine. Whichever type of wood you choose, specify planed square edge timber (PSE), which is planed on three sides and has a smooth finish that needs little extra work.

Man-made boards These often come veneered with a wood grain and with all four edges finished. If it has to be cut, an edging strip can be ironed on to the exposed side later. If the surface is going to be painted use plywood, blockboard or extra-rigid medium density fibreboard (MDF).

Glass This is ideal for display shelving in an alcove or across a window. The edges should be perfectly smooth for safety. The glass merchant will be able to do this when you buy the shelves.

Choosing brackets

When putting up a small shelf on its own, or perhaps a pair, you can use basic L-shaped brackets.

These vary from simple shaped pieces of wood to fancy wrought iron scrolls. Some shops offer a shelf pack with brackets and fixings included, otherwise you have to buy all the items separately.

Shelf fixings

Masonry walls Brackets are securely fixed with screws and wallplugs. To attach heavy shelves to masonry walls use an expanding wall anchor. This is an all-metal fixing that consists of a bolt with an expanding outer shell that grips the sides of the hole as the bolt is tightened.

Hollow walls If possible, screw directly into the wooden framing uprights that lie behind the wall facing. To locate these, tap the wall with your fingers until the sound is more solid and check it is the right spot by piercing the board with a bradawl. Fix the shelf brackets to these uprights (usually spaced at 40cm (16in) intervals) using wood screws at least 3.8cm (1½in) long. A lightweight shelf which is not expected to take heavy loads can be put up on a hollow wall using special screws which open out behind the wall.

Spacing brackets		
Thickness	19mm (¾in)	2.5cm (1in)
Medium load	70cm (27in)	90cm (36in)
Heavy load	50cm (20in)	70cm (27in)

▲ On display
These pine shelves fill the alcove providing useful storage space for many household objects, which look better displayed than hidden away.

◄ Decorated brackets
Plaster corbels have been used to support a simple kitchen shelf adding a decorative leaf design on an otherwise plain wall, and enhancing the overall design of the kitchen.

Materials
Shelves and **brackets**.
Power or **hand drill** with a set of **drill bits**.
Spirit level and **plumb line**.
Screwdriver and **bradawl**.

A **wood saw** if the shelves need cutting to size.
Tape measure, pencil and **ruler**.
Wall fixings, if not supplied with shelf, including the appropriate **screws** and **wallplugs** for the type of wall.

Safety check
When hanging shelves, it is vital to ensure you will not be drilling into electric cables or water pipes. Invest in a cable and pipe finder which gives a signal when passing over a pipe or cable.

PUTTING UP BRACKET SHELVES

1 Positioning the brackets Decide where you would like to position the shelf. The brackets should be placed about 50-75cm (20-30in) apart. Hold a bracket up to the spot and mark with a pencil through each screw hole.

2 Drilling the wall Choose a drill bit suitable for the type of wall and one size larger than the screws you plan to use. Hold the drill up to the first pencil mark, keep it at right angles to the wall and use a steady pressure to drill holes to the correct depth (at least 2.5cm (1in) into solid brick). Do not force the drill in or this will make it wander. Insert the wallplugs then screw the bracket into place.

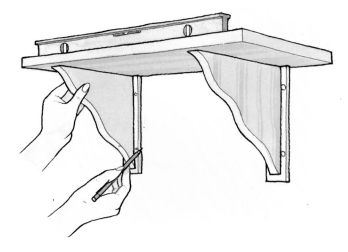

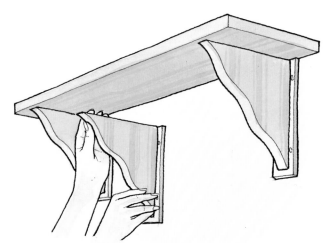

3 Check it is level Hold the second bracket in position against the wall. Place the shelf across the two brackets with the spirit level resting on top. When satisfied that the shelf is straight, mark the screw holes of the second bracket with a pencil.

4 Dealing with longer shelves A centre bracket may be needed to stop a longer shelf from sagging in the middle. Attach the two outside brackets first and place the shelf on them before marking the position of the third bracket.

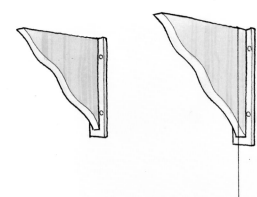

5 Check the line up When hanging two or more shelves, one above the other, screw the top brackets in place first, without fixing the shelf to them. Hang a plumb line over the side and use it as a guide to position the other brackets.

▲ *Homemade brackets With a little skill, and a mitre box for cutting accurate angles, you can make your own brackets from lengths of timber screwed together.*

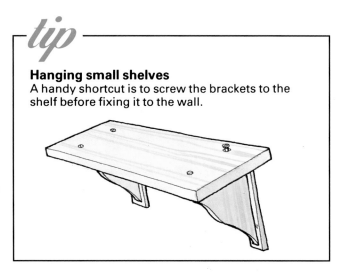

Hanging small shelves
A handy shortcut is to screw the brackets to the shelf before fixing it to the wall.

◄ Green corner
A white corner shelf, with unusual brackets holds a white bowl full of trailing plants.

▼ Lacy detail
Cast iron shelf brackets have an open lacy effect, which fit in with the cut out detail above the hob.

Making the most of storage

As the old proverb says, 'A place for everything and everything in its place' makes for an orderly life. In an ideal world, every item would have a regular home in the house. To ensure this, you need plenty of ever-expanding cupboard space – and a family that puts things back where they belong.

When choosing a cupboard pay attention to the door design. Wood panelled doors will neatly hide the contents from view, no matter how untidily, which is great for the out-of-sight, out-of-mind school of house-keeping. Glass fronts, open metal grilles or chicken wire on the doors create a

display cabinet. Behind either sort of doors, there may be shelves, drawers, hooks, pegs or rails.

▼ *Quilt cupboard*
A gracious old cupboard provides an ideal hideaway or display case for some pretty quilts and blankets.

▲ Fireside recesses
Building a fitted cupboard with shelves into an alcove beside a chimney breast makes sensible use of a rather inaccessible area of the room. Here, wire mesh instead of door panels protects some handsome, valuable volumes from prying fingers and idle curiosity, but still lets them be seen and admired.

▼ Part of the scenery
A run of cupboards along the bedhead wall provides plenty of much-needed storage and hanging space in this bedroom. They have been taken over the bed and become part of the architecture of the room. Some door panels are replaced by mirrors, while fabric behind the glazed doors links with the curtains.

Fitted cupboards

The concept of a fitted kitchen or fitted bedroom, with a built-in assortment of cupboards selected to match your personal taste and specific requirements, is a familiar one. Contrary to popular opinion, fitted furniture has been around a long time, so it is just as appropriate in the traditional, country-style home as the free-standing items. Fitted cupboards are popular because they use space efficiently and give the room a comprehensive, planned look.

Shop round before you make a purchase. There are many different styles and materials, from veneered timber to melamine, in rustic country styles and elegant period designs.

Most self-assembly units can be installed by a competent craftsperson. If you are unsure about your skills, it is worth hiring a carpenter to do the job properly or use the shop's fitters.

Locations

The easiest location for fitting an off-the-peg cupboard system is in a straight run along a wall. Such an ideal situation rarely exists, by the time windows, chimney breasts, doors and radiators are taken into account. You may have to consider a radical solution like moving a radiator, knocking out a chimney breast or blocking a redundant doorway to make room for cupboards.

Alternatively, alcoves provide a neat location for a fitted cupboard. In some cases it is possible to create a cupboard by closing off the recess space with a frame and door. An alcove is usually shallow, so in a bedroom you may need to hang clothes against the wall, rather than along it, since a hanger requires a minimum depth of 56cm (22in).

Kitchen cupboards don't generally need to be as deep as hanging cupboards. They can be fitted with shelves for crockery or foodstuffs or with pegs along the back wall to make a broom cupboard.

For an unusual or awkward location, it is wiser to have a customised cupboard built to fit the space precisely. The oddly shaped area under the stairs can be closed off fairly easily with doors and used for all manner of storage.

Fitting considerations

When planning the location of a cupboard, always allow for the opening swing of the doors, plus space for standing while you open them. Leave a clearance in front of at least twice the width of the doors or on average 90cm (3ft). Check that the door to the room and any open drawers won't block the opening of the cupboard doors either.

A cupboard door should open wide, exposing the entire hanging or shelving space. Sliding doors are a neat solution in a small space, but they can sometimes prevent you from seeing the entire interior at a glance.

Lighting is also important if you are to be able to see what is inside. Opening the cupboard doors can cast the interior into shadow, so you may have to relocate light fittings or fix a light inside.

If a cupboard door has a mirror on the outside or inside, make sure that there is sufficient space for you to see yourself full length, at a distance of about 1½-2m (5-6ft). Mirror-lined doors should open with their backs to the window, so that the light shines on you.

◄ Sat in the corner
A pine corner cupboard makes good use of otherwise wasted space by storing some fine china. When open, the doors create a frame.

▼ Behind closed doors
A wall of tall, narrow cupboards is a splendid solution for those who hanker after an uncluttered kitchen. The empty space above makes a handy shelf for baskets.

▼ Bathing belle
Hung on the bathroom wall, this rustic little cabinet provides compact storage for toiletries. Roughly washed white paint gives it a dreamy, sea-worn quality.

Free-standing cupboards

You may prefer to assemble your kitchen or bedroom furniture piecemeal from a variety of cupboards instead of from a fitted range. This produces an accumulated-over-the-years style of furnishing, which is rich in character.

Free-standing cupboards are often really beautiful, well-made items of furniture. They can be antique and collectable, or contemporary in design. Currently, there is a vogue for siting a bedroom cupboard or wardrobe as major pieces of display furniture in the living room, kitchen or hallway, which can look very exciting and magnificent.

One big advantage of free-standing cupboards over their fitted counterparts is that they can be moved. They can also be taken with you when you move; you won't begrudge spending a fair amount of money on a quality cupboard if you know it is going to stay in the family.

The downside is that separate cupboards do not always make the most efficient use of space. A single wardrobe occupies a certain width and depth, depending on its size, plus equal gaps on either side before the neighbouring piece of furniture can be positioned. There will also often be a dead space between the top of the cupboard and the ceiling. With fitted cupboards you could build in a taller unit, making the room look bigger.

Planning your purchases

A home is very rarely sorted out in one go. In fact most people take about four years before they get things right. You need to live in a place to discover what you really need and want in the way of storage cupboards. Spend time planning your needs – a checklist of your requirements will help to focus your mind. If you are an avid shoe collector, for example, you will need adequate storage for them; a voracious reader requires plenty of bookshelves.

In kitchens

Cupboards, whether ready made, home made, built in or free standing, must suit the goods to be stored in them. In an old-fashioned kitchen, a cupboard can be used for keeping brooms and cleaning equipment, as a larder for dry goods, or simply as a storage cabinet.

If you have a large farmhouse-style kitchen, free-standing cupboards and dressers will look solid and charming. The mellow tones of old pine are always attractive, but staining, woodgraining, stencilling or free-hand painted decorations can be applied to add a splash of colour, disguise the ravages of time, tie the piece in with the decorative scheme

▲ **Hide and seek**
What a difference a coat of paint has made to this small cupboard. The inside glows in a pinkish coral colour and acts as a warm contrast to the cool blue exterior.
   As a result, it has found a delightful new role, displaying a treasure trove of lovely old books and curios. The contents are too interesting to be hidden away, so the doors are left casually ajar and show off the collection.

◄ **Jewel bright**
The current trend for siting bedroom cupboards in the living room is worth copying. This lovely old press has been stained in a brilliant shade of jade, which lends glowing colour and ample storage space to a country-style living room. Treated in this way, it becomes an important decorative feature in the room.

or draw attention to any uniquely fine features.

Old cupboards can be picked up at auctions and house sales for quite reasonable prices, with the best prices being given for the smaller examples which fit most easily into the more confined spaces in contemporary homes. Do check the dimensions of the item before you make a bid, especially if you have a narrow or awkwardly shaped hallway through which you will have to manoeuvre the piece into position.

Some old wardrobes can be so large, in fact, that you may have difficulty in getting it into your home or up the stairs to the bedroom. However, such excellent bargains can be picked up that it might be worth considering carefully dismantling a favourite piece, as long as it is not very valuable, to get it into the room. It can then be reassembled once it is in place.

An attractive cupboard can be a great way of making use of otherwise useless space. In the front hall or lobby, it can be used to store outdoor gear, while a small cupboard on a landing could be useful for storing linen.

▲ Wired for display
The beauty of a wire-fronted cupboard is that the interior is always clearly visible yet ventilated, even when the doors are closed. This opens up umpteen opportunities for some zany decorating ideas. For instance, here, potted paper sunflower heads and candles in glasses, stand proudly and somewhat incongruously in front of the more conventional stacks of china plates and tureens.

▶ Reformed character
Paint techniques are simple devices for transforming the character of an old cupboard. Here, the pine was treated to give it a softly limed effect.
Originally intended for display, this cupboard has also undergone a change of use and now provides attractive hanging space in a country bedroom.

Decorative finishes

A beautiful old polished mahogany or satinwood cupboard, with a wonderfully rich grain and patina, is a lovely object in its own right and will be a significant feature in any decorative scheme. It only needs to be given plenty of space to be seen to advantage.

Less attractive fitted and unfitted cupboards can be finished in a variety of ways, to fit in amicably with their surroundings. Doors may be solid, glazed or filled with lattice work, metal grilles or chicken wire. You can entirely alter the appearance of a cupboard by changing its doors, replacing plain glazing with coloured glass, or painting the glass to emulate a stained glass panel effect.

Glass doors can be screened with gathered fabric, picked up from other soft-furnishings in the room to provide a visual link. Lace pinned against the glass, showing all the intricacy of the design, also looks remarkably pretty.

Paint finishes

There are a host of attractive paint techniques that can be used to incorporate a fitted cupboard into the overall room scheme, or to give an old or plain cupboard a new lease of life. Graining, dragging and sponging provide you with plenty of opportunities to express your creativity and enhance a rather plain piece of furniture.

Some of the prettiest effects are achieved using bright, unusual colour combinations, combined with distressed paint work. You could simply pick a colour from the decorative scheme and use that or go for a bold contrast colour, so that the cupboard becomes an important colour accent.

Scandinavian designs offer inspiring ideas for painted furniture, in lovely shades of blues and greens gently washed and rubbed to give them a time-worn quality. America, too, has a long tradition of painted furniture; the colourful folksy, naïve designs of the Pennsylvania Dutch are especially jolly, and ideal for a child's room or an old-fashioned country kitchen.

Instead of paint, wallpaper can be pasted into the door panels and varnished, again providing a visual link with the rest of the room. Stencils, freehand painting or découpage techniques can also be applied to create charmingly original effects.

Door furniture is also important. Look for pretty ceramic knobs with a floral motif, plain glass or, better still, coloured glass knobs in brilliant colours. Brass is traditional and adds a touch of mellow sparkle.

▲ **Classical designs**
Imaginative motifs, skilfully painted in a sensitive colour scheme, create a masterpiece of a cupboard.

▼ **Blushing trellis**
A spiralling ribbon motif on the border inspires a bold lattice treatment for these cupboard panels.

INDEX

Page numbers in *italic* refer to illustrations
and captions

ACKNOWLEDGEMENTS

PHOTOGRAPHS: 4 Dulux, 7(bl) Marks and Spencer (cr) EM/Steve Tanner, 8(t) Marks and Spencer (b) EM/Steve Tanner, 9 Dorma, 10 Paper Moon, 11,16 Arthur Sanderson and Son, 17 EM/Steve Tanner, 18,19(t) Arthur Sanderson and Son, 19(b) EWA/Spike Powell, 20(t) Tomkinson's Carpets (b) Dorma, 21 EM/Simon Page-Ritchie, 22 Stoddard, 23(tl) EM/Steve Tanner (tr) Laura Ashley (bl) Ken Kirkwood (br) Laura Ashley, 24 Arthur Sanderson and Son, 25(tr) EWA/Spike Powell (cl) Laura Ashley (b) Richard Paul, 26(tl) MFI (br) EWA/Tom Leighton, 27 EM/Simon Page-Ritchie, 28 Arthur Sanderson and Son, 29(tl) Richard Paul (b) Warner Fabrics, 30(t) Richard Paul (b) EWA/Neil Lorimer, 31 EM/Simon Page-Ritchie, 32(tl) EWA/Di Lewis (b) Rene Stoeltie, 33(r) Hill and Knowles (bl) EM/Simon Page-Ritchie, 34(t) Sterling Roncraft (b) EM/Simon Page-Ritchie, 35(tl) EWA/Spike Powell (tr) Ken Kirkwood (bl) EM/Simon Page-Ritchie (br) EWA/Michael Dunne, 36(tl) Anna French (tr) Habitat (b) The Nursery Window, 37 EM/Steve Tanner, 38(t) IPC Magazines/Robert Harding Syndication (b) Richard Paul, 39(t) EWA/Di Lewis (b) EWA/Brian Harrison, 40(t) Mondadori Press (b) EWA/Jerry Tubby, 41(cl) Laura Ashley (cr) EWA/Michael Corbett (b) Laura Ashley, 42(t) EWA/Andreas von Einsiedel (c) Dorma (b) Richard Paul, 43 EM/John Suett, 44(tl) Bo Appeltoft (bl) Laura Ashley 44–45 Crown Paints, 46(tl) Jahres Zeiten Verlag (b) Harriet's House, 47(t) EWA/Tom Leighton (bl) Marie Claire Maison/Girandeau/Postic (br) EM/Steve Tanner, 48(t) Dovedale Fabrics (bl) EM/Steve Tanner (br) Dorma, 49,50(tl) EM/Steve Tanner, 50(tr) Ariadne Holland (b) Sue Atkinson, 51(t) EWA/Michael Crockett (c) EM/John Suett (b) Laura Ashley, 52(tl) EM/John Suett (bl) Textra, 52–3(c) Anna French, 53(t) Ehrman (b) Marks and Spencer, 54(t) Arthur Sanderson and Sons (c) Sue Atkinson (bl) Harris Communications (br) EM/John Suett, 55 EM/Tif Hunter, 56 EWA/June Buck, 57 Arthur Sanderson and Son, 58 Dovedale Fabrics, 61,62(t) Anna French, 62(bl) EWA/Tom Leighton (br) EM/Steve Tanner, 63(tl) Brian Yates (c,b) EM/Steve Tanner, 64(t) Crown Berger (b) EM/Steve Tanner, 65 EWA/Di Lewis, 67 Dulux, 68(l) EM/John Suett, 68–71 Dulux, 72 Arthur Sanderson and Son, 73 Magnet, 74 Crown Paints, 75 IPC Magazines/Robert Harding Syndication, 76 Ametex, 77(tl) Ken Kirkwood (tr) Stencil-itis, 78 Ametex, 79 Pictures Colour Library, 80 EM/Steve Tanner, 82 Jahres Zeiten Verlag, 83 IPC Magazines/Robert Harding Syndication, 84(t) Ronseal (b) Conran Octopus/Simon Brown, 85(t) EWA (b) Cuprinol, 86(l) EWA/Michael Nicholson (r) Cuprinol, 87,90 Junckers. 91 Ken Kirkwood, 92 EM/Sue Atkinson, 93 EWA/Rodney Hyett, 94(t) Crown Paints (b) VPM, 95 EWA/Peter Aprahamian, 96 Jon Bouchier, 97(t) Arthur Sanderson and Son (b) Cuprinol, 98(t) Cuprinol (b) Marie Claire Maison/Eriaud/Comte, 99 Pictures Colour Library, 100 EM/Steve Tanner, 102 Jahres Zeiten Verlag, 103(l) EM/Steve Tanner (r) Insight London/Michelle Garrett, 106(br) Ronseal, 107 IPC Magazines/Robert Harding Syndication, 108(tl) EWA/Neil Lorimer (bl) EWA/Brian Harrison, 109(t,bl) IPC Magazines/Robert Harding Syndication (br) EM/Graham Rae, 110(t,br) Cristal (bl) EM/Graham Rae, 111(t) EWA/Tim Beddow (b) Cristal, 112 Stovax, 113 Cristal, 114 EM/Tif Hunter, 115 Ken Kirkwood, 117 EM/Steve Tanner, 118 Arthur Sanderson and Son, 119 Laura Ashley, 120-122 EM/Tif Hunter, 123 Marks and Spencer, 124 Richard Paul, 127 EWA/Di Lewis, 128–9 EWA/Spike Powell, 129(br) Richard Paul, 130(t) Nets (cr) Marks and Spencer (bl) EWA/Spike Powell (br) Forbo-Mayfair, 131 Ametex, 134 Cooperative Wholesale Society, 135 Crowson Fabrics, 136 Cy deCosse Inc, 137 IPC Magazines/Robert Harding Syndication, 138 Cy deCosse Inc, 139 Crown Paints, 140 EM/Simon Page-Ritchie, 142 Ashley Wilde, 143,145 Hill and Knowles, 146(t) EM/Steve Tanner (b) Marie Claire Maison/Hussenot/Puech, 147,8 Harrison Drape, 149 EM/Marie-Louise Avery, 151 Romo Fabrics, 153 Interior Selection, 154 Osborne and Little, 155 Warner Fabrics, 156 EM/Simon Butcher, 158(t) Crowson Fabrics (b) Bo Appeltoft, 159 Kirsch, 160 EM/Steve Tanner, 161(t,br) EM/Steve Tanner (bl) Anna French, 162(tr,cr) EM/Steve Tanner (br) EM/Marie-Louise Avery, 163 Collins, 164–5 EM/Steve Tanner, 167 EWA/Neil Lorimer, 168 EM/Simon Butcher, 170(t) EWA/Jerry Tubby (b) EWA/Michael Crockett, 171,2 EM/Steve Tanner, 173(t) Ametex, 175 Ariadne, 176(tl) Boys Syndication, (tr,cr,bl) VPM Redakionsservice, 177 Smallbone of Devizes, 179 Richard Paul, 180 Cy deCosse Inc, 181 EM/Simon Page-Ritchie, 182 Arthur Sanderson and Son, 183–186 EM/Steve Tanner, 187 Brooke London Ltd, 188,9 EM/Steve Tanner, 190 Interior Selection, 191,2 Dorma, 193 EM/Eric Crichton, 194 EM/Steve Tanner, 195 Romo Fabrics, 197 Richard Paul, 198 Cy deCosse Inc, 199-201 EM/Simon Page-Ritchie, 201(tr) Ariadne Holland, 202 EM/Simon Page-Ritchie, 203,204 Richard Paul, 205 IPC Magazines/Robert Harding Syndication, 206 Monkwell Ltd, 207–210 EM/Sue Atkinson, 211–214 EM/John Suett, 215 Dulux, 216, 218, 219 Arthur Sanderson and Son, 221 Dulux, 222 Cy deCosse Inc, 223 Dorma, 224–226 EM/Simon Page-Ritchie, 227 Pictures Colour Library, 230 EWA/Michael Dunne, 231 Anna French, 232,3 Osborne and Little, 234 EM/Steve Tanner, 235, 236–7 Richard Paul, 237 Rene Stoeltie, 238 Bo Appeltoft, 239 Dorma, 241 EWA/Di Lewis. 242(t,b) Marie Claire Maison (c) EWA/Michael Dunne, 243 Osborne and Little, 244 Tino Tedaldi, 245(t) Jane Churchill (bl) Barbara and Rene Stoeltie (br) Osborne and Little, 247 EWA/Di Lewis, 248(t) Dorma (bl) Richard Paul (br) Modes et Travaux, 249,250 EM/John Suett, 251,2 EM/Steve Tanner, 253 EM/JS, 255-258 EM/Steve Tanner, 259 EM/Steve Tanner, 260 Arthur Sanderson and Son, 261 Elizabeth Bradley Designs, 262(tl) EWA/Michael Dunne (tr) Modes et Travaux (b) Richard Paul, 263 Ariadne Holland, 265 Richard Paul, 266 Ariadne Holland, 267 Anna French, 268 Ariadne Holland, 269 Anna French, 270 Ariadne Holland, 271 EWA/Andreas von Einsiedel, 273 EM/John Suett, 274(l) EM/John Suett (r) Boys Syndication, 275–278 EM/John Suett, 279 EWA/Spike Powell, 280(cr) EWA/Spike Powell (bl) Marie Claire Maison/Sarramon/de Roquette, 281 Mazda Lighting, 282(tl) Crown Paints (tr) EWA/Spike Powell (bl) EWA/Ed Ironside, 283–286 EM/John Suett, 287 Ariadne Holland, 288 EM/Steve Tanner, 289 Barbara and Rene Stoeltie, 290(t) Liberty (b) EM/Steve Tanner, 291 EWA/Andreas von Einsiedel, 292(t) B&Q (b) Houses and Interiors, 293 Dulux, 294(t) Boys Syndication (b) Smallbone of Devizes, 295 Ariadne Holland, 296(t) IPC Magazines/Robert Harding Syndication (b) Sharps Bedrooms, 297(t) Houses and Interiors (bl) Habitat (br) EWA/Rodney Hyett, 298(t) EWA/Andreas von Einsiedel (b) Grange, 299(t) Ariadne Holland (b) EWA/Spike Powell, 300(t) EWA/Peter Wolosynsky (b) EWA/Kudos/Brian Harrison.

ILLUSTRATIONS: 59–60 Stan North, 63 Tig Sutton, 66–72 Stan North, 73(tl) Jenny Abbot/Garden Studios, 73(b),74 Stan North, 76–7 Christine Hart-Davies, 80–106 Tig Sutton, 116 David Ashby/Garden Studios, 121–2 Stan North, 125–138 Will Giles and Sandra Pond, 140–2 Terry Evans, 144–5 John Hutchinson, 148–50 Terry Evans, 152–8 John Hutchinson, 164–6 Irwin Technical, 168–9 John Hutchinson, 172–9 Terry Evans, 184–6 John Hutchinson, 196–8 Will Giles and Sandra Pond, 200(t) Julie-Anne Burt, 200(b), 201(bl) Terry Evans, 201(br) Julie-Anne Burt, 202 Terry Evans, 204–6 Kate Simunek, 208–9 John Hutchinson, 212–4 Terry Evans, 217–8 Christine Hart-Davies, 220 Will Giles and Sandra Pond, 224–6 John Hutchinson, 228–30 Terry Evans, 232–245 John Hutchinson, 250 Terry Evans, 252 John Hutchinson, 254 Sally Holmes, 256–8 John Hutchinson, 264–6 Christine Hart-Davies/Julie-Ann Burt, 268–278 John Hutchinson, 280–2 David Ashby/Garden Studios, 284–6 Terry Evans, 288–90 John Hutchinson, 293–4 Stan North.